LET'S MAKE A DEAL

Let's Make a Deal

Understanding the Negotiation Process in Ordinary Litigation

HERBERT M. KRITZER

The University of Wisconsin Press

The University of Wisconsin Press
114 North Murray Street
Madison, Wisconsin 53715

3 Henrietta Street
London WC2E 8LU, England

5 4 3 2 1

Printed in the United States of America

Library of Congress Cataloging-in-Publication Data
Kritzer, Herbert M., 1947–
    Let's make a deal: understanding the negotiation process in
ordinary litigation / Herbert M. Kritzer.
    220 pp.   cm.
    Includes bibliographical references (p. 181) and index.
    1. Dispute resolution (Law)—United States. 2. Negotiation.
I. Title.
KF9084.K75   1991
347.73'9—dc20
[347.3079]
ISBN 0-299-12820-2   90-50648
ISBN 0-299-12824-5   CIP

To my parents,
Jean Freisleben Kritzer
and Emanuel Kritzer

Contents

Figures   ix
Tables   xi
Acknowledgments   xiii

Chapter 1. Adjudication, Bargaining,
*   and Settlement*   3

Introduction   3
What We Know about Negotiation in Court—Four Stories   5
Data Sources   14
The Cases and the Lawyers   17

Chapter 2. A Portrait of Negotiation and Bargaining
*   in Ordinary Litigation*   30

Introduction   30
Intensity in the Bargaining/Negotiation Process   30
The Content of Negotiations   41
The Relationship of Negotiation to Results Achieved   52
Summary   54

Chapter 3. Settlement, Negotiation, and Economics
*   in Ordinary Litigation*   57

Introduction   57
Economic Realities in Settling Civil Disputes   58
Bargaining as the Exchange of Economic Information   66

Chapter 4. Power, Games, and Bargaining   72

Introduction   72
Bargaining as the Strategic Manipulation of Power   72
Cooperation and Competition in Bargaining   76
Game-Theoretic Approaches to Bargaining   80
Conclusions   98

Chapter 5. The Structure of Economic Incentives
for the Lawyer   99

Introduction   99
Contingent Fees and the Content of Negotiation   100
Tactical Bargaining and Fee Arrangement   103
A Comparative Perspective: The Impact of
   Fees and Costs on Bargaining in England   105
Conclusion   110

Chapter 6. The Forms of Negotiation:
A "Sociological" Approach   112

Introduction   112
Categories and Typologies for Analyzing Negotiation 113
Three Modes of Negotiation   118
Conclusion   127

Chapter 7. Conclusion: The Need to Keep
Negotiation in Perspective   130

Negotiation and Civil Justice Reform   135

Notes   141
References   181
Index   197

Figures

4.1   The Prisoner's Dilemma Game Matrix   81
4.2   A Multistage Litigation Game   91
4.3   Swanson's Litigation Game   95
6.1   Negotiation Styles   114
6.2   Negotiation Contexts   115
6.3   Negotiation Face-Offs   123

Tables

1.1	Characteristics of the Five Federal Judicial Districts	15
1.2	Percentage Distribution of Kinds of Cases (Areas of Law) in Federal and State Courts, by Judicial District	19
1.3	Percentage Distribution of Lawyers' Perceptions of Stakes	20
1.4	Frequency Distribution of Lawyers' Responses Regarding What Was at Stake	22
1.5	Percentage Distribution of Lawyers' Attitudes toward Their Work	26
1.6	Percentage Distribution and Intensity Ratings of What Litigators Reported to Like and Dislike about Their Work	27
1.7	Percentage Distribution of Lawyers' Responses Regarding the Traits That Make a Good Litigator	28
2.1	Contact Intensity: Percentage Distributions of Lawyers' Responses Regarding the Number of Hours and Percentage of Time Spent on Settlement Discussions	32
2.2	Contact Intensity, by Area of Law	32
2.3	Contact Intensity, by Case Characteristics	33
2.4	Contact Intensity, by Federal Judicial District	35
2.5	Distribution of Offers and Demands in the First Round of Bargaining, by Plaintiffs and Defendants	36
2.6	Distribution of Offers and Demands in the Second Round of Bargaining, by Plaintiffs and Defendants	38
2.7	Percentage Distribution of Exchange Intensity, by Area of Law	38
2.8	Percentage Distribution of Exchange Intensity, by Case Characteristics	40
2.9	Percentage Distribution of Types of Offers and Demands	42
2.10	Percentage Distribution of Negotiation Contents, by Area of Law	43
2.11	Percentage Distribution of Negotiation Contents, by Case Complexity	44
2.12	Percentage Distribution of Negotiation Contents, by Lawyer Experience and Specialization	45

2.13 Percentage Distribution of Negotiation Contents,
by Fee Arrangement   46

2.14 Percentage Distribution of Types of Nonmonetary
Demands and Offers   46

2.15 Percentage Distribution of Ratios of Offers and
Demands to Stakes   48

2.16 Percentage Distribution of Ratio of Demands to Stakes,
by Area of Law   49

2.17 Percentage Distribution of Ratio of Offers to Stakes,
by Case Size and Complexity   49

2.18 Percentage Distribution of Changes in Offers and Demands   50

2.19 Correlations of Offer and Demand Ratios with Case
and Lawyer Characteristics   51

2.20 Percentage Distribution of Relationship of Respondents'
Demand Ratio by Selected Variables   52

3.1 "Risk Analysis" for a Typical Case   60

3.2 Impact of Stakes on Zone of Overlap   62

3.3 Impact of Stakes on Zone of Overlap for
Contingent-Fee Lawyers   64

4.1 Litigant Strategies in P'ng's Litigation Game   85

4.2 Summary of Game-Theoretic Models of
Bargaining in Litigation   88

5.1 Percentage Distribution of Negotiation Contents, by Fee
Arrangement, for Monetized Cases Only   102

6.1 Dimensions of the Negotiation Situation / Context   117

Acknowledgments

The data that form the basis of the analysis in this book were collected by the Civil Litigation Research Project during 1979–80. CLRP, as it was known, was a unique undertaking, both in purpose and in scale. The funding for the project came initially from the Office for Improvements in the Administration of Justice in the United States Department of Justice (Contract No. JAOIA-79-C-0040); after the political winds shifted in 1981, responsibility for the project was transferred to the National Institute of Justice (Contract No. J-LEAA-003-82). Over the years, substantial supplemental support has been forthcoming from the University of Wisconsin Graduate School and the University of Wisconsin Law School. In the time since funding from the Department of Justice came to an end, support for specific pieces of work and analysis was provided by the National Institute for Dispute Resolution (NIDR) and the National Science Foundation (Grant No. SES-8320129), which funded the negotiations analysis which I report in the pages that follow. With additional support from the National Science Foundation (Grant No. SES-8511622) the data collected by the project have been archived for use by other researchers; data and accompanying documentation are available from the Interuniversity Consortium for Political and Social Research (ICPSR), University of Michigan, P.O. Box 1248, Ann Arbor, Michigan, 48106.

The work that I describe in the following pages reflects substantial contributions by a number of people. David M. Trubek (professor of law, University of Wisconsin–Madison, and former director of the Institute for Legal Studies) served as project director, taking on the burden of day-to-day administration of the project during the years when large numbers of people were involved. Along with David Trubek, William L. F. Felstiner (distinguished research fellow and former director of the American Bar Foundation), Joel Grossman (professor of political science and law, University of Wisconsin–Madison), and Austin Sarat (professor of political science, Amherst College) were collaborators in the tasks of thinking through the design of the research and planning the data collection and the early analyses.

Most of the survey data were collected on our behalf by Mathematica Policy Research in Princeton, New Jersey. Lois Blanchard and Joey Cerf worked on a day-to-day basis insuring that the data collected would meet our requirements; the work at Mathematica was under the general supervision of Paul Planchon. The court records data were coded by law students working under the direct supervision of Stephen McDougal and Judith Hansen; collection of data from alternative dispute-processing institutions was handled in the field by Jill Anderson. In Madison, Laura Guy, Richard Miller, Jeannette Holz, Kristin Bumiller, Elizabeth McNichol, Dan Krymkowski, George Brown, and Mary Pfister carried out much of the day-to-day work of the project. I was assisted by Karen Holst, Thomas Schmeling, and Jung Il Gill in the preparation of the open-ended data used in the negotiations analysis. Many other persons, both students and nonstudents, worked on the project over the years. To all of them I owe a debt of appreciation for their hard work.

Much of chapter 5 appeared previously, and I would like to thank the journals where the material originally appeared for their permission to include it in this book:

"Fee Arrangements and Negotiation: A Research Note," *Law & Society Review* 21, 2 (1987): 341–348; reprinted by permission of the Law and Society Association.

"A Comparative Perspective on Settlement and Bargaining in Personal Injury Cases" (a review essay of *Hard Bargaining: Out of Court Settlement in Personal Injury Actions,* by Hazel Genn), *Law & Social Inquiry* 14 (1989): 167–185.

Additionally, a version of Table 1.1 appeared in:

"Studying Disputes: Learning from the CLRP Experience," *Law & Society Review* 15, 3–4 (1980–81): 514; reprinted by permission of the Law and Society Association.

Several persons read and commented on portions of the manuscript at various stages of its development: Tim Swanson, Malcolm Feeley, Carrie Menkel-Meadow, and Craig McEwen. Their comments have led to a much more interesting book, and I greatly appreciate their time and effort. The manuscript benefited tremendously from Robin Whitaker's excellent editing. In a less specific way, this work has benefited from my opportunity to interact with the large Law and Society community at the University of Wisconsin–Madison, including Marc Galanter, Stewart Macaulay, Jack Ladinsky, Howard Erlanger, Laurie Edelman, Malcolm Feeley, Martha Fineman, Dirk Hartog, Donald Downs, Steve Penrod, and the many graduate students who "did time" at Wisconsin during the 1980s. The initial draft of the manuscript was prepared while I was a visiting fellow at the Faculty of Law, University College London, and a guest of the Institute for Advanced

Legal Studies in London; the opportunity to escape the phone calls and committees of Madison allowed me the relaxed context needed to conceptualize and draft the manuscript. Of course, the final responsibility for the analyses and conclusions rests with me.

Finally, to my wife, Amelia Howe Kritzer, who has put up with this research project for too long: Amy, the publication of this book means it's over!

LET'S MAKE A DEAL

CHAPTER 1

Adjudication, Bargaining, and Settlement

Introduction

Americans have a long-standing reputation for relying upon the legal system to deal with all manner of problems and issues.[1] In recent years we have been described as having reached new heights of litigiousness (Lieberman, 1981; Rosenberg, 1972); we suffer from the disorder of "hyperlexis" (Manning, 1977). The correctness of this diagnosis is vigorously debated, with prominent judges (Burger, 1982; Posner, 1985: 59–93), policy-makers and researchers (Marvell, 1987, 1985), and academics (Barton, 1975; Tribe, 1979; Galanter, 1983, 1986a) marshaling personal experiences, anecdotes, and statistics to buttress one side or the other of the argument.

Although the resolution of this debate is not in sight, all observers agree that very few of the cases on the dockets of America's courts will be resolved by the full, formal adjudication of the issues presented. Of the vast majority of the cases started in the courts, perhaps 90 percent will be settled by the parties, many without ever seeing the inside of the court*room*.[2] If one were to include the cases that never get through the door of the court*house*—cases that are settled between the parties before a formal court action is even started—the settlement figure approaches 99 percent![3] Does this mean it is time to consider replacing the phrases chiseled in stone above America's courthouse doors, phrases like that appearing on the United States Supreme Court Building in Washington, D.C.:

Equal Justice under Law

with something that more accurately reflects the realities of what happens in the civil justice system? A cynic might suggest the following as a more apt epigram:

Let's Make a Deal!

3

But is there an inconsistency between "justice" for an aggrieved party achieved through adjudication and "deals" arrived at by parties in a dispute through negotiation? What is the significance of the dominance of settlement over adjudication for the civil justice system's goal of providing justice for aggrieved parties?[4]

Although settlement and adjudication can be cast as contrasting methods of resolving disputes, they are by no means unrelated within the context of actual or potential civil litigation: there is always the option to forego settlement and allow the dispute to be adjudicated.[5] Marc Galanter goes one step further, arguing that the combination of *liti*gation leading to formal adjudication and ne*gotiation* to achieve an out-of-court settlement should be thought of as "a single process of disputing in the vicinity of official tribunals that might [be] call[ed] *litigotiation,* that is, the strategic pursuit of a settlement through mobilizing the court process" (Galanter, 1984: 268).[6] What is interesting about this characterization is that it recognizes the interrelationship between litigation and negotiation while preserving the analytic distinction between adjudication and settlement. From the recent work of the Civil Litigation Research Project (Trubek, Grossman, et al., 1983; Trubek, Sarat, et al., 1983; Kritzer, Sarat, et al., 1984; Kritzer et al., 1985, 1987; Kritzer, 1990) we now know a great deal about the litigation and adjudication side of this process in ordinary cases. Much less is known about the nature of the negotiation and settlement side; the purpose of this book is to fill in this gap.

In the pages that follow, I will draw upon data collected through interviews with lawyers involved in a sample of federal and state court cases from five federal judicial districts to present a portrait of the negotiation and settlement process in *ordinary* litigation. Because of the data source, the discussion is oriented toward the lawyer's perspective rather than the litigant's. The first goal of this book is to describe the day-to-day negotiation and settlement of cases in America's civil justice system. With the portrait in place, I will examine several ways to explain the patterns I describe. To do this, I will turn to the large theoretical literature on negotiation and settlement. I argue that much of that literature is of little help in accounting for the realities of what happens in ordinary civil cases. This is not to say that theories of settlement and negotiation are of no value; rather, there is a narrow element among those theories that can account for much of what is observed. From this discussion of existing theories, I will posit a typology that I believe is helpful in understanding what types of theoretical approaches can be usefully pursued in advancing our knowledge of negotiation and settlement in ordinary litigation. Lastly, in the concluding chapter, I will examine the implications of the analysis, both theoretically and practically:

—Given an empirically based portrait of settlement and negotiation, what are the implications for court reform, both now and in the future (and what does this tell us about the impacts of past efforts to reform the civil litigation process)?

—With a better understanding of the realities of the settlement process, how can the litigotiation image be refined and extended?

What We Know About Negotiation in Court—Four Stories

The perception of a justice system frustrated by deals made in the corridors of the courthouse[7] certainly arises in part from a popular dissatisfaction with the criminal side of the justice system, which is commonly seen as being subverted by rampant so-called plea bargaining. Plea bargaining is attacked both by those who see it as a process by which defendants become the victims of injustice because of a natural fear of the consequences of insisting upon their right to a full trial (e.g., Alschuler, 1968, 1975, 1976, 1981, 1983) and by those who see it as symptomatic of the failure of the criminal justice system to mete out the harsh penalties that criminals justly deserve (e.g., van den Haag, 1975: 171–173; Fine, 1986). The criticisms of settlement in the civil justice system neatly parallel those of the criminal side. Some people attack the deals that are made by way of settlement as evidence that victims of legally compensable injuries are forced (by delay, uncertainty, and the like) to accept resolutions far short of what the law entitles them to (Fiss, 1984; Alschuler, 1986). Others see the civil justice process as a vehicle by which undeserving persons (and their contingent-fee lawyers) extort payments by filing frivolous lawsuits which defendants choose to settle because the cost of defending the case in court exceeds the amount that the plaintiff is willing to accept in settlement.

In fact, as suggested by Galanter's notion of litigotiation, there is a growing realization that both the criminal and civil justice processes involve a complex mix of adversary advocacy, threatened and actual adjudication, and cooperative and competitive bargaining. On the criminal justice side, analyses show that the large numbers of dispositions through guilty pleas may reflect a combination of bargaining with strong cooperative overtones and client advocacy; this combination produces an adversarylike process through which the prosecutor and defender arrive at a common perception of what the case represents and what constitutes an appropriate sanction (see Utz, 1978; Feeley, 1979a). This revisionist view of the "guilty-plea process" is supported by the fact that there is little systematic evidence to support the proposition that guilty pleas reflect wholesale reductions in charges and/or sanctions (see Maynard, 1984a; Nardulli, Flemming, and Eisenstein, 1985; Nardulli, Eisenstein, and Flemming, 1988; Eisenstein, Flemming, and Nardulli, 1988). Furthermore, the fact that at least one very large urban court disposes of most of its cases through trials rather than guilty pleas (Schulhofer, 1984, 1985) confirms previous research questioning the argument that plea bargaining is an inevitable result of heavy case loads (Heumann, 1977; Feeley, 1979b).

Our understanding of civil settlement is about where our knowledge of the guilty-plea system in criminal cases was 20 years ago. We know that settlement negotiations take place, and we know that they more often than not succeed (at least in the sense that some settlement is agreed to[8]); however, we know little about how or why they succeed. What we do know is dominated by an image of cases that are much bigger than those that make up the bulk of the work of state and federal trial courts (see, for example, Raiffa, 1982: 66–77; Wallach, 1979), particularly those kinds of cases that capture substantial media attention.

THE PENNZOIL VERSUS TEXACO CASE

In a 1980's multibillion-dollar case, Pennzoil sued Texaco in a Texas state court, claiming that Texaco had illegally interfered with a deal Pennzoil had negotiated to buy Getty Oil. In November 1985 a jury found in Pennzoil's favor, awarding approximately $10.5 billion in damages.[9] Texaco went to federal court to seek relief from the Texas law requiring it to post a bond in the full amount of the judgment in order to appeal the jury's verdict; in February 1986, a federal judge in White Plains, New York, issued an order allowing Texaco to post an appeals bond of $1 billion (in stock) rather than the required $12 billion (the higher amount reflecting accrued interest). A year later, Texaco obtained a $2 billion reduction in punitive damages from a Texas appeals court, but was shocked by a United States Supreme Court ruling two months later (April 6, 1987) that the New York federal judge had erred in reducing the appeal bond amount. Six days later, April 12, 1987, Texaco filed for protection under the federal bankruptcy statutes (*National Law Journal*, December 28, 1987, p. 18).

Although the public reports of the settlement negotiations are sketchy, it is clear that a complex dance between Texaco and Pennzoil started soon after the initial jury verdict. This dance included executives of Texaco and Pennzoil, attorneys representing Texaco shareholders (some of whom had filed suit against the Texaco board of directors), plus outside players such as Carl Icahn (who purchased a large block of Texaco shares and exerted substantial pressures to try to bring about a settlement) and Texaco's general creditors who had been put on hold through the bankruptcy filing (and who were owed approximately $2.5 billion by Texaco). Reported potential settlement figures ranged from $1 billion to $5 billion, and were discussed in the shadow of three different courts: the Texas Supreme Court, the United States Supreme Court, and the federal bankruptcy court in New York. Negotiations were accelerated in November 1987, after the Texas Supreme Court refused to review the Texas appeals court decisions, leaving the United States Supreme Court as Texaco's only hope.

Particular plans included both outright settlement as well as a possible agreement that Texaco would pay a fixed, nonrefundable amount prior to Supreme Court review to purchase what in effect would be a fixed maximum payment; i.e., Texaco would pay Pennzoil $1 billion before filing with the Supreme Court, and Pennzoil would agree that if it (Pennzoil) prevailed at the Supreme Court, Texaco would not have to pay more than $3 billion to satisfy its liability to Pennzoil (*National Law Journal*, December 21, 1987, p. 10). On December 19, 1987, Texaco announced a settlement in which it would pay Pennzoil $3 billion to settle the case, as well as paying other creditors $2.5 billion in order to emerge from the Bankruptcy Court (*Chicago Tribune*, December 20, 1987, p. 6).

This very general chronology suggests a complex, behind-the-scenes process where the costs, risks, and likely outcomes of continuing the fight through the courts were constantly weighed against the results that could be achieved by settlement. The negotiations clearly involved many parties with both conflicting and complementary interests that had to be balanced. Since we do not have a detailed account of actions and responses for individual players, we cannot do more than speculate on how those actors and actions led to the ultimate result.

THE AGENT ORANGE CASE

Peter Schuck (1986) does provide that kind of detailed look at the complexities involved in settling the Agent Orange class action case. This case involved claims by a large number of Vietnam veterans (and their families) against a group of chemical manufacturers and the United States government for a variety of health problems alleged to be associated with exposure to dioxin-based defoliants used in Vietnam. Three key groups were involved in the negotiations: a group of attorneys representing claimants (known as the Plaintiffs' Management Committee, or PMC), attorneys representing companies that had manufactured the chemicals, and Federal Judge Jack B. Weinstein, plus three attorneys working with Judge Weinstein as special masters.

Soon after Judge Weinstein assumed responsibility for the case, he asked the first special master, Kenneth Feinberg, to draft a plan to guide the settlement discussions. This 80-page document, which avoided any references to specific settlement amounts, laid out the three primary areas where resolution was needed:
—in determining the aggregate amount of the settlement;
—in setting the amounts to be paid by each defendant;
—in dividing the settlement among the claimants.
Each of these areas raised many thorny issues. For example, concerning the amount of the settlement, there was no information available on the total number of claims that might be made, nor was there any information on the distribution of the various types of injuries that had been alleged.

The second special master, David Shapiro, had responsibility for working directly with the two sides to try to reach agreement on the specific issues. These negotiations dealt with questions such as:
—Should the proportion of the settlement to be paid by each defendant be proportional to market shares, dioxin content of their chemicals, litigation cost, or some combination of these?
—Should potential claimants be permitted to "opt out" of any settlement that was reached, or should all claimants be required to accept the settlement under provisions of the federal rules governing class actions; if opt-outs were to be permitted, to what degree should their claims be paid out of the settlement fund?
—How should claims of children and the unborn be handled?
—Should American and Vietnamese civilians plus soldiers (and their families) from American allies (Australia and New Zealand) be included?
—When should interest on the settlement fund begin to accrue?
—What role, if any, should the federal government be required to play in funding the settlement?[10]
—What kinds of fee awards should be made to attorneys representing claimants?
—What kinds of information should claimants be required to provide to obtain compensation?

The negotiations started with the two sides far apart on settlement issues, particularly the amount of the settlement. The defendants were willing to settle, but the amount they typically mentioned was $25 million. The PMC was thinking in terms of $700 million. A week before jury selection was slated to start, the two sides were still $260 million apart ($100 million versus $360 million). As jury selection neared, Shapiro decided to engage the two sides in marathon negotiation sessions; participants were told to come to the federal courthouse in Brooklyn on Saturday morning at 9 A.M., and be prepared to stay through Saturday and Sunday nights (jury selection was to begin Monday morning).

Shapiro and Feinberg met with all the lawyers in one room to begin the marathon. Shapiro then proceeded to shuttle back and forth between the two sides, alternately encouraging and badgering the players. Judge Weinstein came in and gave a pep talk to the two sides on the importance of achieving a settlement, and then met with each side. As solutions to specific issues were proposed, Judge Weinstein indicated which positions he would support. When needed, Shapiro and/or Feinberg met with lawyers for individual chemical companies, trying to resolve issues that divided the defendants.

On Sunday, divisions among members of the Plaintiffs Management Committee began to become acute. At least one lawyer believed that the defendants would become more flexible after the trial had begun; others were concerned that potential weaknesses in the plaintiffs' case would in fact stiffen the defense. Late in the afternoon, the masters took the PMC's current position to the defendants. By that time, the difference between the two sides had been narrowed to about $50 million ($150 million versus $200 million). After talking with Judge Weinstein, the masters took $180 million as their target figure. In discussions with the PMC, the masters pointed out that a $180 million settlement would grow to something over $200 million with accrued interest by the time the settlement was finalized.[11] Then, with the masters present, Judge Weinstein met with the PMC and urged the acceptance of the $180 million figure; when the judge asked each of the lawyers to indicate where he or she stood on the offer, some indicated a willingness to accept it, but most were still resistant. While the lawyers were leaving Weinstein's chambers, the judge raised the specter of the responsibility that would fall on members of the PMC if the case went to trial and the defendants won.

A heated two-hour discussion among members of the PMC resulted in a near complete collapse of those opposed to the $180 million figure; only one lawyer held out. Judge Weinstein personally presented the PMC's position to the defendants' lawyers late Sunday evening: $180 million with interest to accrue starting that day. After the judge warned the defendants once again of the vagaries of trial, the defendants caucused. A few hours later, early Monday morning, the defendants reconvened with the judge to review the agreement that apparently had been reached. After one more discussion with the PMC, and only hours before jury selection was to begin, Weinstein called the two sides in to read to them the outline of the settlement ($180 million with interest starting that day, plus details on inclusions, exclusions, expenses, etc.). It took another two weeks of intensive, frequently fractious talks, often going around the clock, to agree fully on the many details.

These examples, plus many others I might cite (the AT&T antitrust settlement, the Westinghouse uranium case settlement, etc.) indicate a complex process involving multiple players' participation in a game of give and take, leading toward an eventual compromise. This picture has many parallels to the image of the guilty-plea process in high profile *criminal* cases (see, for example, Cohen and Witcover's [1974] description of the plea negotiation that occurred in the case leading to Vice President Spiro Agnew's resignation in 1973). However, in the criminal arena, we know that most guilty pleas do not arise from such a process; there is little give and take, there is little subtlety, and often there is little compromise (see Maynard, 1984a; Nardulli, Flemming, and Eisenstein, 1985; Nardulli, Eisenstein, and Flemming, 1988; Eisenstein, Flemming, and Nardulli, 1988).

In contrast with a rich, empirically based picture of the process by which everyday criminal cases are resolved (see Heumann, 1977; Mather, 1979; Feeley, 1979a; Utz, 1978; Eisenstein and Jacob, 1977; Eisenstein, Flemming, and Nardulli, 1988; Nardulli, Eisenstein, and Flemming, 1988; Maynard, 1984a, b), we have little systematic empirical knowledge concerning the resolution of civil cases. Although there is a growing body of theoretical work on the settlement of civil cases, there have been few efforts to use those theories in empirical analyses of data drawn from actual cases sampled from the civil dockets of courts in the United States.[12] Regarding many of the other aspects of ordinary litigation, the work of the Civil Litigation Research Project has show that day-to-day civil cases bear little resemblance to the image derived from the mammoth (or silly) cases that tend to be discussed in the media.[13] Is it possible that the settlement process in day-to-day civil disputes is a fairly cut-and-dried process?

THE CASE OF MICHAEL'S WRIST

Consider the following actual experience of an acquaintance I will call Michael: On a spring day several years ago, Michael was bicycling to the University of Wisconsin campus in Madison when he was struck by a car turning left as he crossed through an intersection on a green light. Michael's injuries were minor but troublesome: several abrasions to his forehead (he had not been wearing a helmet) and his leg, and an injured tendon in his wrist.[14] Several days after the accident he was contacted by a representative of the driver's insurance company; the company was clearly anxious to reach a settlement as quickly as possible. Michael explained that he was having difficulty with his wrist, and that he wanted to wait several weeks to be sure that it would heal without significant problems. The wrist brace that he was wearing allowed him to do most usual activities, but it did make it more difficult to handle the spring gardening and to ride his repaired bicycle. He began to consider what he should ask for in the way of a settlement, and reached the tentative conclusion that $300 sounded like a fair figure.

During this period Michael encountered an acquaintance in the neighborhood grocery store whom he knew to be an attorney who handled personal injury cases. Waving his wrist in the air (still in the brace), Michael asked the lawyer, "Allen, what's it worth?" After hearing a brief description of what had happened, the lawyer indicated that he was getting around $700 for injuries of the type Michael had suffered. The lawyer recommended that Michael ask the insurance company for $1,700, explaining that if Michael were to ask for $2,000, it would sound like a round number pulled out of the air, but $1,700 sounded like a figure that had been arrived at after some deliberation.

Shortly after the discussion, Michael wrote to the insurance company, detailing the difficulty that he had had with his wrist. Michael indicated that he had "consulted with his attorney" and that "after some consideration" the attorney had recommended that an appropriate settlement would be $1,700. Michael further stated that he hoped the matter would be resolved without the necessity of formally turning the case over to his attorney. An adjuster called Michael soon thereafter to set a time to meet to discuss the claim.

Shortly before the adjuster arrived, Michael extracted the wrist brace from the drawer where it had been residing for several weeks, and put it back on his wrist. After several minutes of pleasantries, the adjuster got out Michael's file and began thumbing through the materials in it. She acknowledged the "demand" for $1,700 but indicated that it was quite a bit above what they usually paid in such cases; the top figure, she said, was more like $1,000. Given the difficulties Michael had had with his wrist, she felt that the company would be willing to settle the claim in that higher range of $1,000. After considering this offer for a minute or two, Michael agreed. The adjuster wrote out a check on the spot, and a release form. Michael signed; the adjuster left; Michael took the check to the bank (after removing the wrist brace).[15]

THE CASE OF THE KRITZER'S CAR

In the case of "Michael's wrist," the only issue was how much should be paid in compensation for Michael's loss and his pain and suffering; the bargaining that occurred concerning those damages was minimal and straightforward. As a second example of an everyday case, where the issue was one of liability rather than damages, consider the following personal experience:

A family member was turning left onto a main street, when a car driven by an elderly woman (whom I will call Mrs. Jones) ran a red light and struck our car. No one was injured, but Mrs. Jones was badly shaken up. Several witnesses stopped; one reported that the same driver (Mrs. Jones) had almost side-swiped his car a block or two up the street. When it became apparent that the police would be delayed in arriving at the accident scene, the two witnesses left their names and phone numbers and departed. The police officer took statements from both drivers, and assisted Mrs. Jones in contacting someone to come and take her home; our damaged car was operable, and the driver and passengers were able to use it to get back to our house.

When I contacted Mrs. Jones's insurance company, the adjuster told me that "their insured" had reported the accident but was claiming that she had the green light when she entered the intersection. When I said this was contrary to what had happened, and that we had witnesses to back up our version, the adjuster told me she would obtain a copy of the police report. In the meantime, she advised me to get an estimate from a body shop. When I called the adjuster back two weeks later, she had received my damage estimate (which came to about $1,300) but she had not yet obtained the police report (nor had she been able to contact either of the witnesses). I told her I would go down to the police station, get a copy of the police report, and mail it to her.

I contacted the police department, and was told where I could pick up a copy of the police report. When I went to that office, the clerk was unable to locate the report in the files, although he was able to identify the investigating police officer. The clerk suggested that I call back later that afternoon when the officer came on duty and speak directly with him. When I called the officer, I explained what had transpired, and asked if he had retained a copy of the accident report; he had not, having submitted it 10 days earlier in the normal course of his duties. I asked if there was much chance that the report would show up within a few days, and he said that he had no way of telling. Not knowing what else to do at this point, I did think to ask whether he could check his citation book to see if a citation had been issued to Mrs.

Jones; he called me back later that day to report that Mrs. Jones had been cited for failure to obey a traffic signal.

With that information, I recontacted the insurance adjuster. I explained that the police report apparently had been lost. When the adjuster reported that she still had not reached either of the witnesses, I asked whether Mrs. Jones had notified the insurance company that she had been cited in connection with the accident. The adjuster said no such information had been received, but she would do some additional checking. At the adjuster's request, we arranged for one of the insurance company's estimators to inspect the damaged car.

Several days later, after the company's inspection and with no further contact from the insurance adjuster, I received a check in the mail for about $1,500. The check was for more than the body shop's estimate because the insurance company's inspector had found some additional damage that the body shop had missed, and had worked out a revised figure in consultation with the owner of the body shop.

BIG CASES VERSUS EVERYDAY CASES:
TOWARD AN UNDERSTANDING OF THE ROUTINE

Analysis by anecdote is always dangerous, and I do not propose to generalize from the experiences of two people. Nonetheless, the images of negotiation one would take away from these last two examples is far from the image one would draw from the descriptions of the settlement of major, newsworthy cases. What then is the nature of negotiation in ordinary litigation? Is it more like the complex interaction in the Texaco and Agent Orange cases, or is it fairly cut and dried as in the cases of Michael's wrist and the Kritzer's car? The answers to these questions are the foci of much of the analysis presented in chapter 2.

The remainder of this chapter is devoted to a brief description of the data that I will use in the empirical analysis, plus brief sketches of the nature of the cases that compose the day-to-day work of America's civil justice system and the lawyers who handle ordinary litigation. This will set the context for the discussion in chapter 2 of the parameters of the negotiations that take place in ordinary, everyday civil cases. In chapters 3 through 6, I will examine a variety of potential explanations for the broad patterns developed in chapter 2.[16] The first three of these chapters rely entirely upon a variety of existing theoretical frameworks, and the fourth relies partly on existing theories:
—the economic analysis of settlement;
—bargaining as an exercise in the economics of information;

—game theory and power analysis;
—the lawyers' economic incentives and the theory of agency;
—typological analyses of bargaining contexts and bargaining styles.
In chapter 6, I propose my own typology of negotiation, which places the patterns described in chapter 2 in a perspective that is easily understood. That typology includes many elements of previous works, but combines them in a way that is particularly useful in the context of negotiation and settlement in ordinary litigation. Three general categories emerge from my analysis:
—maximal-result, concessions-oriented negotiation;
—appropriate-result, consensus-oriented negotiation;
—*pro forma* negotiation.
Chapter 7 concludes the book with a summary and a discussion of the implications of the analysis for civil justice reform.

Data Sources

The data used in the following chapters were collected by the Civil Litigation Research Project in 1979–80.[17] These data come from a sample of state and federal court cases that were terminated during 1978 in five federal judicial districts: Eastern Wisconsin, Eastern Pennsylvania, South Carolina, New Mexico, and Central California. Although any sample of five federal judicial districts cannot be said to be strictly representative of the 90 districts that cover the entire country,[18] these five were selected to be broadly representative of the variations that exist in the country. Table 1.1 shows a variety of selected characteristics of the districts from which cases were sampled; there is no reason to believe that this set of districts is systematically unrepresentative of the country as a whole, and for that reason the patterns described in chapter 2 are probably generalizable to ordinary litigation in the United States as a whole.[19]

In each of the five federal judicial districts, random samples consisting of approximately 150 cases were selected from the federal court and from the state courts.[20] In each of three of the districts (South Carolina, New Mexico, and Central California), cases were selected from a single state court, the court serving the county in which the federal district court is based.[21] In each of the other two districts, approximately 120 cases were selected from the court serving the urban center, with the remaining 30 cases chosen from an outlying rural or suburban county.[22] For the federal courts, a list of cases terminated in 1978 was obtained from the Administrative Office of the United States Courts, and a random sample of cases was chosen for each district from that list; the sampling method used in each state court varied

Table 1.1. Characteristics of the Five Federal Judicial Districts[a]

Characteristic	Central California	New Mexico	Eastern Pennsylvania	South Carolina	Eastern Wisconsin
Population, 1975 (in 1,000s)	10,759	1,144	5,092	2,816	2,831
Population change, 1970–75 (%)	3.9	12.5	-0.5	8.7	2.3
Net migration, 1970–75 (%)	-0.5	5.8	-2.6	3.4	-0.2
Population, 1970 (in 1,000s)	10,343	1,016	5,112	2,591	2,768
Population growth, 1960–70 (%)	29.3	6.8	7.7	8.7	12.2
Black population, 1970 (in 1,000s)	838	18	767	788	119
Population of spanish heritage, 1970 (in 1,000s)	1,768	407	nil	nil	nil
Urban population, 1970 (in 1,000s)	9,990	711	4,287	1,232	2,128
Median years of education, 1970	11.9	11.8	11.4	10.0	11.6
Number of farms over 10 acres, 1969	8,568	10,563	12,845	27,080	34,648
Percent of land area on farms	25.1	60.2	42.0	37.1	53.6
Percent of labor force in blue-collar occupations	43.9	27.4	53.1	58.8	54.3
State court organization[b]	multi-tiered	unified	overlapping multi-tiered	multi-tiered	unified
State court use of federal rules of civil procedure[c]	no	yes	no	no	yes
Number of federal judges, 1975[d]	16	3	19	5	5
Weighted federal caseload per judge, 1975[d]	414	385	242	520	383
Civil only	270	264	193	402	282
Median disposition times of federal civil cases (in months)[8]					
With no court action	6	4	5	5	7
During or after pretrial but before trial	16	10	13	12	21
All civil cases	6	7	9	7	11
Number of lawyers[f]	190,360	13,190	90,420	23,790	48,120

[a]Unless otherwise noted, data were compiled by the author.
[b]Data from the National Survey of Court Organization (LEAA, 1973) and supplements.
[c]Data from personal inquiries.
[d]Data from the Report of the Administrative Office of the U.S. Courts, 1975: Table X-1.
[e]Data from the Report of the Administrative Office of the U.S. Courts, 1978: Table C-5.
[f]Data collected by Carroll Seron and Wolf Heydebrand.

depending upon the information available on cases terminated.[23] Certain types of cases were excluded from the sample or otherwise restricted in some way: cases involving uncontested collections (where the defendant made no appearance and a default judgment was entered), prisoner petitions, one governmental unit suing another governmental unit, probate, bankruptcy, judicial review of administrative agency decisions except if the case involved a trial *de novo* or involved federal court reviews under the Administrative Procedure Act, deportations, Narcotic Addiction Recovery Act (NARA) Title II cases, and labor law cases that arose out of grievance procedures normally covered by collective bargaining agreements (e.g., appeals from the decisions of arbitrators). Also excluded were "small claims" cases, which were defined as cases involving only monetary claims of less than $1,000, and those cases that were clearly "nonordinary" as shown by the magnitude of the court file (a total of 36 nonordinary cases were ultimately excluded; all but 4 of these were from the federal court[24]). In addition, domestic-relations (primarily divorce) cases were arbitrarily limited to no more than 20 percent of the sample of cases in any state court and were excluded entirely in Pennsylvania, where they were maintained on a docket separate from the primary civil docket. Although I will make some specific references to divorce cases, the restrictive sampling of them limits my ability to draw generalizations that fully take into account the peculiarities of negotiation arising in the divorce context.[25]

Two different kinds of data were collected. The first kind consists of information extracted from the documents on file with the court for each of the cases in the sample; these data were coded in the field by law students trained and supervised by CLRP staff members. The information collected includes names, addresses, dates of filings, causes of action, pleadings and motions filed, discovery, judicial actions, appeals, and so on. Court record information was collected for a total of 1,649 cases. With this information in hand, telephone interviews were conducted with all the primary partici-pants (lawyers and litigants) who could be identified and located. Not all the cases in the records sample were included in the interview sample; no inter-views were sought for 226 cases.[26] The interviews were conducted by Math-ematica Policy Research (MPR) of Princeton, New Jersey. The typical full interview ran about one hour in length. All the participant interviews focused on the specific court case in the sample, including information about the background of the case, what was at stake or issue in the case, time and money spent on the case, relationships with other case participants, negotia-tions among the parties, outcome of the case, and the participant's evaluation of how well the court had handled the case. Additional background and attitudinal questions were asked of each participant as well.

The primary set of interview data used in the analysis in the following chapters comes from 1,382 lawyers;[27] this by no means exhausts the total number of lawyer interviews that might have been completed, given that interviews were actually sought for 1,423 court cases (out of the original sample of 1,649). One problem encountered was that some lawyers were involved in two or more cases in the sample. It seemed unreasonable to ask an individual to go through an entire hour-long interview more than once, so these lawyers were interviewed in depth about only one of their cases, with some brief questions about the additional cases. These brief sets of questions constitute another 430 short interviews that are not used in the analysis presented in chapter 2.

An entirely separate survey was conducted with government lawyers involved in the court cases; these represent another 96 interviews that I will draw on for one or two specific points in the analysis. (Another 136 short interviews, which will not be used in the analysis, were also conducted with government lawyers.) Of the lawyers that should have been interviewed but were not, some outright refused, but more begged off, claiming to have been only minimally involved in the cases or to have no recollection of the cases. This is borne out by comparisons between the cases for which lawyer interviews were obtained and those for which no interviews were obtained. The cases without interviews tend to have involved fewer docket entries, to have taken less time to dispose of, and to have more often involved domestic-relations issues (see Trubek, Grossman, et al., 1983: I-120). Thus, if anything, the lawyers interviewed tended to be involved in longer, more complex, less routine cases than those who were not interviewed.

The Cases and the Lawyers

In this section I will sketch, very briefly, pictures of the ordinary, everyday cases and the lawyers who handle them. Substantial additional detail can be found in Trubek, Sarat, et al., 1983, Trubek, Grossman, et al., 1983, and from my book, *The Justice Broker: Lawyers and Ordinary Litigation* (1990), from which this discussion is drawn.

THE CASES: ISSUES AND STAKES

There is a great variety of issues that can be raised in a lawsuit, and categorizing those issues involves a great deal of ambiguity. Because of this problem, the law student coders were asked to make their own judgments, based upon the complete case file, regarding the kinds of issues raised by each case in the sample; the coders were permitted to identify up to four different types of legal issues that were raised by the case. For purposes of discussion, I collapsed the 130 detailed areas of law used by the coders into eight broad categories: real property, contracts/commercial, torts, domestic-relations, business regulation, discrimination/civil rights, government benefits (disability, social security, black lung, welfare), and government action (taxation, zoning, political process, governmental financial obligations, freedom of information, voting rights, immigration/naturalization, and abuse of governmental authority).[28]

In the information displayed in Table 1.2, one can see the variation, by court and by location, in the kinds of issues raised.[29] Probably the most striking difference is the relative concentration of tort (injury to persons and/or property) cases within the state courts (with the exception of New Mexico) and the lack of any similar such concentration in the federal courts as a set. At the extreme, one finds that 98 percent of the sampled cases in the Pennsylvania state courts involved tort issues compared with only 16 percent of the cases in the Wisconsin federal court. It is interesting to note, however, that the Pennsylvania federal court was also dominated by cases involving tort issues (77 percent). The modal category of cases in the federal courts varies from district to district: it is torts for Pennsylvania and South Carolina, and contracts/commercial for Wisconsin, California, and New Mexico. Four of the categories found in the federal court—business regulation, discrimination, government benefits, and government action—are virtually nonexistent in most of the state courts in the study; real property is an important category in state courts (except in Pennsylvania) but of much less importance for the caseload of the federal courts. None of these trends should be particularly surprising, because they tend to follow jurisdictional rules. What does stand out is the dominance of torts in the state courts and the greater diversity of issues in the federal courts.

One of the first questions that is likely to be asked about a case is, How much is at stake? This apparently simple question starts to become complicated as soon as one tries to define what one means by "stakes." When I use the term I do *not* mean the amount of damages requested by the lawyer at the time she[30] initiates the court action; that demand is usually the outside figure of what might be recovered, and may in fact bear little resemblance to the actual amount in controversy. Also, I do *not* mean the amount that is ultimately recovered by the plaintiff, because that figure may be substantially less than what the case is worth (at the extreme, the case may ultimately go to a jury that finds for the defendant, awarding nothing to the plaintiff). I do *not* mean

Table 1.2. Percentage Distribution of Kinds of Cases (Areas of Law) in Federal and State Courts, by Judicial District

Area of Law	Federal Courts					State Courts				
	Eastern Wis.	Eastern Penn.	South Car.	New Mex.	Central Calif.	Eastern Wis.	Eastern Penn.	South Car.	New Mex.	Central Calif.
Torts	16	77	55	40	35	70	98	70	45	95
Contracts/ commerical	50	32	46	49	39	40	26	20	55	29
Real property	13	5	8	8	3	24	5	23	12	12
Business regulation	34	17	6	12	29	1	<1	5	12	2
Civil Rights/ discrimination	16	9	10	19	22	<1	0	1	<1	<1
Government actions	13	4	3	9	8	1	0	3	<1	2
Government benefits	13	5	10	12	10	0	0	<1	0	0
Other	5	0	1	7	3	<1	<1	2	1	2
Number of cases	177	151	155	172	155	149	147	140	157	128
Number of issues	277	225	216	266	229	207	192	175	182	183

Note: Any case may be coded to as many as four areas of law.

demands or offers that might be mentioned in the course of negotiation, because such offers and demands may simply reflect negotiating strategy or tactics. I define "stakes" in terms of what an interviewed lawyer felt her client should have been willing *to accept or give to settle a case*. For example, a person who has been injured in an auto accident might file a lawsuit demanding $10,000 in damages. His or her lawyer might believe that, based on prior cases, the injured party has a moderate to good chance of winning a jury verdict in the amount of $5,000. However, the lawyer might advise the client to accept a settlement of $2,000 for the following reasons: the settlement can be obtained immediately, and it would take two or more years to get the case to trial; and/or a jury might return a much smaller verdict or even a verdict in favor of the defendant, and it is better to have the certainty of the $2,000 settlement than risk obtaining much less or nothing at all. As I have defined "stakes," the stakes in this example are $2,000, because that is what the lawyer believed the client should accept to settle the case.[31]

Using this conception of stakes, lawyers involved in the individual cases were asked to respond to the following:

Now I'd like to ask some questions about what you thought your client(s) should take or do to settle the case. In these questions we are interested in your view of the stakes

Table 1.3. Percentage Distribution of Lawyers' Perceptions of Stakes

Amount at Stake ($)	State Cases	Federal Cases	All Cases
0–5,000	55	26	40
5,001–10,000	18	15	16
10,001–25,000	16	23	20
25,001–50,000	7	17	12
50,001 and up	4	19	12
N	411	448	859
Median $ amount	4,500	15,000	

in the case, not in actual negotiations, which we will get to in a few minutes. Did you ever form an opinion about what the case was worth in terms of what your client(s) would be willing to take or do to settle the case?

If the response to this was yes, the lawyer was then asked:

Based on that opinion, what did you think at the time should have been done to settle the problem?

Those lawyers whose responses involved something other than or in addition to money were then asked:

Suppose there could have been a settlement at that time which involved only a lump sum payment of money. What would you think it should have been?

Of the 1,382 lawyers interviewed, 859 were able to describe the stakes entirely in monetary terms; of the remaining 523 respondents, 331 said that they had never formed an opinion about what the case was worth, and 192 had an opinion but it involved a significant nonmonetary component which could not be translated into monetary terms.[32]

Table 1.3 provides a summary of the stakes involved in the cases in the sample, *as described by the lawyers.* The largest value for stakes reported by the lawyers was $2.5 million, which is quite consistent with the popular image of the dockets of our courts being dominated by big cases.[33] However, this amount was not only the largest but was also very atypical. Most state cases are quite small, involving less than $5,000; if the median is used as a measure of typicality (the median being the middle case when the cases are sorted from smallest to largest), the "typical" case in state court involves $4,500.[34] Very few cases in state court (4 percent) exceed the "moderate" level of $50,000. In federal court the cases are larger, as one would expect given the jurisdictional minimums in those courts: the median case involves $15,000, and 19 percent of the caseload involves more than $50,000.[35] If one is interested in the characteristics of most cases in American courts, the state figures are quite representative,[36] because over 95 percent of the civil cases (of the type I am interested in) filed in the United States are litigated in the state courts;[37] the "All Cases" column in Table 1.3 is included primarily to give an overall picture of the data I will be using as the discussion proceeds.[38]

What about cases where the lawyers were not able to monetize the stakes, or where they were unable to describe what their clients were willing to take or do to settle the cases? What were those cases about? For the "nonmonetized" cases, I looked at the lawyers descriptions of the nonmonetary elements, and, where the lawyers had no opinion regarding what to take or do to settle, I looked at their responses to the question "What was at stake from the viewpoint of your client?" Table 1.4 summarizes information regarding both what was at stake for those who had not formed an opinion about settlement and the nonmonetary elements for those who had formed an opinion. As is evident from the table, money was at stake in most of the cases where the lawyers had not formed an idea of exactly what their clients should take or do to settle the cases. The first three categories in both columns relate directly to money and constitute 69 percent of the responses. Even the ostensibly nonmonetary stakes tended to involve money (if one assumes that cases where the lawyer described the stakes as "dismissal of the case" or "dismissal of my client from the case" were primarily about money); 47 percent (204 of 437) of the responses fell into the first three categories. Thus, although lawsuits can raise questions that are not easily expressed in dollars and cents, the vast majority of lawsuits are about money, but not about large sums of money.

Lawyers see most cases in terms of money, but this does not necessarily mean that all the cases which lawyers described in monetary terms started out on those terms. A potential litigant who comes to a lawyer may not describe what he or she wants in monetary terms. Interestingly though, looking at litigants' responses to a stakes question similar to what was asked of lawyers, one finds these responses also tend to be of a nature that is overwhelmingly monetary. For individual respondents who were plaintiffs, 55 percent (N = 172) initially described the stakes in terms of specific monetary amounts, and an additional 14 percent did so in response to a follow-up probe that asked what they would take if only money were involved. Furthermore, another 9 percent mentioned only nonspecific sums of money in their open-ended responses, and many of the others made reference to things like repairs, completion of unfinished work, and other services or actions which could reasonably be converted to sums of money. A conservative estimate based on these data would be that 78 percent of indi-

Table 1.4. Frequency Distribution of Lawyers' Responses Regarding What Was at Stake[a]

Stakes	Respondents Who Had Not Formed an Opinion about an Appropriate Settlement	Respondents Whose Desired Resolutions Involved Nonmonetary Components
Money[b]	233	62
Dismissal of case or client	33	121
Divorce:		
Support/property	6	21
Custody/visitation	5	17
Interpretation of law, contract, or insurance policy	21	4
Vindication	28	0
Obtainment of compromise or agreement	0	33
Cessation or prevention of action or practice	10	2
Continuation of action or practice	0	8
Obtainment of action (or permission for action)	16	48
Restoration of status quo ante[c]	10	26
Modification of action or practice	0	45
Forfeiture of property/reclamation of goods/enforcement of decision	0	20
Nothing/don't recall	19	15
Other	13	15

[a]This table is based on those cases in which stakes were not entirely monetized or the lawyer had no opinion regarding what should be done to settle the case.

[b]This category includes responses like "denial of liability" or "payment of as little as possible," which were given to the stakes questions in the interviews.

[c]For example, reinstatement of job.

vidual plaintiffs wanted to be paid sums of money by the defendants. An equivalent analysis for individuals who were defendants (N = 45) produced similar results: 71 percent were willing to settle by paying sums of money to the opposing parties. Organizations were even more likely to see the cases in monetary terms: almost 90 percent of organizational defendants (N = 142) were willing to pay sums of money to resolve the cases, and 81 percent of organizational plaintiffs (N = 90) were seeking the payments of sums of money. Most organizational representatives' responses that were open ended and not explicitly monetized dealt with money-related issues like patent or trademark infringement, franchising, or fulfillment of the terms of a contract.

Regardless of how stakes are initially framed by a potential litigant, both the lawyers and the litigants come to see most cases in monetary terms. As I will discuss in chapter 5, this probably has something to do with the need of many lawyers to monetize stakes in order to facilitate the calculation of a percentage-based contingent fee. Lawyers may also seek to monetize stakes because they perceive that the litigation process is most successful in delivering remedies that are expressed in terms of sums of money. Of course not *all* cases are monetized, and for many more a creative litigator could devise solutions that involve nonmonetary components (or, in some cases, that involve no exchange of money). However, the current reality is that the bulk of ordinary litigation, with a couple specific exceptions (e.g., divorce cases involving children, prisoner petitions), is explicitly framed around a monetary payment or can readily be expressed in those terms.

Some analyses of dispute processing (e.g., Merry and Silbey, 1984; Merry, 1990; Conley and O'Barr, 1988; Hoffer, 1989: 306) have suggested that it is often the case that disputants are seeking some nonmonetary result (i.e., an apology, an acknowledgement of responsibility, vindication of some sort, prevention of similar behavior in the future, etc.). My data provide no indication that a large fraction of the cases that compose ordinary civil litigation involve goals other than money.[39] It could well be that some of the cases in the sample were initially phrased in terms of nonmonetary goals,[40] but those goals were transformed (see Felstiner, Abel, and Sarat, 1980–81; Mather and Yngvesson, 1980–81; Menkel-Meadow, 1985a) by the litigants and/or their lawyers.[41] There is little evidence that such is the case for those disputes that become ordinary litigation. As Merry and Silbey pointed out (1984: 172), for their respondents, turning to the courts and police with problems was a last resort. They did so only if the problems were very serious, if doing so couldn't be avoided, or if they had tried everything else. For their respondents the perceived costs, stated in nonmonetary terms, were very high ("antagonizing the people they live with every day," "loss of control"). Given the kinds of cases Merry and Silbey examined (interpersonal, neighbor, and family disputes), this is to be expected. Moreover, those kinds of cases make up a very small fraction of the cases in courts of general jurisdiction. Whether it is because of the kinds of remedies offered by general jurisdiction courts or because disputants are unwilling to expend the private resources needed to pursue cases in civil courts, individuals with grievances that are not readily monetized seek resolutions outside the general civil justice system (perhaps by going to the police or initiating criminal proceedings).[42]

Given the monetary costs involved in the litigation process, few potential litigants, particularly individuals, are going to be willing to expend resources unless there is a potential for financial return.[43] Furthermore, the primary mechanism by which individuals obtain legal representation (outside of divorce) to file lawsuits—the contingent fee—virtually insures that the resulting cases will be resolved in monetary terms.[44] Thus, with the likely exception of divorce cases, concerns about the nonmonetary goals of litigants in ordinary civil cases are probably misplaced. Disputes involving nonmonetary issues are no doubt quite common and important (both to the individuals involved and to the larger community), but those disputes are handled through mechanisms other than the civil courts that process "ordinary civil litigation."

THE LAWYERS: TRAINING, EXPERIENCE, AND ATTITUDES

Since the focus in this book is on negotiations conducted by lawyers, it will be helpful to have a portrait of the lawyers who are litigating the kinds of ordinary cases described above. What kinds of training, experience, and expertise do they bring to their work? What are their attitudes toward their work? There are many dimensions along which one could describe any occupational group; I have selected two general dimensions to use in briefly describing the lawyers handling ordinary litigation: background (including training, experience, and expertise) and attitudes toward law practice.[45]

Virtually all the lawyers in the sample were graduates of law schools. Only four lawyers reported that they had not completed law school. A total of 127 law schools were attended by these lawyers. I have divided the schools into five groups:[46] "elite" law schools (Harvard, Yale, Chicago, University of Michigan, Columbia, and Stanford), "prestige" law schools (University of Pennsylvania, University of Virginia, University of California at Berkeley, UCLA, University of Texas, Northwestern, Cornell, Duke, and New York University), other state-supported law schools (typically affiliated with major state universities), other private nonproprietary law schools (typically affiliated with private universities), and a residual category of "other" law schools, including proprietary (for profit) law schools, foreign law schools, and schools no longer in existence. Not surprisingly, the largest group of lawyers (48 percent) attended state-supported law schools outside the elite and prestige groups; the second largest group (30 percent) attended private law schools outside the elite and prestige groups; only about a fifth of the lawyers graduated from one of the law schools in the upper echelons (8 percent from elite schools and 13 percent from prestige schools). Only a little over 1 percent of the lawyers in this sample reported having attended a law school in the residual category (proprietary, foreign, or now-defunct schools).[47]

How did these lawyers do in law school? Let me look at two indicators of performance: self-reported rank in class, and membership on the law review. By their own reports, these litigators were, as a group, better-than-average law students. Almost three-quarters (74 percent) of them claimed ranks in the top half of their law school classes, 35 percent reported being in the top quarter, and 16 percent in the upper decile. This high level of performance appears to be borne out by the relatively frequent reports of participation on the law review (26 percent, over half holding positions as officers).[48]

How much experience did this group of lawyers bring to their work? Experience can be judged in at least two different ways: how long a lawyer has been practicing law and how many "similar" cases a lawyer has handled. As is well known, there was, starting in the early 1970s, a major influx of persons into law school and then into careers as lawyers. This influx is clearly reflected in the group of lawyers handling ordinary litigation: in this sample over a third (34 percent) of the lawyers had been in practice for 5 years or less; the remaining lawyers were fairly evenly divided (20–24 percent) among those who had been practicing 6–10 years, 11–20, and more than 20.[49] What about experience with actual cases? The lawyers were asked to identify the fields of law into which the cases they were working on fell. Each was then asked how many cases in that field he or she had handled prior to taking on the sampled case. Most of the lawyers indicated that they had previously handled many cases in the same substantive areas. Only about 25 percent had handled 25 or fewer cases in the given area; more than half (54 percent) had handled over 100 "similar" cases. As with years of experience, one finds that most of the lawyers had extensive specific substantive experience, though there was clearly a group with less such experience.[50]

Experience is a fairly objective concept; expertise, on the other hand, is more subjective. Each lawyer was asked for an assessment of his or her expertise in the legal field in which the sampled case fell. Most of the lawyers viewed themselves as being an "expert" (42 percent) or "somewhat of an expert" (41 percent) in the fields named; very few (17 percent) described themselves as "not an expert." These figures are consistent with the lawyers' reports of the significant amounts of activity, outside of handling cases for individual clients, in the substantive fields of the sampled cases. Each lawyer was asked whether, since being admitted to the bar, he or she had taken or taught courses or workshops in the field, written articles or books about it, or served on any bar association or government committees that dealt with the field. Five specific activities were asked about, and only 16 percent of the respondents reported no outside activities. More than half (54 percent) had

Table 1.5. Percentage Distribution of Lawyers' Attitudes toward Their Work[a]

Aspect	Very Important	Somewhat Important	Not Important	N
Intellectual challenge	63	35	2	1,361
Winning	67	31	2	1,360
Serving the community and public	39	51	10	1,360
Making a decent living	64	35	1	1,360
Helping individual people with problems	66	31	3	1,358
Being your own boss	75	22	3	1,359
Having a high standing in the community	42	42	16	1,357
Having the respect of family and friends	64	30	6	1,358
Working with pleasant and interesting people	57	38	5	1,356
Making a lot of money	16	62	22	1,356
Having comfortable work surroundings	46	50	4	1,361

[a]The wording of the question was, "Overall, in looking at your legal work, how important is each of the following considerations for you?"

been involved in two or more of the activities.[51] Thus, the general picture of training and experience that one sees in the figures presented above is that of a group of lawyers with solid legal training from well-regarded law schools and a substantial expertise in the legal fields that constitute ordinary litigation.

The type of practice these lawyers engaged in tended to be litigation oriented. About two-thirds of the lawyers spent more than half their time working on court cases, and 45 percent reported spending more than three-quarters of their time on such cases. Although court cases dominated the activities of these lawyers, the actual trying of cases tended to consume a small portion of their time. Only 3 percent of the lawyers reported spending as much as half their time actually trying cases, and 81 percent spent less than a quarter of their time on this activity. However, even though many (if not most) of the lawyers could be fairly characterized as litigation specialists, there was not an overwhelming trend for the lawyers to specialize in one substantive area of the law for their litigation work, even though they tended to have a lot of experience with cases in the substantive area of the sampled case that each reported. When asked to estimate the percentage of their cases that were in the same substantive area as the case in the sample, 39 percent of the lawyers reported that over half their caseload was in that area compared with 38 percent who indicated that less than a quarter of their cases fell into that area.

What kinds of attitudes toward their work do lawyers bring to ordinary litigation? Lawyers rated the importance of 11 considerations related to why

Table 1.6. Percentage Distribution and Intensity Ratings[a] of What Litigators Reported to Like and Dislike about Their Work

Aspect	Most Liked (%)	Intensity[a]	Least Liked (%)	Intensity[a]
Negotiating	25	2.0	33	1.6
Planning and research	18	1.9	47	1.7
Arguing and trying	53	2.3	16	1.7
Combination[b]	4	c	4	c
	100		100	
N	1,290		1,236	

[a]The computation of the intensity scale is based on a follow-up question that asked whether the preference was "very strong," "strong," or "slight." The intensity columns are the average of these responses, with very strong coded as 3, strong coded as 2, and slight coded as 1.

[b]Two or more aspects.

[c]Intensity ratings were not obtained when the responses included a combination of aspects.

they were pursuing their legal practice. The 11 "goals," as they might be described, included such things as making money, having an enjoyable and challenging work situation, and providing service to people and the community.[52] The lawyers described each of the 11 goals as "very important," "somewhat important," or "not important." The responses are summarized in Table 1.5. As the table shows, very few of the goals received more than a handful of "not important" ratings. Almost a quarter of the respondents (22 percent) said that "making a lot of money" was not important; the only other goals to be rated as unimportant by 10 percent or more of the respondents were the two that referred to the community: "serving the community and public" and "having a high standing in the community." The most highly rated goal, with 75 percent of the lawyers describing it as very important, was "being your own boss." Five of the other goals were rated as very important by about two-thirds of the lawyers, with two other goals, both having to do with the specifics of the work situation (physical surroundings and co-workers), being somewhat less important to the respondents.[53]

Given the description of their goals, what aspects of their litigation work do lawyers particularly like or dislike? Lawyers were asked which of the following they most liked and which they most disliked: negotiating, planning and research, and arguing and trying. Each respondent also indicated how intense those likes and dislikes were ("very strong," "strong," or "slight"). Responses to the likes and dislikes are summarized in Table 1.6. As

Table 1.7. Percentage Distribution of Lawyers' Responses Regarding the Traits that Make a Good Litigator[a]

Trait	Very Important	Somewhat Important	Not Important	N
Being firm	66	30	4	1,342
Being fair	75	19	6	1,345
Being thorough	91	8	1	1,350
Being consistent	61	30	9	1,325
Being willing to compromise in order to resolve a problem	43	46	11	1,342

[a]The wording of the question was, "To be a successful litigator, how important do you think it is to have a reputation for each of the following?"

one can see in the table, by far the largest group of lawyers (over half, 53 percent) like arguing and trying cases the best, with negotiating coming in a poor second. Planning and research was both least often the most liked and most often the least liked.[54] It is also noteworthy that the preference of those who most liked arguing and trying was more intense (typically somewhere between "strong" and "very strong") than was the preference of those who first preferred either negotiating or planning and research.

Finally, what do the lawyers believe it takes to be a successful litigator? Lawyers rated five traits (being firm, being fair, being thorough, being willing to compromise in order to resolve a problem, and being consistent) as "very important," "somewhat important," or "not important" (Table 1.7). Thoroughness clearly stood out in the eyes of these litigators, with 91 percent of them rating that trait as very important.[55] At the other end of the ordering of importance was the willingness to compromise, with only 43 percent rating it "very important" and another 46 percent rating it "somewhat important." There was strong agreement that the remaining three traits—firmness, fairness, and consistency—were very important, but the views regarding these traits did not approach the near unanimity found for thoroughness.[56]

SUMMARY

This picture of ordinary litigation and the lawyers who handle it can best be described as showing relatively modest endeavors undertaken by experienced practitioners. The cases involve moderate sums of money and fairly routine kinds of issues. The lawyers have seen many similar cases in the past and will probably see many similar cases in the future. These are the cases that make up the bread-and-butter work of the lawyers who handle the vast bulk of the cases in America's civil courts. These are the lawyers who form the core of the local legal communities who service individuals, small businesses, and the companies that insure individuals and small businesses. What is the nature of the bargaining and settlement process carried out by these lawyers in these cases? That is the question addressed in the next chapter.

CHAPTER 2

A Portrait of Negotiation and Bargaining in Ordinary Litigation

Introduction

The anecdotal examples presented in chapter 1 represent contrasting images of negotiation in civil litigation. On the one hand, the example of the Agent Orange litigation showed a complex, richly textured process involving substantial give and take in the context of extended contact. On the other hand, the story of Michael's wrist portrayed a cut-and-dried affair involving the establishment of an initial position followed by a quick "compromise" resolution. In this chapter, I turn to the extensive body of data described in the last half of the previous chapter to provide a more systematic description of the negotiation process and content in ordinary litigation.

In the discussion that follows, I will concentrate on two key descriptive dimensions of the bargaining/negotiation process. The first of these is the quantity—or, as I will term it, the *intensity*—of activity involved in the process. The analysis will show that bargaining and negotiation in ordinary litigation is a low-intensity activity. The second descriptive dimension will be the *content* of the offers and demands. This analysis will show that the negotiations that take place in ordinary litigation are overwhelmingly about money,[1] and that the amount of actual movement in the negotiation process is small, in both relative and absolute terms. Overall, the discussion will show that the negotiation process in ordinary litigation is consistent with the image of modesty presented in the description of the cases in chapter 1. In the last section of the chapter, I will briefly consider what differences the various dimensions of the negotiation process make for the outcome of the litigation.

Intensity in the Bargaining/Negotiation Process

I begin with what might be described as the most basic question: How much negotiation/bargaining is there in the typical case? As I said above, I will refer to this "how much" question as intensity. For purposes of discussion, let me distinguish between two different kinds of negotiation/bargaining intensity. The first of these I label *contact* intensity; this refers to the amount of time, both in relative and absolute terms, spent on settlement discussions. The second I label *exchange* intensity; this refers to the number of exchanges of demands and offers that take place.

Each of the lawyers interviewed was asked about the negotiations that took place in his or her sampled case. Specifically, the interviewers asked the lawyers to describe up to three exchanges of offers and counteroffers (the first, the last, and the "most important" intermediate). The specific questions used were patterned on the following language:

> Now I'd like to ask about any negotiations attempting to settle the case which you may have had on behalf of your client(s). At any point did you negotiate with the opposing party(s) or his/her/their lawyer?

Respondents answering yes, were then asked:

> Can you briefly describe what happened the first time you discussed what would be necessary in order to settle the case? What did you ask them to do and/or what did you offer to do to settle the problem?

The lawyers were also asked:

> During your first discussion with the opposing party, did he/she/they make a settlement offer or demand?

Respondents answering yes to this latter question were asked:

> What did they offer to do or ask your client to do to settle the problem?

In addition each lawyer was asked how much of his or her time on the case was spent on "discussions aimed at settlement." The responses to these questions form the basis of the tables I present below.

CONTACT INTENSITY

Let us first consider what I have labeled contact intensity—the time lawyers spend on discussions aimed at settlement. Table 2.1 shows the overall breakdowns and the summary statistics for the number of hours and the percentage of their time that the sample lawyers spent on these discussions. In looking at these figures, one should keep in mind that in the median case in the CLRP sample the lawyer put in only 30.4 hours (Trubek, Sarat, et al., 1983: 90), and that the activity which takes, on average, the highest percentage of the lawyer's time (discovery) had a mean percentage of only 16.7 (ibid.: 91). In the median case, the lawyer reported spending 10 per-

Table 2.1. Contact Intensity: Percentage Distributions of Lawyers'
Responses Regarding the Number of Hours and Percentage of
Time Spent on Settlement Discussions

Hours on Settlement	Percent of Cases	Percent of Time on Settlement	Percent of Cases
0	17.7	0	17.0
>0–1.5	18.4	1–5	23.3
>1.5–3.5	23.9	6–10	20.0
>3.5–5.5	13.2	11–20	19.6
>5.5–19.5	20.0	21–30	9.8
>19.5 or more	6.6	31 or more	10.3
N	1,253		1,308

cent,[2] or three hours, on settlement discussions. Only a fifth of the respondents reported that more than 20 percent of their time had been spent
on settlement discussions; about three-quarters reported spending five hours
or less. Thus, it is clear that actual settlement discussions do not constitute a
dominant part of the activities of lawyers engaged in civil litigation, though
many of the other activities (e.g., conferring with the client, discovery, other
factual investigation), which together typically take almost half the lawyers'
time (ibid.), are often closely related to settlement discussions.[3]

    When one looks at the relationships between contact intensity and case
characteristics, there are some interesting patterns to be found. Table 2.2
shows the median number of hours and the mean percentage of time devoted
to settlement discussions for the summary eight areas of law discussed in
chapter 1: torts, contracts/commercial transactions, real property, business
regulation, civil rights/civil liberties/discrimination, domestic relations,

Table 2.2. Contact Intensity, by Area of Law

	Torts	Contract/ Commercial	Domestic Relations	Real Property	Business Regulation	Civil Rights/ Civil Liberties/ Discrimination	Government Action	Government Benefits
Median number of hours	2.7	2.7	3.0	2.9	3.0	3.0	3.0	0.0
N	528	435	40	99	154	88	32	38
Average percent of Time	13.2	15.2	18.7	14.6	17.0	9.1	4.2	1.9
N	562	446	41	102	160	91	33	38

government action/political process, and government benefits.[4] Most of the areas of law (torts, contracts, domestic relations, real property, and business regulation) have similar means and medians.[5] The area that stands out is the one that tends to pit individuals against government agencies: government benefits (and to a lesser degree government action); relatively little time is spent on negotiations when one of the litigants is a government actor.[6]

Using the CLRP data, there are several possible ways of assessing case size and complexity. The relationships (summarized in Table 2.3) between these variables and contact intensity are not surprising. For stakes,[7] there is a sharp increase in the median number of hours as the stakes increase, from 2 hours for cases involving less than $5,000 to 10.5 hours for cases involving more than $50,000. This is to be expected, because the overall amount of time goes up as the stakes go up (Trubek, Sarat, et al., 1983; Trubek,

Table 2.3. Contact Intensity, by Case Characteristics

	Stakes				
	$5,000 and Under	$5,001– $10,000	$10,001– $25,000	$25,001– $50,000	over $50,000
Mean percent of time	16.8	13.6	15.7	14.2	11.7
N	331	136	164	95	101
Median number of hours	2	3	4	5	10.5
N	319	133	156	90	90

	Subjective Complexity				
	Simple ———————————————————→ Very Complex				
	1	2	3	4	5
Mean percent of time	18.4	15.0	10.8	9.6	9.8
N	307	391	312	191	88
Median number of hours	2	2	3	4	6
N	298	364	306	182	85

	Docket Entries			
	Number of Entries			
	0–4	5–9	10–19	20 and More
Mean percent of time	23.6	18.4	12.6	9.4
N	107	283	428	490
Median number of hours	2.5	2	2	3
N	100	274	414	465

Grossman, et al., 1983; Kritzer, Sarat, et al., 1984; Kritzer et al., 1985). As for the percentage of time, the mean tends to decline slightly as the stakes go up.[8]

One measure of complexity is the lawyer's subjective judgment; each lawyer was asked to rate the case on a five-point scale from "simple" to "very complex."[9] When one looks at this subjective measure of complexity, one sees that, as complexity increases, the percentage of time decreases and the absolute amount of time increases.[10] An alternate measure of complexity can be obtained by looking at the level of court-oriented activity in a case: the more docket entries, the more complex the case. Although this measure is, by nature, crude (things other than complexity can influence the number of docket entries), it does provide a measure that is "objective." When this measure is used, the same pattern described for the subjective complexity measure holds: the absolute amount of time increases but the proportion of effort decreases as the number of docket entries goes up.[11] In summary, what one finds is that, for bigger, more complex cases, lawyers spend a smaller percentage of their time but more actual hours on settlement discussions.

What about lawyer characteristics? Can one find any relationship between contact intensity and variables like lawyer attitudes or lawyer experience? I looked at one of the attitudes described in the previous chapter—what the lawyers like and/or dislike about their litigation-related work[12]—and an indicator of the lawyers' risk preferences, which I measured by an index that combined the responses to four questions concerning the lawyers' willingness to undertake risky activities.[13] There was only one detectable relationship between contact intensity and these two lawyer attitudes: those lawyers who like negotiation spend a greater proportion of their time doing it. Of lawyers whose favorite activity was negotiation, 30.8 percent reported spending more than 20 percent of the case time on settlement negotiations compared with only 12.5 percent of those who least liked negotiation. Those who neither most nor least liked negotiation fell in between, with 20.5 percent reporting that they spent more than a fifth of their time on settlement discussions. It is interesting to note that, although one can find a relationship between attitudes toward the tasks involved in litigation and proportion of time spent on them, one finds no relationship between attitudes and the number of actual hours. Also, I had tentatively hypothesized that lawyers with negative attitudes toward risk would make an effort to avoid trial by more intensive efforts at reaching a settlement, but there was no evidence to support that hypothesis.

I looked at a variety of other lawyer characteristics (specialization, expe-

Table 2.4. Contact Intensity, by Federal Judicial District

	All Cases		Federal Cases		State Cases	
	Mean Percent	Median Hours	Mean Percent	Median Hours	Mean Percent	Median Hours
Eastern Wisconsin	13.0	3	10.3	3	15.6	3
N	272	261	130	125	142	136
Eastern Pennsylvania	13.9	2	12.8	3	14.9	1
N	278	257	144	129	134	128
South Carolina	10.7	2	10.2	2.5	11.7	2
N	259	250	160	154	99	96
New Mexico	11.5	2	10.5	3	13.7	2
N	242	236	163	161	79	75
Central California	18.6	3	16.5	4	21.0	3
N	257	244	165	131	118	113

rience, type practice), but only one relationship between those characteristics and contact intensity was evident. This relationship follows directly from the complexity-size relationships reported previously: lawyers in large firms (which are likely to be involved in the bigger, more complex cases) tend to spend more hours on settlement discussions.

To what degree does the percentage of time or number of hours devoted to settlement discussion vary with location? Is contact intensity affected by "local legal culture"—the local norms governing the actions of the key actors in the court system (Church et al., 1978; 53–62; Church, 1982, 1985; Sherwood and Clarke, 1981)? Table 2.4 shows the mean percentage of time and the median number of hours lawyers in each of the five federal judicial districts reported. On the percentage measure, the Central California District stands out as almost five percentage points higher than any of the other districts; Eastern Wisconsin and Eastern Pennsylvania have somewhat higher percentages than South Carolina or New Mexico.[14] The further breakdown by federal and state courts shows that California stands out from the other districts for cases in both types of courts, with no clear discernible pattern among the other districts.[15] The distinctiveness of California in the percentage of time devoted to negotiation stands up when separate comparisons (which are not shown) are done for torts, contracts, and cases that involve neither tort nor contract issues. In only one comparison does a single other district even approach the percentage reported by the California lawyers. The findings are much more ambiguous with regard to the median number of hours devoted to negotiation. Only in federal cases does Central

Table 2.5. Distribution of Offers and Demands in the First Round of Bargaining, by Plaintiffs and Defendants

Actions of Respondent	Number Who Made a Demand *and*:		Number Who Made No Demand *and*:	
	Made an Offer	Made No Offer	Made an Offer	Made No Offer
Plaintiff-Respondents				
Actions of Opposing Defendant				
Made a demand *and*:				
Made an offer	10	5	11	27
Made no offer	6	16	194	236
Made no demand *and*:				
Made an offer	1	8	3	8
Made no offer	0	0	5	154
Defendant-Respondents				
Actions of Opposing Plaintiff				
Made a demand *and*:				
Made an offer	9	18	1	13
Made no offer	0	33	3	38
Made no demand *and*:				
Made an offer	4	229	3	39
Made no offer	0	27	1	153

California evidence greater contact intensity than the other districts in terms of absolute hours, and statistical analyses cast doubt on whether this difference is significant.[16]

Why does California stand out from the others in its level of contact intensity? The state court in Los Angeles is well known as one in which there is an extreme backlog of cases awaiting trial (see Selvin and Ebener, 1984); one could speculate that the inability to obtain a trial in a reasonable period of time might account for the greater effort devoted to negotiations. Since the number of state cases far exceeds the number of federal cases, the pattern in the state courts might establish the norms vis-à-vis contact intensity in negotiation. These norms then become a part of the local legal culture of the regular players in the civil justice system.[17] This kind of pattern is consistent with prior work on the local legal culture, though the statistical analysis indicates that location accounts for only about 4 percent of the variation in contact intensity.[18]

EXCHANGE INTENSITY: DEMANDS AND OFFERS

Because the CLRP data contain a maximum of three exchanges of offers and counteroffers, one might question the usefulness of the data to examine the numbers of demands and offers. However, this limitation introduces minimal distortion: only 15 percent of the lawyers reported that their cases involved as many as three exchanges; the largest proportion of lawyers (41 percent) reported two exchanges of offers/counteroffers, 11 percent reported one exchange, and 23 percent reported no exchanges of settlement offers at all.[19] In fact, given the ambiguity as to what constitutes an "exchange," these figures probably *overstate* the exchange intensity of bargaining in ordinary litigation.

Each exchange in a prototypical case involving one plaintiff and one defendant can involve both an offer and a demand from each side; that is, the plaintiff can demand something from the defendant *and* offer something in return, and the defendant can offer something to the plaintiff *and* demand something in return. Table 2.5 shows the full configuration of offers and demands for the first exchange (which is also the last exchange if there is only one round of bargaining), controlling for whether the respondent was a plaintiff or a defendant. As the table shows, when the respondent was the defendant, most of the first exchanges involved both a plaintiff's demand and a defendant's offer.[20] However, when the respondent was a plaintiff, the first-round pattern is fairly evenly divided between those who reported that the other side did respond with an offer and those who reported no responding offer. This apparent asymmetry between plaintiffs and defendants probably reflects two primary factors. First, there may be some response bias, with a defendant being likely to associate his or her initial response with the plaintiff's first demand; second, and closely related, if the bargaining is conducted by correspondence, a defendant who responds immediately to the plaintiff's demand will see the demand and response as a unit, whereas the plaintiff may see them as being separate because of the time interval between sending the demand and receiving the response.[21] For purposes of counting exchanges as reported by plaintiffs, the latter situation shows up as two exchanges rather than one.

Table 2.6 shows the corresponding set of figures for the second round of bargaining. The asymmetry of the first round is missing here; most cases involved both a demand by the plaintiff and an offer by the defendant. In fact, for most cases the second round was the last round, and the offer and demand represented the settlement that the parties agreed to. Thus, the two most frequent patterns of bargaining are a demand and an immediate responding offer, followed by a settlement (probably representing a compromise of some sort), or a demand followed sometime later by an offer which is accepted as the settlement (the pattern represented in the case of Michael's wrist, described in chapter 1).

Table 2.6. Distribution of Offers and Demands in the Second Round of Bargaining, by Plaintiffs and Defendants

Actions of Respondent	Number Who Made a Demand *and*:		Number Who Made No Demand *and*:	
	Made an Offer	Made No Offer	Made an Offer	Made No Offer
Plaintiff-Respondents				
Actions of Opposing Defendant				
Made a demand *and*:				
Made an offer	9	0	54	4
Made no offer	2	2	279	26
Made no demand *and*:				
Made an offer	9	7	35	5
Made no offer	0	0	1	271
Defendant-Respondents				
Actions of Opposing Plaintiff				
Made a demand *and*:				
Made an offer	4	0	3	2
Made no offer	0	1	8	1
Made no demand *and*:				
Made an offer	44	233	44	20
Made no offer	0	0	0	250

How do the figures on the number of exchanges vary depending upon case characteristics? Table 2.7 shows cross-tabulations between the number of exchanges and area of law. The area that stands out as having the highest level of exchange intensity is torts (with both the lowest percentage of cases with no exchanges and the highest percentage with three or more). Government-benefits cases (e.g., social security, welfare benefits, etc.) clearly stand out as having the lowest level of exchange intensity, with almost three-quarters of the respondents reporting no exchanges at all. Civil rights/civil liberties/

Table 2.7. Percentage Distribution of Exchange Intensity, by Area of Law

Number of Exchanges	Torts	Contract/ Commercial	Domestic Relations	Real Property	Business Regulation	Civil Rights/ Civil Liberties/ Discrimination	Government Action	Government Benefits
0	18.4	27.3	25.0	25.5	25.6	33.7	34.4	74.4
1	10.0	10.8	30.6	17.6	12.8	18.6	25.0	17.9
2	45.0	49.4	38.9	47.1	51.9	37.2	34.4	7.7
≥ 3	26.6	12.5	5.6	9.8	9.6	10.5	6.3	0.0
N	522	417	36	102	156	86	32	39

discrimination and government actions/political process are lower in exchange intensity than other kinds of cases but not as low as government benefits. Lastly, domestic-relations cases stand out by having the highest percentage of cases with a single offer-counteroffer exchange. Even with these variations, the single most striking aspect of Table 2.7 is the low percentage of cases involving three or more exchanges, regardless of the area of law; one could not characterize any of the areas as involving a high level of exchange intensity: in the most intensive area, torts, only about a quarter of the cases involved as many as three exchanges.

There are some interesting connections between case characteristics that indicate size and/or complexity and the number of offers/demands. When exchange intensity is correlated with stakes there appears to be no relationship at all (Pearson's r = .02). This result masks an intriguing, albeit modest, relationship which can be seen in the top panel of Table 2.8: there is a slight curvilinear relationship, with larger-stakes cases having a higher likelihood of involving no exchanges, or one, or three or more, whereas smaller cases are more likely to involve two exchanges. With the subjective measure of complexity (i.e., the lawyer's subjective assessment), there is no apparent linear relationship between exchange intensity and subjective complexity (r = -.05). However, as with stakes, one can better see the nature of the relationship (again modest) in tabular form (middle panel of Table 2.8): the proportion of respondents reporting two exchanges declines as the complexity of the cases increases, from 54 percent for simple cases to 33 percent for very complex cases. The alternate measure of complexity, that which is based on the number of docket entries, shows the same pattern yet again: the linear relationship is weak, in fact it is inverse (r = -.090, p < .001), but the likelihood of two-exchange bargaining situations goes up as the number of events goes down (see the bottom panel of Table 2.8).

When I looked for relationships between exchange intensity and location, lawyer characteristics (experience, expertise, specialization, and nature of law practice), and lawyer attitudes, I found only one interesting linkage: as the lawyer's degree of specialization[22] decreased, the likelihood of there being no exchanges of demands and offers increased (from 16.5 percent for the most specialized lawyers to 31.6 percent for the least specialized group). This suggests that lawyers who are "unfamiliar with the territory" may be more reluctant to engage in bargaining, perhaps because of the fear that they will be bested by the opposition. Alternately, it may simply be that the nonspecialist lawyer does not have a feel for the "going rate" and consequently does not know what to ask for in negotiations.

Table 2.8. Percentage Distribution of Exchange Intensity, by Case Characteristics

| | Stakes | | | | | | |
Number of Exchanges	$5,000 or less	$5,001– $10,000	$10,001– $25,000	$25,001– $50,000	Over $50,000	$25,000 or less	Over $25,000
0	13.6	9.0	14.6	16.7	18.5	12.9	17.6
1	12.1	16.4	10.2	16.7	12.0	12.5	14.3
2	53.9	51.2	53.5	36.7	37.0	53.3	36.8
≥ 3	20.4	23.1	21.7	30.0	32.6	21.3	31.3
N	323	134	157	90	92	614	182

$\chi^2 = 21.84$ $\chi^2 = 16.16$
$p = .04$ $p = .001$

| | Subjective Complexity | | | | |
| Number of Exchanges | Simple ⎯⎯⎯⎯⎯⎯⎯⎯⎯⎯⎯⎯⎯→ Very Complex | | | | |
	1	2	3	4	5
0	24.1	20.7	27.7	27.0	27.6
1	10.3	11.4	11.7	15.1	20.7
2	53.5	45.7	45.0	40.5	33.3
≥ 3	12.1	22.3	15.7	17.3	18.4
N	318	409	331	204	93

$\chi^2 = 29.74$
$p = .003$

| | Docket Entries | | | |
| | Number of Entries | | | |
Number of Exchanges	Fewer than 5	5–9	10–19	More than 20
0	16.2	20.5	27.5	28.0
1	7.1	7.7	12.0	16.7
2	55.6	52.0	43.9	40.6
≥ 3	21.2	19.8	16.7	14.8
N	99	273	408	461

$\chi^2 = 33.03$
$p < .001$

SUMMARY

The thrust of the data presented above is clear. The level of intensity in bargaining in everyday civil cases is modest: Most cases require few exchanges of offers to arrive at a settlement, and most cases require a relatively modest amount of lawyer time devoted specifically to settlement discussions. There are some interesting variations in contact intensity depending upon location and in both contact and exchange intensity depending upon case type, size, and complexity, but the basic finding of there being modest to low intensity holds up even when controls for these kinds of variables are included. There is no evidence that lawyer attitudes or characteristics exert a major influence on either of the types of intensity examined in the precedingpages.

The Content of Negotiations

The second dimension of litigation, the content dimension, concerns the substance of the offers and counteroffers that are advanced during the negotiation sessions.[23] There are at least three issues that can be examined as part of the content dimension. First, what is actually offered or demanded? Is it money, something other than money (if so, what?), or some combination of the two? Second, to what degree are opening offers and demands tactical in nature (i.e., what is the relationship of the offers and demands to the actors' perceptions of what they are actually trying to get; do negotiators tend to ask for twice as much or offer half as much, or is there no apparent "formula" governing selection of starting positions)? Third, how do offers and counteroffers change over the course of negotiations; that is, comparing the first and last exchanges, are there any clear patterns? For all three of these content-related questions (the nature of the exchanges, the relationship of the initial offer/demand to stakes, and the change in offers/demands), are the variations related to case characteristics or to negotiator characteristics? These are the questions that I turn to in this section.

CONTENT OF DEMANDS AND OFFERS

For purposes of the initial examination of the substance of the demands and offers, I have categorized the contents of the bargaining exchanges as monetary, nonmonetary, and mixed. In creating this trichotomy, I looked at all the offers/demands reported by the lawyer. If only specific monetary amounts were indicated across all offers and demands, the trichotomy was coded as "monetary"; if only nonmonetary actions were indicated, the trichotomy was coded as "nonmonetary"; and if both were indicated, the trichotomy was coded as "mixed."

In looking at these overall figures, it is important to keep in mind the absence of offers and/or demands. Consequently, Table 2.9 shows the trichotomy I defined above, plus the number of respondents who reported that there were no demands or offers. As the table shows, about a quarter of the respondents indicated that there were no demands/offers exchanged. When

Table 2.9. Percentage Distribution of Types of Offers and
Demands

Type of Offer/Demand	All Cases	Only Cases with Offers and Demands
No exchanges	28	
Monetary only	52	72
Nonmonetary only	7	9
Mixed	13	18
N	1,228	885

Note: Columns may not add to 100 percent because of
rounding.

I exclude that set of respondents, there are 885 lawyers who reported the
content of the offers and demands in their cases; of that group, 72 percent
reported that the offers/demands concerned only money, 9 percent that the
offers/demands were nonmonetary, and 18 percent that there was a mixture
of money and other things included. Thus, money is clearly the dominant
feature of the offers/demands exchanged in this sample of civil cases, though
it is certainly not the only item of concern. Let me now turn to variations in
the nature of the offers and demands.

The first variable that one would identify as being likely to relate to the
content of offers and demands is the area of law that the case concerns. It
should not be surprising that the content of negotiation is closely related to
the area of law. Table 2.10 shows that tort cases stand out as having negotiations most dominated by money; together the monetary and mixed categories constitute virtually all the cases described by the lawyers.[24] The offers
and demands in contract/commercial cases are slightly less monetary in
nature, but money is still the dominant feature (only about 5 percent of the
respondents reported no monetary component to the offers and demands).
At the other extreme are domestic relations, business regulation, and government action cases; for these types of cases, many more cases are nonmonetary: 26–36 percent compared with 2 percent and 6 percent for torts and
contract/commercial, respectively. Falling in between are property cases and
civil rights cases, in which around 80–90 percent of the cases involve a
monetary component in the offers and demands.

Given the dominance of monetary concerns reflected in the participants'
descriptions of the stakes in these cases, the dominance of money in negotiations should not be surprising. One possible exception is the heavy monetary component in negotiations in civil rights/discrimination cases.[25] There
are a number of possible explanations for the monetary concern in civil

Table 2.10. Percentage Distribution of Negotiation Contents, by Area of Law

Area of Law	Monetary	Nonmonetary	Mixed	N
Torts	87	2	11	405
Contract/commercial	75	6	19	295
Domestic relations	22	26	52	27
Real property	60	16	24	75
Business regulation	39	36	26	106
Civil rights/discrimination	58	21	21	53
Government action	48	38	14	21
Government benefits	(2)	(6)	(1)	9

Note: Percentages are not computed when N is less than 10; figures shown in parentheses are actual frequencies. A respondent is counted in more than one row if the case involved two or more different areas of law.

rights/discrimination cases. First, it may be that *by the time a lawsuit is filed*, it is frequently too late for the parties to resolve the underlying problem, and the only workable remedy is to compensate the plaintiff for the "injury" that was experienced and for the two parties to go their separate ways. Alternately, it might be that potential discrimination plaintiffs must have a monetizable claim in order to get representation, which is often paid for on a contingent-fee basis. Lastly, the legal remedies available may be structured in a way that forces the parties to think in terms of money rather than alternative kinds of resolutions. Although all three explanations probably have some merit, I lean more toward the first two. Particularly in discrimination cases, there are nonmonetary remedies available, but I suspect that neither plaintiffs' lawyers nor defendant litigants really want those remedies—the former because they need a monetary resolution in order to collect a fee, the latter because they do not want to have an ongoing relationship with someone who has forced them into court.[26]

Is the content of the offers/demands related to the other two major case characteristics—stakes and complexity? The only relationship that appeared between stakes and the content of offers/demands was the natural consequence that lawyers who were not able to express the stakes in unambiguous monetary terms were more likely to report that the offers/demands had nonmonetary components (55 percent) than were those lawyers who were able to provide an estimate of stakes in monetary terms (19 percent). Of those lawyers who were able to express stakes in unambiguous monetary terms, only 2 percent indicated that the offers/demands lacked clear monetary components. The magnitude of the monetary stakes had no impact on the nature of the offers/demands (though the magnitude of the stakes was strongly correlated with the magnitude of the offers/demands).

Table 2.11. Percentage Distribution of Negotiation Contents,
by Case Complexity

Complexity	Monetary and Mixed	Nonmonetary	N
Simple 1	94	6	211
2	90	10	279
3	92	8	208
4	86	14	121
Complex 5	84	16	61
$\chi^2 = 9.88$			
$p = .04$			

The relationship between complexity (measured using the lawyer's subjective evaluation) and offers/demands is shown in Table 2.11. As the table indicates, there is a clear, steady shift toward nonmonetary offers and demands as the complexity of the cases increases, going from 6 percent for the simplest cases to 16 percent for the most complex. Again, this is not particularly surprising, because in more complex cases there *may* be greater possibilities for "creative" solutions. If the case is cut and dried, the solutions are likely to be cut and dried, and the most cut-and-dried solution involves the simple exchange of money.[27] Even if a small case is not straightforward, the economics of working on a contingent-fee basis encourage lawyers to seek quick resolutions in modest cases, and the quickest resolutions are likely to involve payments of sums of money.

There are some interesting relationships between lawyer characteristics and the monetary/nonmonetary content of the offers and demands.[28] There is a clear and consistent relationship between specialization/experience and the likelihood that the negotiations will focus on money. The top panel of Table 2.12 shows that the more specialized the lawyer,[29] the more likely the offers/demands are to be monetary in nature. Similarly the bottom panel of Table 2.12 shows that the lawyers who devote the most time to litigation are the ones most likely to report that the offers and demands exchanged in negotiations are entirely monetary in nature. These findings run somewhat counter to what one might expect to find: that the more specialized and experienced lawyers would be the most able to come up with creative resolutions. What is unclear from this analysis is the degree to which this "experience" effect is indicative of the kinds of cases the most experienced, more specialized lawyers take, and to what degree it might reflect a "routinization" that comes with experience. That is, lawyers who have handled many cases of a particular type are able to see more easily the kind of monetary

Table 2.12. Percentage Distribution of Negotiation Contents,
by Lawyer Experience and Specialization

	Degree of Specialization			
	Monetary	Nonmonetary	Mixed	N
Low 1	61	20	19	125
2	70	81	22	269
3	74	9	17	339
High 4	80	50	15	210

$\chi^2 = 25.09$
$p < .001$

	Percent of Concentration on Litigation		
	Monetary	Nonmonetary and Mixed	N
0–25%	65	35	102
26–50%	69	31	189
51–75%	72	28	213
76–90%	73	27	210
91–100%	78	22	171

$\chi^2 = 21.83$
$p < .001$

resolution that is likely to be arrived at, and thus avoid searching for non-monetary solutions.[30]

There is one final lawyer characteristic that is potentially important in accounting for the kinds of offers and demands that are made, and that is fee arrangement. Contingent-fee lawyers have a strong reason to concentrate on dollars and cents: it is difficult to take a percentage of something else (e.g., a third of a house, or a third of an apology, or a third of a job). Table 2.13 shows the kinds of offers and demands made by the respondents (i.e., it ignores the offers and/or demands of the opposing parties) broken down by fee arrangement: hourly, contingent, and other (flat, house counsel, legal aid, third-party payment, etc.). Seventy-seven percent of the contingent-fee lawyers reported that their demands (contingent-fee lawyers almost always represent plaintiffs, so there were very few offers) were entirely monetary; this compares with entirely monetary demands and/or offers by 51 percent of hourly fee lawyers and 44 percent of lawyers retained on some basis other than hourly or contingent fees. As one might expect, only 3 percent of the contingent-fee lawyers reported demands that were entirely nonmonetary; nonmonetary. Clearly, having a stake in the outcome has some impact on the nature of the outcome that is sought.[31]

Table 2.13. Percentage Distribution of Negotiation Contents, by Fee Arrangement

	Monetary	Nonmonetary	Mixed	N
Hourly	51	19	29	547
Contingent	77	3	20	349
Other	44	28	28	109

$\chi^2 = 90.55$
$p < .001$

What is the nature of the nonmonetary demands and offers that are made? Because a respondent could report more than one kind of nonmonetary demand and/or offer, the tabulations may count a single respondent more than one time. In coding the substance of the demands and offers that were made, approximately 100 categories were used; in tabulating those responses, an offer/demand was counted singly if the same kind of offer/demand was made more than once in a given case. In order to make the analysis more manageable, the original categories were combined to form 12 broader categories.

Table 2.14 shows the distribution of the nonmonetized demands and offers reported by the lawyers. As the table shows, many of the demands/offers related more to the processing of the case than to settling the case (one could argue that these types of demands/offers should simply be excluded). Perhaps what is most striking, in light of some of the discussions of what

Table 2.14. Percentage Distribution of Types of Nonmonetary Demands and Offers

Demand/Offer	Percent of All Demands/Offers[a]	Percent of Cases Involving Nonmonetary Demands/Offers[b]
Apologize	1	1
Acknowledge liability	2	3
Agree on meaning of law	1	2
Grant coverage or benefits	4	6
Employment related	7	9
Property related	13	16
Divorce related	11	14
Enforce, modify, or release from contract	10	13
Stop or modify	14	18
Agree to injunction	1	2
Do something specific	16	20
Process related	21	27

[a]Number of responses = 287
[b]Number of cases = 220

plaintiffs want (e.g., Merry and Silbey, 1984; Merry, 1990; Conley and O'Barr, 1988), is that very few lawyers reported offers or demands centered on simple acknowledgements of interpersonal obligations (e.g., apologies or acknowledgements of liability). This may mean any of several different things:

—The cases that get to court are not concerned with such things.
—It is not in the lawyer's interest to spend time negotiating on such things.
—Such matters are seen by the lawyers as so secondary that they were forgotten by the time the interviews were conducted.
—The lawyers "transform" cases that involve interpersonal grievances so that they can be dominated in dollars (see Felstiner, Abel, and Sarat, 1980–81; Mather and Yngvesson, 1980–81; Menkel-Meadow, 1985a).

When I looked at variations in the substance of the nonmonetary content by area of law, I found little that was surprising: divorce cases deal with divorce matters, property cases deal with property matters, contract/commercial cases deal with contract matters (or property matters, because many property matters are directly related to contract issues, e.g., contracts to sell, lease, build, etc.), civil rights/discrimination cases deal with employment issues (because most such cases arise out of employment discrimination), and business-regulation cases deal with stopping, starting, or modifying business activities of various sorts.[32]

FIRST-OFFER, FIRST-DEMAND TACTICS

In the practical literature on negotiations, much attention is devoted to first offers or demands; the first offer or demand is viewed as the key tactical decision in the overall bargaining strategy. Yet little is known about the nature of actual first offers or demands in relation to what is at stake. In this section, I will examine the connection between offers/demands and stakes, focusing only on the explicit monetary component of offers and demands (because there is no obvious way to compare nonmonetary offers/demands with stakes).

For purposes of this discussion, I constructed two ratios: highest demand (which is almost always the first, and frequently the only, demand) to stakes, and lowest offer to stakes. As before, stakes are operationalized as the respondent's evaluation of the appropriate resolution of the case from the client's viewpoint; where that evaluation changed during the case, the highest evaluation was used as the denominator of the ratio. Obviously, if stakes were not expressed in monetary terms, or if stakes were given as $0, the ratio could not be constructed and the respondent had to be excluded from the analysis discussed in this section.

Table 2.15. Percentage Distribution of Ratios of Offers and Demands to Stakes

Proportion of Stakes Offered	Percent of Offers Made	Percent of Demands Made	Proportion of Stakes Demanded
0–39%	20	15	<100%
40–69%	29	37	100%
70–99%	17	25	101–150%
100%	25	9	151–199%
>100%	10	14	>199%
N	247	374	

Table 2.15 summarizes the distribution of the two types of ratios I constructed. What is particularly striking is the relatively high percentage of respondents who bargained in a nontactical fashion by offering or demanding the exact stakes figure: 37 percent of the highest demands were exactly equal to stakes, and 25 percent of the lowest offers equaled stakes. An additional 15 percent of the lawyers reported that the highest demand was less than stakes; 10 percent reported that the lowest offer was more than their view of the stakes. Only 14 percent of the lawyers indicated that their highest demand was at least twice their view of stakes; 37 percent reported that their lowest offer was half or less of their view of stakes (not shown in the table).

How does the ratio of offers/demands to stakes vary by lawyer and case characteristics? The "demand" ratio varies substantially by area of law. Because of the small number of cases involved, I collapsed the areas of law into four categories: tort, contract/commercial, other (including domestic relations, real property, business regulation, civil rights/discrimination, government action, and government benefits), and "mixed" (involving two or more areas of law). As Table 2.16 shows, lawyers in tort cases stand out as being different from lawyers in the other categories: only 41 percent demanded payments equal to or less than stakes compared with 61 percent or more for the other areas of law (the dominant element of the "mixed" category is the contract/commercial area, with 77 percent of the cases involving issues in this area). The demand ratio does not vary systematically with any of the other variables I looked at (stakes, complexity, location, experience/expertise, and the lawyers' attitudes toward litigation).

As for the "offer" ratio, it does not vary systematically with area of law, but it does vary with stakes and complexity, as shown in Table 2.17. As cases get bigger and/or more complex, offers tend to be proportionately smaller in relation to what the lawyers view as appropriate resolutions. As with the ratio of demand to stakes, the ratio of offer to stakes does not vary systematically with location, lawyer characteristics, or lawyer attitudes.[33]

Table 2.16. Percentage Distribution of Ratio of Demands to Stakes, by Area of Law

	Percent of Stakes Demanded					
	<100%	100%	101–150%	151–199%	>200%	N
Tort	11	30	30	11	18	200
Contract/commercial	18	46	21	7	7	95
Other	25	36	20	2	16	44
Mixed	14	49	20	9	9	35

$\chi^2 = 24.67$
$p = .016$

THE EVOLUTION OF OFFERS AND DEMANDS

In the previous section, I looked at the relationship of offers and demands to stakes. I now turn to the relationships between first and last offers and between first and last demands. That is, how do offers and demands change over the course of negotiations? Is there really much give and take, or, as is suggested by the previous section, is it that, in a large percentage of negotiations, the demands and offers simply reflect what the participants deem to be appropriate resolutions in the cases? Are the variations in the changes in offers and demands systematic (in that they are related to the

Table 2.17. Percentage Distribution of Ratio of Offers to Stakes, by Case Size and Complexity

	Percent of Stakes Offered					
	0–39%	40–69%	70–99%	100%	>100%	N
	Amount of Stakes					
≤$5,000	16	20	14	36	14	119
$5,001–10,000	13	43	26	13	6	47
$10,001–25,000	29	36	10	21	5	42
$25,001–50,000	24	35	24	12	6	17
>$50,000	40	35	20	0	5	20

$\chi^2 = 40.57$
$p < .001$

	Complexity of Case					
Simple 1	16	17	21	33	13	70
2	17	42	12	21	9	77
3	18	26	18	30	8	61
Complex 4 & 5	38	30	14	11	8	37

$\chi^2 = 23.95$
$p = .02$

Table 2.18. Percentage Distribution of Changes in Offers
and Demands

Ratio of First to Last Demand	Percent of Demands Made by:	
	Respondent	Opposing Party
< 1.00	6	6
1.00[a]	16	8
1.01–1.50	28	19
1.51–2.00	19	19
> 2.00	31	49
N	339	231

Ratio of First to Last Offer	Percent of Offers Made by:	
	Respondent	Opposing Party
0–0.33	13	27
0.34–0.66	30	34
0.67–0.99	24	19
1.00[a]	27	12
> 1.00	6	8
N	223	146

[a]Represents no change.

kinds of variables I have been examining throughout this chapter—case characteristics, location, lawyer characteristics, and lawyer attitudes)? To look at the changes in the monetary component of offers and demands, I constructed four ratios, two for demands (one for respondent demands and one for opposing-party demands), and two for offers (again, one each for the respondent and the opposing party).

The overall patterns for the four ratios are shown in Table 2.18. For the demands, only 22 percent of respondents reported that their own first demands were equal to or less than their own final demands; this figure drops to 14 percent for the opposing parties' demands. A second difference in patterns between the two ratios for respondent and opposing-party demands is that only 31 percent of the respondents reported that their own first demands were more than twice their final demands; in comparison, respondents reported that almost half the first demands of their opponents were twice the opponents' final demands. A comparable pattern shows up for the offer ratios: 27 percent of the respondents report that their own final offers were the same as their first offers compared with 12 percent for opposing parties' offers that remained unchanged; only 13 percent of the respondents indicated that their first offers were less than a third of their final offers compared with 27 percent of the opposing parties. Clearly, the

Table 2.19. Correlations of Offer and Demand Ratios with Case and Lawyer Characteristics

	Demand-Ratio Correlations				Offer-Ratio Correlations			
	Respondent		Opposing Party		Respondent		Opposing Party	
	Orig.	Log	Orig.	Log	Orig.	Log	Orig.	Log
Lawyer Characteristics								
Specialization	.02	.05	.10	.12*	.06	.08	.05	.01
Years of experience	.06	.05	.03	.03	.12*	.08	.10	.05
Concentration on litigation	.03	.06	.13*	.16**	-.04	.05	-.05	-.10
Case Characteristics								
Stakes	.08	.07	-.07	-.06	-.11	-.13*	-.03	-.06
Complexity	.19***	.21***	.15*	.15**	.06*	-.02	-.08	-.18*
Docket entries	.21***	.23***	.08	.11*	-.02	.02	-.08	-.13
Duration	.07	.08	-.04	-.01	-.08	-.06	-.03	-.06

*$p < .05$
**$p < .01$
***$p < .001$

Note: The columns headed "Orig." employ the ratios on their original scale; the columns headed "Log" employ the natural logarithm of the ratios.

respondents presented themselves as being more reasonable than their opponents were. This asymmetry is strongly suggestive of a process of either selective recall or response patterns influenced by social desirability effects (i.e., trying to present oneself as a reasonable person). Given the time lapse between the interviews and the events being described (typically at least two years), it is not surprising that such biases would be evident. Because of the asymmetry shown in Table 2.18, caution is necessary when making comparisons across the four different ratios.

When I look for systematic relationships between the variables discussed in previous sections (case characteristics, location, lawyer characteristics, and lawyer attitudes), what is most striking is the *lack* of relationships. This set of results is summarized in Table 2.19, which shows Pearson product moment correlations between the ratios (both in their original scales and on the natural logarithm scale) and a variety of other variables.[34] The only ratio that shows much in the way of correlations with other variables is the respondent's demand ratio; this is also true when I look for nonlinear relationships using tabular displays. The only ratio with a meaningful relationship with area of law is the respondent demand ratio (top panel of Table 2.20), and the same is the case for what the lawyer likes most about litigation (bottom panel of Table 2.20). Tables 2.19 and 2.20 indicate that the

Table 2.20. Percentage Distribution of Relationship of Respondents' Demand Ratio by
Selected Variables

	0–0.99	1.00	1.01–1.50	1.51–1.99	≥2.00	N
			Area of Law			
Torts	4	8	27	24	37	195
Contract/commercial	8	30	34	11	17	83
Other	11	23	23	14	29	35
Mixed	8	23	19	23	27	26
$\chi^2 = 39.77$						
$p < .001$						
		Lawyer's Preference among Litigation Activities				
Negotiating	4	24	32	23	18	84
Planning and research	2	22	26	22	29	55
Arguing and trying	8	10	28	19	35	176
$\chi^2 = 18.31$						
$p < .019$						

respondent's demand ratio is higher for complex cases, for cases with a lot of
litigation activity, and for tort cases; it is also higher for lawyers who most
like arguing and trying cases (as compared with negotiating, or planning and
researching). The lawyer's attitude toward risk taking, as I have measured it,
has no relationship to any of the ratios.

The Relationship of Negotiation to Results Achieved

A description of what goes on in negotiation in ordinary litigation would
not be complete without at least some consideration of what difference that
negotiation makes. Dealing with success is a difficult question (see Kritzer et
al., 1987; Kritzer, 1990: 135–161). Here I will simply define measures of
relative outcomes for three different actors in litigation, and report the relationship between those indicators and key negotiation characteristics.

MEASURING RELATIVE OUTCOMES

For a plaintiff, the simplest measure of "success" is net outcome (i.e.,
outcome minus expenses such as lawyer's fees[35]) divided by what was at
stake (measured in the same terms I have used in the previous discussion):

$$PS = \frac{(outcome - expenses)}{stakes}$$

This indicator can take on both positive and negative values, with a negative value indicating that there was an actual net loss for the plaintiff.[36]

For defendants, measuring success is much more difficult. What is the appropriate baseline? The goal of the defendant in litigation is to reduce or avoid a payment to the opposing party, and to the degree that the expenses incurred in the litigation are less than the amount saved, that litigation has been "successful." The problem here is to ascertain how much was saved. One could use the amount initially demanded by the plaintiff, but this is potentially contaminated by the plaintiff's negotiating strategy. A better indicator is the amount that the plaintiff was actually prepared to accept to resolve the case. Although the defendant will not normally know what this figure is, the CLRP data set includes stakes information from the opposing plaintiffs' lawyers for 140 defense lawyers. For this group of defense lawyers, one can construct the following indicator of success:

$$ds = \frac{\text{plaintiff's stakes} - (\text{payment} + \text{expenses})}{\text{plaintiff's stakes}}$$

A simple algebraic manipulation of this measure yields an indicator that neatly parallels that for the plaintiff:[37]

$$DS = \frac{\text{plaintiff's stakes}}{\text{payment} + \text{expenses}}$$

This second indicator takes on only positive values, with values greater than 1.0 indicating success in the sense that the defendant was able to reduce the payment to the plaintiff by more than what he had to pay out in legal fees and expenses.

The third actor with a direct stake in the outcome of the case is the contingent-fee lawyer. Because virtually all the contingent fees paid in the United States are simple percentage fees, the more the lawyer recovers, the greater the fee the lawyer receives. This does not mean that getting the maximum payment is necessarily in the lawyer's best interest, because the lawyer must weigh any increase in payment against the opportunity cost that must be expended to achieve that increase;[38] when lawyers have other fee-generating uses of their time, quickly achieved but relatively small settlements are frequently more lucrative than larger settlements achieved with substantially greater commitments of the lawyers' resources.[39] Consequently, the best indicator of success for the contingent-fee lawyer is the effective hourly rate achieved:

$$LS = \frac{\text{fee received}}{\text{number of hours worked}}$$

There is no implicit baseline for this ratio, though it is worth noting that the median effective hourly rate for contingent-fee lawyers in the sample was $42 compared with an effective hourly rate (computed in the same fashion) of $50 for hourly fee lawyers.[40]

IMPACT OF NEGOTIATION ON SUCCESS[41]

First, does exchange or contact intensity of negotiation/bargaining make any difference in the relative outcomes for the plaintiff, the defendant, or the contingent-fee lawyer? The *only* statistically significant relationships that are revealed by the analysis are between the two measures of intensity and the effective hourly rate achieved by the contingent-fee lawyer. Both of these relationships are positive (i.e., more intensive negotiations lead to higher effective hourly rates), but both are also quite weak (the correlations are .16 and .18) and in fact disappear when control variables (such as stakes and the number of hours worked) are introduced. Thus, there appear to be no meaningful relationships between intensity and success.

The picture is quite different with regard to the tactical content of negotiations. High initial demands (relative to stakes) by plaintiffs and low initial offers (again, relative to stakes) by defendants are related to success for the relevant side. The relationship is particularly strong for defendants ($r = .56$), and clear but weaker for plaintiffs ($r = .21$). When control variables are introduced, these relationships do not disappear, and in fact stand out as the strongest predictors of success for each of the two sides (see Kritzer, 1990: 143–155, 159–161). On the other hand, tactical bargaining is unrelated to the effective hourly rate achieved by the contingent-fee lawyer, either in a bivariate sense or when potential control variables are introduced (ibid.: 137–142). This lack of relationship for the lawyer will have important implications for the discussion in chapter 5.

Summary

The image of negotiation in ordinary litigation that emerges from the data collected by the Civil Litigation Research Project is quite clear. That negotiation process has little in common with the rich, complex interaction portrayed in the Agent Orange example presented in chapter 1. Clearly, negotiation is not a high-intensity activity. Relatively little time is spent in direct contact between the opposing lawyers, and the actual exchanges of offers and demands are few in number. No doubt a good bit of the time spent in investigation and consultation with clients is intended to develop the information needed to frame the offers and demands, but the negotiation itself appears to be simple and straightforward.

Negotiations in ordinary litigation center strongly on monetary payments. For a large proportion of cases there appears to be no effort to engage in tactical bargaining (making particularly high demands or low offers). However, for those who do engage in this kind of bargaining, there is a clear payoff: they achieve better results than those who make demands or offers at or near the amount at stake.

This image of bargaining in litigation is quite consistent with a recent study of the settlement of tort claims in Great Britain (Genn, 1988). That research, which was based on interviews with solicitors, barristers, and insurance company officials, found that the emphasis in bargaining was not on intensive or extensive exchanges between the parties. Many lawyers played down the important of *any* face-to-face contact in the negotiation process. Furthermore, there was a clear recognition on the part of the insurance claims inspectors (who would have the title of claims adjuster in the United States) that the best results were achieved when "hard bargaining" took place. Some plaintiffs' solicitors (particularly those who had been retained by unions on behalf of members who had been injured on the job) were recognized by the insurance claims inspectors as tough bargainers who were able to obtain better settlements than were solicitors who approached the negotiation in what Genn characterized as a more cooperative fashion. The inspectors also made it clear that they would not hesitate to obtain the best results from their perspective (i.e., the lowest payments) that they could get the claimants' solicitors to agree to.

Genn's portrait of bargaining is consistent with Williams' study of legal negotiation (1983), in which he found that some lawyers adopted what he characterized as a cooperative style, whereas others adopted a more competitive or adversarial approach to the process of settling cases.[42] Drawing on the social-psychological literature, Williams (1983: 48) describes the competitive approach as being characterized by:[43]

—making high initial demands and maintaining a high level of demands in the course of the negotiation; and

—making few concessions, and only small ones when concessions are made. In assessing the impact of the different styles on outcomes, Williams concludes that neither approach produces uniformly better results than the other (1983: 41).[44] Genn, on the other hand, argues that a lawyer approaching negotiation with a cooperative style may be disadvantaged if the opposing lawyer sees the process in more competitive terms (see also Lowenthal, 1982: 82–83). To the extent that tactical bargaining, as indicated by making relatively high demands or relatively low offers, is an indicator of a competitive stance in the bargaining process, my analysis is more consistent with Genn's conclusion than with Williams'.

CHAPTER 3

Settlement, Negotiation, and Economics in Ordinary Litigation

Introduction

Chapters 1 and 2 make it clear that one of the dominant themes in ordinary litigation is money: litigants seek to obtain payments from or to avoid making payments to the opposing parties. Additionally, attorneys carry out the work of litigation to earn a living, and governments pay to build and staff courthouses in order to provide a forum in which litigants and their representatives can process civil cases. One study of the costs and compensation paid in tort litigation alone estimated that, in 1985, taxpayers and litigants devoted from $29 billion to $35 billion to the civil justice system (Kakalik and Pace, 1986: 69).[1] If one triples this figure to obtain a crude (and probably conservative) estimate of the amount of money involved in the entire civil justice system, Civil Justice America is approximately a $100 billion-per-year enterprise.[2]

With these sums of money involved, it seems natural to look to the tools of economics as a vehicle for understanding aspects of the civil justice process that are as central as settlement and negotiation. In this chapter, I examine two different lines of theoretical investigation from economics that appear relevant for explaining the patterns I reported in the previous chapter:

—the economics of settlement decisions; and

—bargaining as a method for obtaining economically relevant information.

In this chapter's discussion, I will explore the relevance of existing economics-based theories for explaining the patterns that exist in ordinary litigation; the typical discussion of such theories in the litigation context presumes considerably larger cases than were described in chapter 1 (Raiffa, 1982: 66–77), and the difference of magnitude may pose difficulties for some of the theoretical frameworks.

Economic Realities in Settling Civil Disputes

In this section I will describe an approach to understanding the settlement process in litigation that draws upon the tools of economic analysis; the approach is well established and is represented by the work of Friedman (1969), Posner (1973), Gould (1973), and Ross (1980: 144–146).[3] As I will detail below, based on this framework, one would expect that modest cases of the type that constitute ordinary litigation would tend to be settled quickly and with little give and take. This does not mean that ordinary cases are "simple" or involve unimportant issues. The dollar-and-cents realities of such cases create a situation that leads economically rational actors to settle without protracted negotiations.

The thrust of the theoretical analysis is that settlement should occur if the parties' settlement expectations, after adjusting for uncertainty, risk preference, and potential transaction costs, create a *zone of overlap;* such a zone will exist if the minimum amount that the plaintiff will accept is less than the maximum amount that the defendant will pay.[4] In the litigation context, this analysis involves computing an *expected* outcome by multiplying the gross outcome by the probability that it will occur,[5] and then adjusting for transaction costs by subtracting (for plaintiffs) or adding (for defendants) the costs that would be incurred in obtaining that outcome.[6] For example, a plaintiff estimating a 70 percent chance of winning $10,000 at a processing cost of $1,000, has an expected gain of $6,000; the defendant, on the other hand, might think there is only a 50 percent chance of losing $10,000, but at a processing cost of $2,000, which leads to an expected loss of $7,000. In this example, there is a $1,000 zone of overlap between $6,000 (the plaintiff should be happy to settle for anything greater than $6,000) and $7,000 (the defendant should be happy to settle for anything less than $7,000).

One problem with this kind of analysis is that it presumes that there is some systematic basis for arriving at evaluations of what cases are "worth." However, there are several indications that case valuations involve much more uncertainty than the notion of "case worth" suggests. Williams (1983: 5–6) conducted an experiment with 20 pairs of lawyers, all of whom practiced in the same community—Des Moines, Iowa. The assembled group was given information about the same case. After examining the information, each pair undertook, in private, to arrive at a settlement through negotiation. The disparity among the results was impressive, from a high of $95,000 to a low of $15,000,[7] with the other settlements scattered in essentially a random fashion between the high and low values.[8]

Much the same problem is demonstrated in a study of lawyer-client relations in personal injury cases. As part of that study, Rosenthal (1974) assembled a panel of five experts experienced in evaluating personal injury claims, and had each member of the panel independently evaluate the cases in his study. There was substantial disagreement among these experts concerning the worth of specific cases: in 52 of the 59 cases for which evaluations were made, the ratio of the highest to the lowest was 2 or more, and in 19 cases (i.e., *almost a third*) it was 4 or more.[9] Although there is no doubt substantial uncertainty about what cases are worth,[10] the kinds of cases that have demonstrated the uncertainty are typically substantially larger than the median case in ordinary civil litigation. As I will suggest below, the range of uncertainty may be such that, in more typical cases, it does not negate the usefulness of the standard economic analysis of settlement based on the existence of a zone of overlap.

As shown by the problems of ambiguity connected with defining what a case is worth, the standard economic analysis of settlement described above neglects many of the problems inherent in the litigation process. In spite of the rather simplistic assumptions made in the usual presentations of this standard analysis, a variety of components can easily be added to bring the analysis more in line with the real world. First, the ambiguity inherent in case valuation can be taken into account by viewing each player as considering a variety of possible outcomes,[11] rather than limiting the individual players to a single figure (e.g., the $10,000 in the example above). This extension can be most easily considered in the framework of what is sometimes called risk analysis (see Victor, 1985; Raiffa, 1982: 66–77). This involves each party specifying a set of likely outcomes and associating a probability with each. Table 3.1 is a simple example of such an "outcome set" for a plaintiff and a defendant. The "expected value" for each side is obtained by multiplying each possible outcome by its associated probability, summing, and adding (for defendants) or subtracting (for plaintiffs) the transaction cost.[12] Thus, for the example in Table 3.1, the expected outcome for the plaintiff is $4,170, and for the defendant $5,715. Because in this example there is a range of overlap, one would expect a settlement somewhere in the $1,545 gap between the two expected outcomes.[13]

This simple example of a risk analysis does not take into account one other area of uncertainty in litigation—the uncertainty concerning transaction costs. That is, not only must litigants consider a range of possible outcomes, they must also extend the risk analysis model to take into account the possible variations in the cost of achieving those outcomes.[14] This additional uncertainty could easily be factored into the computation shown in Table 3.1 by specifying the probability associated with each of a number of

Table 3.1. "Risk Analysis" for a Typical Case

Amount at Stake ($)	Plaintiff		Defendant	
	Probability[a]	Expected Value[b] ($)	Probability[a]	Expected Value[b] ($)
0	0.300	0	0.400	0
1,000	0.010	10	0.015	15
2,000	0.030	60	0.030	60
3,000	0.040	120	0.040	120
4,000	0.040	160	0.050	200
5,000	0.050	250	0.060	300
6,000	0.060	360	0.125	750
7,000	0.070	490	0.100	700
8,000	0.080	640	0.080	640
9,000	0.120	1,080	0.070	630
10,000	0.200	2,000	0.030	300
	1.000	5,170	1.000	3,715
Transaction costs		–1,000		+2,000
Expected result		4,170		5,715

[a]Probability of the respective outcome.

[b]Expected value is equal to the amount multiplied by the probability.

possible values for transaction cost, then summing to get an "expected cost"; this expected cost could then be added (for defendants) or subtracted (for plaintiffs) to obtain the expected result.[15]

A second problem that can be incorporated into the model is that each side must consider its own evaluation in light of what it thinks the other side might be prepared to accept. Cooter and Marks (1982), for example, introduce the notion of optimal hardness to refer to what they see as the central problem in the dynamic process of offers and demands: the players must decide what their individual offer/demand strategies should be in light of their hoped-for result and the impression they desire to convey to the other side. In effect, when making a settlement offer or demand, a party that strongly prefers to settle must take into account the fact that the greater the demand, the less likely the opposing party will be to see the demand as realistic; thus in making a demand or offer, a party must try to gauge the amount in such a way that the opposing party will either accept it or respond with a counter that is acceptable (or is moving in the direction of acceptability).[16]

Regardless of whether one uses the simplistic model or any of the more refined images, the driving force of the analysis is the "surplus" generated by the potential cost of going to trial (see Cooter and Marks, 1982: 228–229) and the ways the risks associated with those costs are distributed (see Shavell, 1982). This surplus derives in part from the nonvoluntary nature of the bargaining which occurs in the context of civil litigation (or other civil disputes). Bargaining in the context of a dispute takes place in the "shadow of adjudication" (see Eisenberg, 1976) and in the "shadow of the law" (Mnookin and Kornhauser, 1979; Galanter, 1988: 61–62).[17] These shadows have several implications. First, aggrieved parties who fail to obtain settlements may seek authoritative judgments on their claims; thus the bargaining takes place under a clear threat of coercion. Second, the law may set the framework for negotiation or even dictate the possible settlement alternatives,[18] though the "law" has historically provided little guidance for establishing the amount of compensation for things like pain and suffering.[19] Third, the processes that compose litigation can be used to impose costs on the opposing party (though usually this requires that the party imposing the costs must itself be prepared to incur some costs). In cases involving relatively small amounts of money, this can deter a potential claimant from seeking compensation by making it uneconomical to do so.[20] This can also serve to increase the uncertainty for the participants,[21] which in turn may increase the size of the zone of overlap, thus making settlement still easier. As I will show in the next section, this is particularly important in the relatively modest cases that constitute ordinary litigation.

SETTLEMENT IN ORDINARY LITIGATION

For purposes of understanding bargaining and settlement in ordinary litigation, the shadow of the law may be less important than the shadow of adjudication and the costs that lurk behind that shadow. Specifically, the potential transaction costs may be so great relative to the amount at issue that the zone of overlap is very large in relative terms. In the first example used above, I presumed a $10,000 case. Although, strictly speaking, the cost of bringing a case to trial is related more to the complexity of the issues in dispute than to the amount at stake, it seems to be a fair assumption that there would be relatively little systematic variation in the costs of trial for cases involving stakes of $2,000–$10,000. Table 3.2 makes exactly the same assumptions about transaction costs that I made for the $10,000 case, and shows the calculation of the zone of overlap for cases in what can be thought of as the ordinary range, given that, excluding small claims, the median case is around $5,000 in the state courts, which handle the vast bulk of civil litigation.

What the table shows is that, the smaller the amount at stake, the wider

Table 3.2. Impact of Stakes on Zone of Overlap[a]

Amount At stake ($)	Expected Value		Zone of Overlap	
	Plaintiff ($)	Defendant ($)	Absolute size ($)	Relative size[b]
1,000	–300	2,500	2,800	2.80
2,000	400	3,000	2,600	1.30
3,000	1,100	3,500	2,400	0.80
4,000	1,800	4,000	2,200	0.55
5,000	2,500	4,500	2,000	0.40
6,000	3,200	5,000	1,800	0.30
7,000	3,900	5,500	1,600	0.23
8,000	4,600	6,000	1,400	0.18
9,000	5,300	6,500	1,200	0.13
10,000	6,000	7,000	1,000	0.10

[a]This table assumes that the plaintiff estimates a .7 chance of winning with $1,000 in transaction costs, and the defendant expects a .5 chance of winning (and a .5 chance of losing) with $2,000 in transaction costs.

[b]Relative size equals the absolute size of the zone of overlap divided by the stakes.

the zone of overlap, in both absolute and relative terms.[22] The specific figures shown in the table depend upon the parameters that generated them (i.e., the probability and cost for each party), but conditional generalizations can be drawn. First, the costs need not be constant; given the probabilities used above, as long as the costs decline at a rate slower than the amount at issue, the zone of overlap will narrow as stakes increase.[23] Second, so long as the defendant's estimate of the probability that the plaintiff will prevail is lower than the plaintiff's own estimate, both the relative and absolute size of the zone of overlap will increase as stakes decrease. This is the most likely situation, because there is probably a tendency for the plaintiff to view his own case more positively than the defendant will view the plaintiff's case and vice versa.[24] However, if the two sides' estimates of the probabilities are equal, the absolute size of the zone of overlap will be constant, and if the defendant thinks it more likely that the plaintiff will succeed than does the plaintiff, the absolute size will decrease as stakes decrease. However, in both of these situations, the relative size of the zone of overlap will increase as stakes decrease.[25]

In effect, what this means is that, for the kinds of cases that constitute ordinary litigation, there would be little need to fine tune evaluations of stakes, costs, and probabilities in order for the parties to arrive easily at some figure that both sides are willing to accept. That is, as the costs of pursuing a case rise relative to the amount at issue, the acceptable settlement ranges for the two parties increase in width, making it increasingly likely that a demand or offer will fall in the other side's acceptable range.[26] For example, using the figures for a $4,000 case in Table 3.2, a plaintiff who demands $3,600, which is twice his expected outcome of $1,800, will still be in the defendant's acceptable range of $4,000 or less; likewise, a defendant who offers $2,000, which is half of his expected outcome of $4,000, will still be in the plaintiff's range of acceptability.[27]

One might question the validity of this analysis as applied to ordinary litigation in the United States, because the plaintiff is usually an individual who has retained a lawyer on a contingent-fee basis (i.e., the lawyer is paid a fee only if a recovery is made). Under the American contingent-fee system, the plaintiff will almost always face transaction costs equal to a fixed proportion of what is recovered, regardless of whether the recovery is obtained through trial or settlement (see Johnson, 1980–81; Kritzer et al., 1985).[28] Although this does in fact complicate the applicability of the analysis, it does not undermine it in any fundamental fashion. Because it is the contingent-fee lawyers who must effectively bear the transaction costs (in terms of the effort that must be invested in resolving the case), they will normally be very sensitive to those costs; this arises because it is often the situation that the marginal return to the lawyer from the increased recovery that might be achieved by going to trial is insufficient to cover the value of the lawyer's time that would be required by the trial. From the lawyer's viewpoint, the best return can often be achieved through a quick resolution that requires a minimum effort on the lawyer's part (see Rosenthal, 1974; Miller, 1987). Although it is true that the client must consent to the settlement (and thus in theory can force the lawyer to take the case to trial if the settlement terms offered are unsatisfactory), it is also true that the client is usually entirely dependent upon the lawyer's assessment of the appropriateness of the settlement that has been offered.[29]

If one assumes that it is the contingent-fee lawyer who will make the decision whether to accept a settlement offer, the zone-of-overlap argument is substantially strengthened in the ordinary case. Table 3.3 replicates Table 3.2, except that it relates to the contingent-fee lawyer rather than to the plaintiff. The only change in the computation that makes up the table is that it is assumed the lawyer will get a third of the recovery; that is, each entry in the "Expected Value, Contingent-Fee Lawyer" column is computed by multiplying the amount at stake by the probability of winning *and* the percentage the lawyer will receive before the transaction cost is subtracted.[30] When comparing Tables 3.2 and 3.3, it is immediately clear that the zone of overlap is considerably wider for the contingent-fee lawyer than it is for the

Table 3.3. Impact of Stakes on Zone of Overlap for Contingent-Fee Lawyers[a]

Amount at Stake ($)	Expected Value			Zone of Overlap	
	Contingent-Fee Lawyer ($)	Defendant ($)		Absolute size ($)	Relative size[b]
1,000	−767	2,500		3,267	3.27
2,000	−534	3,000		3,534	1.77
3,000	−301	3,500		3,801	1.27
4,000	−68	4,000		4,068	1.02
5,000	166	4,500		4,335	0.87
6,000	399	5,000		4,601	0.77
7,000	632	5,500		4,868	0.70
8,000	865	6,000		5,135	0.64
9,000	1,098	6,500		5,402	0.60
10,000	1,331	7,000		5,669	0.57

[a]This table assumes that the plaintiff's lawyer, who will be paid a third of the recovery, estimates a .7 chance of winning with $1,000 in transaction costs, and the defendant expects a .5 chance of winning (and a .5 chance of losing) with $2,000 in transaction costs.
[b]Relative size equals the absolute size of the zone of overlap divided by the stakes.

client; the calculation of the contingent-fee lawyer's expected value involves a second fractional multiplier that always makes the lawyer's expected value substantially less than the client's. For the contingent-fee lawyer there is a consideration, in addition to the expected value, that may be of significance in deciding *when* to propose or accept a settlement: the effective hourly return that *has been* achieved at a given point must be compared with the effective hourly return that *might be* achieved with the expenditure of additional effort. Nonetheless, the point of the analysis here is that the conditions for settlement are enhanced as the amount at stake goes down, and this is even more the case for the contingent-fee lawyer than it is for the plaintiff who has retained a lawyer on an hourly (or fixed) fee basis.

STAKES, COSTS, AND SETTLEMENT: MOVING THE BUSINESS

Although I have described this analysis as economic in nature, it might be more appropriate to describe it as an accounting analysis. By this I mean to suggest that in looking at settlements in ordinary litigation one has to keep in mind the realities of dollars and cents with which participants must be concerned. In ordinary litigation the potential costs involved in processing the cases are inevitably going to constitute a substantial fraction of the amount at issue, and when combined with the uncertainties inherent in litigation, this creates powerful incentives to move cases through quickly with as little investment of expensive resources as possible. This is facilitated by costs that are large relative to stakes, creating wide, greatly overlapping zones of acceptable settlements. Thus first offers, or, failing that, second offers, are very likely to fall within those zones of acceptability, usually resulting in settlements after only one or two exchanges of demands and offers.[31]

This argument is consistent with Ross's study (1980) of the way insurance companies process claims arising from automobile accidents, most of which never become actual lawsuits. His analysis points out the simple, routine nature of most injury cases,[32] and consistent with that, the process Ross describes emphasizes simplicity, routinization, speed, and the like. For many cases, even when at least one of the parties is represented by a lawyer, the negotiations that go on are minimal, reflecting a combination of factors:

—the lack of significant issues of liability:

—the ability of both parties to arrive easily at an agreement regarding what the case is "worth"; and/or

—the realization by the parties that the potential transaction costs are high relative to what might be at stake.

One point emphasized by the insurance adjusters in Ross's study (1980: 59–62) is the pressure to move cases through the system as opposed to "toughing out" cases to get the best results possible. In light of the analysis here, it is clear why that approach to claims processing makes sense for most run-of-the-mill cases that adjusters handle: it is simply not worth the expenditure of substantial resources to process modest claims. At the same time, when stakes begin to get high relative to potential processing costs, a tough stance by the insurance company may be the best strategy.

Carlin's description (1962: 71–91) of how solo-practice lawyers in Chicago in the late 1950s handled personal injury cases is consistent with Ross's portrayal of the process from the insurance company side.[33] Carlin emphasized the importance that the lawyers attached to assembling the information needed to arrive at settlement figures with the insurance companies. Typically this involved documenting the "special" damages (e.g., medical expenses, lost wages, etc.). Based on this documentation and the specific nature of the injuries the client had suffered, the lawyer would then have tried to reach an agreement with the insurance company, handling much of the contact with the adjuster over the telephone. Although some attorneys filed lawsuits as a matter of routine, many tried to resolve the cases without taking that step. Carlin distinguished between the "upper-level" personal injury practitioners and the "lower-level" practitioners; the former group was more "effective" in negotiating with insurance companies, and Carlin attributed this to a combination of having established relationships with the insurance company adjusters and having a reputation for being able and willing to take a case to trial if pressed.[34] Perhaps what is most striking about Carlin's analysis, particularly for lower-level personal injury practitioners, is the relatively minimal emphasis on either the legal context in which the settlement is taking place or the needs and desires of the client. The emphasis is clearly on "moving the business."[35]

Bargaining as the Exchange of Economic Information

A second major line of economic theory concerning negotiation, this one directly concerned with the process of bargaining rather than the striking of deals, is much less helpful in accounting for the patterns described in chapter 2. The bargaining problem as conceptualized by these theories revolves around the need for two parties to learn something about one another's preferences where there is some potential conflict of interest between the two sides. The models that flow from these theories concerned with information sharing are typically based on some general economic problem such as the establishment of prices in the context of bilateral monopoly. Prominent theorists of this approach include Zeuthen (1930), Pen (1952), and Cross (1969). The applicability to ordinary litigation of the mathematically derived principles based upon these theories is questionable given the theories' heavy reliance upon the important distinction between bargaining situations that are distributive in nature and those that are integrative.

In distributive bargaining the outcomes are characterized by a "zero sum" nature: what one side gains, the other side must by definition lose, and there is no way to modify the outcome so that both sides are better off than they were before the settlement. That is,

. . . in distributive [bargaining] one single issue, such as money, is under contention, and the parties have almost strictly opposing interests on that issue: the more you get, the less the other party gets. . . . and you want as much as you can get. (Raiffa, 1982: 33)

When the bargaining situation is integrative, positive-sum results, where both sides may be made better off than before the resolution is achieved, are possible. That is,

. . . [in] such bargaining, in which there are two parties and several issues to be negotiated, . . . [t]he parties are not strict competitors. It is no longer true that if one party gets more, the other necessarily has to get less; they both can get more. They can cooperate in order to enlarge the pie that they eventually will have to divide. (ibid.: 131)

Typical examples of integrative bargaining are found in situations where one party has something to which it attaches substantially less value than does the other side; a common example arises in bargaining in the labor arena, where, because of tax laws, fringe benefits may have greater value to the employee than they have cost to the employer.[36]

LEARNING MODELS, BARGAINING, AND ORDINARY LITIGATION

Most of the economic theories of bargaining that are based upon problems like price setting in the context of bilateral monopoly rely heavily upon an assumption of integrative bargaining.[37] This assumption does not apply to much of the real world of bargaining in ordinary litigation, where the situation is usually defined as zero sum or, because of the possible costs of litigation, potentially negative sum. In fact, it is the potentially negative-sum nature of litigation, as described extensively in the previous section of this chapter, that creates the conditions for settlement even when the two sides' estimates of likely gross outcomes differ substantially. Although avoidance of potential transaction costs can create a commonality of interest between the opposing sides, this does not create an integrative bargaining situation in the sense used in the economic theories of bargaining based on a learning model.

The payment of plaintiffs' lawyers on a contingent-fee basis might make possible, at least in theory, solutions that are integrative. Since the contingent fee represents an uncontrollable (albeit variable) cost to the plaintiff, both plaintiff and defendant would benefit if that cost could be eliminated (for example, by splitting the savings). I describe this as a theoretical possibility because it assumes that there is a way of terminating the contingent-fee retainer agreement, which in fact is not normally possible; there is no way to return to the prerepresentation state. There are also problems with this kind of integrative solution prior to retaining a contingent-fee lawyer, because it assumes that the defendant will value the case in the same way regardless of whether or not the plaintiff is represented by counsel; the validity of such an assumption is dubious.[38] In fact, this kind of approach is most likely to occur in situations where the plaintiff has strong support from some other kind of representative (e.g., a union) and where there is an aggregate of cases (e.g., in some types of mass tort cases), which makes large-scale bargaining practical; this quickly moves outside the realm of ordinary litigation.

There are some specific situations involving individual cases, usually falling outside the realm of ordinary litigation, in which integrative solutions do occur in litigation. One such situation occurs when tax laws make possible "structured settlements" (i.e., payments made over a period of years rather than in a lump sum) that offer advantages to both sides in a dispute.[39] Such arrangements make little sense for cases involving the amounts at stake in the vast majority of ordinary cases.[40] Integrative solutions may also be possible where goods which are valued by the payer at wholesale prices but by the recipient at retail prices are provided in lieu of cash. One recent example of such a resolution was reported in a class-action case filed by former employees of a large meat-packing company; a quarter of the settlement in that case was to be paid in the form of coupons for products made by the defendant (see *National Law Journal*, March 9, 1987, p. 8). Such settlements are much more problematic in cases involving individual plaintiffs;[41] as I will discuss in chapter 5, this is in part a function of the way that individual plaintiffs commonly pay their lawyers.

Even if the strict application of economic models derived from the information-sharing problem cannot be applied to the ordinary litigation context, one would think that the core issue raised by these models would be useful for understanding the bargaining that occurs in ordinary litigation. Surely each side must learn something about the preferences of the other from offers and/or demands the opposing parties make. Can the economists' learning models, such as the one articulated by Cross (1969), help in understanding the kind of learning that occurs during negotiation in everyday litigation?

The central notion of Cross's theory is that each party in the bargaining must offer concessions from a starting point in order that a settlement can be reached (unless of course one party simply accepts the other's initial demand/offer). The resulting "concession rates" form a basis of "learning" for the two parties.[42] That is, Party A will adjust his or her concession rate depending on the concession rate of Party B; the faster B concedes ground, the more slowly A will concede, and vice versa. This interactive image suggests that there may be an equilibrium point for the two concession rates (though, as Cross [1969: 51] points out, there is also a strong potential instability), and if so, given a knowledge of the starting points and the equilibrium point, one can predict where the settlement will occur. Obviously, under this model, who concedes first and the size of the initial concession are of central importance. There are a variety of complicating factors and variations that can be introduced into the basic model, and there are a number of additional interesting conclusions that can be drawn from the model; these are described in some detail by Cross (ibid.). The identification of concession and concession rates as a focal point in research on the bargaining process (the "main problem" according to Bartos [1974: 26]) has led to a substantial body of research on factors that influence that rate (see especially the book by Pruitt [1981] which summarizes much of this literature).

In a less formal sense, this kind of learning-theory model underlies Ross's description of bargaining between attorneys and insurance adjusters (1980: 152):[43]

> The initial offer and demand in a bodily injury negotiation are seldom meant to be accepted by the other party. They are rather made almost entirely for their communicative value. The initial demand of $25,000, for example, is a way of saying, "I think this is a serious case, which deserves a settlement in the thousands and not in the hundreds of dollars." A following offer of $2,000 would be a way of communicating agreement on the more general principle, whereas an offer of $400 would most likely be meant and construed as a disagreement. *The communicative function of proposals is also evident in the meanings attached to changes in them through the course of negotiation* [emphasis added]. An attorney reducing his demand from $25,000 to $15,000 and then to $14,500 is saying something different from one whose third proposal is $10,000.

Clearly, the image of bargaining incorporated into these perspectives involves a series of exchanges of demands and offers. However, *bargaining in ordinary civil litigation usually is not characterized by a series of exchanges of this type.* As I spelled out in chapter 2, the most common pattern is for there to be two rounds, which probably means that there is a demand and an offer (round one), followed by a compromise settlement (round two), or a demand (round one) followed sometime later by an offer that is accepted (round two). It is worth noting that a series of exchanges that extends beyond two rounds is most common in the kinds of tort cases that Ross was concerned about (27 percent of cases compared with 12 percent in the next highest category—contracts), but even in that area it is much more likely that negotiations will stop at two exchanges (45 percent of cases).

A second problem with Ross's supposition as applied to ordinary litigation is that his suggested image of an initial demand that is several multiples of the desired result does not appear to reflect what goes on in most cases. Only 14 percent of the initial demands that were made were even as much as twice the amount that the lawyer believed to be an appropriate settlement, and 52 percent of those demands were in fact equal to or less than what was sought; defendants' offers were only slightly more in line with the image suggested by the learning-theory model: 20 percent of the initial offers were for less than 40 percent of what the defendants were prepared to pay, and only 35 percent were equal to or more than that amount.

In summary, the learning-theory/information-exchange image of bargaining appears, on its face, to be a framework that would be a valuable tool for understanding bargaining in ordinary litigation. The problem with this approach, however, is that the realities of what usually happens in ordinary litigation do not look anything like the world that the framework presumes. This leaves the important issue of *why* the realities of bargaining in civil litigation deviate so greatly from what is portrayed by the models in question. It is unlikely that the deviation is accounted for by the conflict between the presumption of integrative bargaining in the model developed by Cross (and others) and the fact that in ordinary litigation most bargaining is distributive; Ross, when he described negotiation in tort cases, was clearly not thinking in terms of integrative bargaining. As I will spell out in chapters 5 and 6, I believe that this deviation reflects a combination of the incentives confronting the lawyers handling the cases and the function that the bargaining is meant to serve.

One interesting question raised by this discussion has to do with the choice of bargaining tactics: is it best to allow the other side to make the first move, thus revealing something about its position, or is it best to move first to establish a bargaining range? The first position is premised upon the view—as described by Ross (see also, Genn, 1988: 136) and supported by Cross's analysis of the way information is used—that the initial offer or demand serves largely to provide information to the other side. The presumption is that it is better to receive than to give when it comes to information. However, if the most common pattern is for there to be two rounds consisting of either one offer and one demand followed by a compromise solution or a demand followed sometime later by an offer that is accepted, whoever makes the first move will be in the advantageous position of setting the parameters of the compromise or the realistic range for the response (see, for example, Raiffa, 1982: 128)[44] In effect, the party who first imparts information may benefit by sharing information which previously had been private or possibly by being in the position to mislead the opposing party.[45]

Of course, as I discussed in the first part of this chapter, there is always the danger that an initial demand or offer is so far away from the acceptable range of the other side that it serves to reduce the likelihood of achieving a negotiated resolution. There is a clear trade-off here between the advantages of locking in a range that is higher (but still acceptable) than the opposing party was considering and the disadvantages of locking in a range that is much lower than what the opposing party was prepared to accept. These advantages and disadvantages must be considered in the context of the uncertainties associated with case valuation and the likelihood that the opposing party is going to tend to evaluate the worth of the case in a way that is more favorable to that party's position (i.e., high for plaintiffs and low for defendants.) Overall, the advantages of making the first move are likely to outweigh the disadvantages.

LEARNING FROM NEGOTIATION: IS THERE AN ALTERNATIVE
TO THE POSITION-ORIENTED PERSPECTIVE?

It is hard to reject the view that at least part of the bargaining process can be characterized as learning through information exchange. However, the kinds of exchange of information envisioned by the major theorists of the economics of bargaining do not occur in ordinary litigation. It is possible that processes of the type considered by those theorists do occur in big-time litigation; the kinds of concessions that occurred in the Agent Orange negotiation probably had a substantial impact on each side's perception of how far the other side was willing to move.

The type of learning that occurs in ordinary litigation appears to be very different from the concession-oriented learning described in the economic literature. Although the economic literature presumes that negotiations convey information about *positions* (where each side is starting, how much importance each side attaches to the case, how far and how fast each side is prepared to move), the patterns described in chapter 2 are geared to communicating information about the *case* (e.g., the appropriate range for discussions for the case). Whereas "position-oriented" negotiations require give and take, "case-oriented" negotiations have no such requirement: the goal is to locate the case within a set of norms and expectations.[46] The first move, regardless of which side makes it, will serve to do this, unless that offer/demand is seen by the other side as inappropriate. The economists' models of learning through bargaining do not provide a framework for analyzing this kind of information exchange. Some of the models developed in chapter 6 will build upon this distinction between position-oriented negotiation and case-oriented negotiation. I will suggest that the bargaining process in ordinary civil litigation has important parallels to the guilty-plea process in criminal cases, with the idea of "going rates" serving to link the two processes together.

CHAPTER 4

Power, Games, and Bargaining

Introduction

Bargaining and negotiation involve interaction among two or more parties. This interaction, and the relationship that it creates, normally involves cooperation, competition, and the manipulation of power asymmetries. These aspects of bargaining have attracted attention from theoreticians and researchers from a wide variety of disciplines. How, if at all, do these perspectives help account for the pattern of negotiation in ordinary civil litigation? That is the question addressed in this chapter.

The issues of power, cooperation, and competition are interrelated in a variety of ways. However, to highlight key issues, I have organized this chapter around three topics: power, cooperation and competition, and game theory. The last of these topics serves to integrate issues raised by the first two. As will become evident, many of the arguments concerning power, cooperation, and competition build upon the key theoretical issues raised by the two approaches considered in the previous chapter: the combination of the evaluation of stakes and estimated probability of success that establish the presence or absence of a settlement range, and the role of uncertainty arising from the strategic situation. It should not be surprising then that most of the approaches in this chapter suffer from the same key deficiency that I identified regarding the learning models in the last chapter: they do not envision the kind of minimal contact and exchange that appears to characterize ordinary civil litigation. However, although many of the approaches "undersimplify," others appear to oversimplify and fail to consider what *could* happen as well as what *does* happen.

Bargaining as the Strategic Manipulation of Power

POWER AS DEPENDENCE

In their analysis of bargaining, Bacharach and Lawley argue that "power is the essence of bargaining" (1981: 43). They define power in terms of dependence: the power of Party A over Party B reflects the dependence of the latter on the former (ibid.: 60–61). The perspective developed by Bachrach and Lawley builds upon, among other work, Schelling's seminal paper "An Essay on Bargaining" (1956), in which Schelling examines the impact of commitment, promise, threat, and power, on the ability of parties in a bargaining relationship to achieve their goals. As applied to the litigation context, the key elements of power are found in: the ability to force a party to adjudication and thereby to invoke specific legal norms that can govern the outcome, the ability to impose costs on the other party through the legal procedures that are a part of litigation, and the parties' capacities for absorbing costs that can be imposed.[1] These elements reflect a combination of what Bachrach and Lawley (1981: 209) called "absolute bargaining power" (the dependence of Party B on Party A) and "relative bargaining power" (the ratio of *A's dependence on B* to *B's dependence on A*).

One of the unique aspects of litigation is that it allows one party to force the other into a dependency relationship. The power of the state, through the courts, imposes on the defendant an obligation to answer the plaintiff's claim; failure to respond will typically result in a judgment of default in favor of the plaintiff, which can then be enforced through the mechanisms of the state.[2] This can be thought of as the shadow of adjudication. In addition, the legal norms that are invoked serve to define the extent of the dependency and to create the context in which negotiation proceeds; Mnookin and Kornhauser (1979), as mentioned previously, referred to this as the "shadow of the law."[3] In principle, the two related shadows might allow for the examination of the ability of one party to exploit the power obtained through the invocation of the legal process. The ability of a shadow theory to provide testable hypotheses will depend upon the distinctness of the shadows cast by the law and by the threat of adjudication. For tort cases, which make up the largest single subset in the sample of cases considered in chapter 2, the standards of judgment that are produced through the adjudicatory process in the United States confer *relatively* little basis for prediction, particularly with regard to the level of monetary damages that can be achieved through litigation.[4] This makes it difficult to use the power implications of the shadows to derive testable hypotheses related to negotiation of tort disputes. One can posit that the ambiguity of power produced by the legal shadows should have implications for whether or not settlement does in fact occur; that is, as the uncertainty concerning who will win increases, the differences in relative bargaining power between the two sides decrease, making it difficult for the more powerful side to obtain the settlement it wants. This analysis is similar to that advanced by Priest and Klein (1984), who present evidence in support of the hypothesis that cases which actually go to adjudication over issues of liability tend to involve situations where outcomes are relatively unpredictable.[5]

The power conferred by the legal shadows may be clearer in other areas of the law, such as contracts or divorce (the latter was the area considered by Mnookin and Kornhauser),[6] and in such situations hypotheses concerning the implications of the shadows for the bargaining process may suggest paths for analysis. In their discussion of "bargaining in the shadow of the law," Cooter and Marks (1982) present what they describe as "a testable model of strategic behavior." They presume that the bargaining problem is one of dividing fixed and known stakes; the effect of invoking the legal process, either through extended negotiation in the shadow of possible adjudication or by adjudication (trial) itself, is to destroy part of the stakes by diverting part of what could be shared by the contending parties to cover legal expenses.[7] The example that is used in Cooter and Marks is drawn from the divorce context, and involves the division of the value of a house between the divorcing spouses; obviously, the stakes here are fixed and known, and the problem is simply one of division. This is a very different problem from that typically confronted in American tort litigation, where much of the uncertainty is over the stakes themselves.[8] In Cooter and Marks's analysis, the power conferred by the legal shadows in the division problem comes down to the ability of one party to take advantage of certain characteristics of the other party (e.g., the other party's possible need for a quick resolution) and the ability of each party to impose costs on the other.[9]

The analysis of the legal shadows leads then to the other two aspects of the traditional approach to power in the negotiation context: the ability to impose costs on the opponent and the capability of absorbing costs; these aspects suggest several questions for potential analysis. First, to what degree do disparities in the capability to absorb costs account for how negotiation is conducted? Stated simply, there is no systematic evidence to suggest that, in the negotiations that do occur in ordinary litigation, one side uses a capability of this type to disadvantage the other side.[10] This in part reflects, at least in the United States, the predominant use of contingent-fee attorneys by individual plaintiffs. These attorneys effectively provide a resource capability in ordinary litigation that appears to offset advantages that might be possessed by organizational defendants.

The other element of power created through litigation is the ability of one party to impose costs on the other. As was discussed in detail in the previous chapter, this cost calculation is one of the key elements creating the zones of overlap that constitute acceptable settlement ranges. Beyond this, however, does the ability to impose costs provide plaintiffs with major bargaining resources in marginal or frivolous cases? Clearly, a defendant must be prepared to incur the costs of a defense unless he or she is prepared to suffer a default judgment; for the typical organizational defendant with resources that can readily be seized to satisfy such a judgment, there is little choice but to respond to the claim that is brought through the formal legal process.[11] This leads to the potential that marginal or frivolous claims can be settled for less than the cost of fighting them, or that the valuations of small meritorious claims are inflated by some fraction of the potential litigation cost to the defendant.[12] The debates over litigation reform often refer to the problem of frivolous lawsuits whereby plaintiffs take advantage of their ability to impose costs on defendants in order to extract settlement offers where the claim has no real basis, and there have been several theoretical analyses that examine how such claims might come about (P'ng, 1983: 584–585; Rosenberg and Shavell, 1985; Bebchuk, 1988). However, there is no evidence to support contentions that large numbers of such cases actually lead to litigation. It may be that individuals make such claims in the hopes of extracting settlement offers,[13] but the incentive structure for contingent-fee lawyers would not lead one to expect them to take cases that have little chance of success if they go to trial.[14] Repeat-player defendants have clear motivation to litigate such cases to insure that contingent-fee lawyers know that frivolous suits that are brought will be forced through to adjudication. Consequently, the ability to impose costs is important insofar as it widens settlement ranges, but I doubt that a significant fraction of cases in ordinary civil litigation are built solely on the defendant's fear of litigation expense.

POWER AND RISK PREFERENCE

Wittman (1988: 322) suggests a second approach to power in bargaining: differentials in risk preference. That is, if one party is risk averse and the other is risk neutral, the risk-neutral party should be able to exploit that difference to its own advantage. This ties in neatly with Galanter's (1974) distinction between "one-shot" and "repeat" players in litigation. Galanter developed this distinction in response to patterns reported by Wanner (1974, 1975), patterns which appeared to show that, in most cases filed in civil courts, an organizational plaintiff was seeking to recover from an individual defendant, and that according to the court record, the organizational plaintiff usually prevailed. Galanter pointed out that most of these organizational plaintiffs were repeat players in litigation, whereas the individual defendants tended to be infrequent or one-shot players. He attributed the organization's apparent advantage at least partly to the knowledge and resources available to them as repeat players.

We now know that most ordinary litigation, outside of divorce and uncontested debt-collection cases,[15] actually involves an individual plaintiff seeking to recover from an organizational defendant (see Grossman et al., 1982).[16] This allows the repeat-player defendant to take advantage of differing views of risk. Specifically, in ordinary litigation a repeat player can be expected to be risk neutral,[17] meaning that the outcome of any one case is relatively unimportant, because the player can expect that wins and losses across cases will average out at some level. In contrast, the one-shot player will tend to be risk averse, because the outcome of the instant case is all important; there is no averaging out of wins and losses over a series of cases.[18] If there is a disparity in risk preference, the player with the lower aversion to risk can use that as an advantage over the other player, and thus can be said to have a degree of power.[19]

The primary implication of this theoretical approach is to focus attention on the role of bargaining tactics and the bargaining situation (both the individual situations of the parties and the situation in which the actual bargaining takes place), and how in conjunction with disparities in risk preference these can be used to the advantage of one side or the other. In the last section of this chapter, I will discuss one recent model (Swanson, 1988) that explicitly incorporates the use of risk preference as a conscious element of bargaining strategy.

Cooperation and Competition in Bargaining

A related approach involves comparing two common alternative styles or strategies in bargaining—those founded on cooperation versus those founded on competition. This distinction, which was discussed briefly in chapter 2, underlies Williams (1983) work specifically on "legal negotiations." Williams' goal is to account for what he terms "negotiator effectiveness." To examine this issue, he takes a "process" approach to describing and accounting for negotiation of legal disputes.[20] The process he describes involves a series of stages:
—orientation and positioning,
—argumentation,
—emergence and crisis, and
—agreement or final breakdown.[21]

Within this framework, Williams (1983: 9) seeks to account for the factors affecting negotiator effectiveness. This variable is in reality a complex and very rich *concept* involving:
—costs of negotiations,
—comprehensiveness of resolution,
—satisfaction to both parties,

—quality of outcome,
—observance of the rules of the game, and
—nature of resources utilized.

In carrying out the analysis, Williams concentrates his attention on the impact of whether a negotiator adopted a *cooperative* or a *competitive* approach (or strategy) to the bargaining.[22]

Williams relies upon a rich set of empirical materials—simulations, in-depth interviews, case studies, and mail questionnaires—to draw conclusions about the effectiveness of cooperative versus competitive negotiating styles. Although the actual categorization of attorneys as cooperative or competitive relies upon statistical analyses of survey data,[23] Williams links his definition of "competitive," and by implication "cooperative," to what has been called a tough approach in the social psychological literature. According to Williams (1983: 48), the elements of this approach include:
—making high initial demands;
—maintaining a high level of demands in the course of the negotiation;
—making few concessions;
—making small concessions (when concessions are made);
—having a generally high level of aspiration.

Williams (ibid.: 53) described the cooperative negotiator in the following terms:

The cooperative negotiator [seeks] to move psychologically toward the opposing attorney. Cooperative negotiators seek common ground. They communicate a sense of shared interests, values, and attitudes using rational logical persuasion as a means of seeking cooperation. . . . The explicit goal is to reach a fair resolution of the conflict based on an objective analysis of the facts and law. . . . [T]he cooperative negotiator show his own trust and good faith by making unilateral concessions. Making unilateral concessions is risky, but cooperative negotiators believe it creates a moral obligation in the other to reciprocate. The cooperative strategy is calculated . . . to induce the other party to reciprocate: to cooperate in openly and objectively resolving the problem; to forego aggression, and to make reciprocal concessions until a solution is reached.

In one of the samples he looked at, Williams estimated that 65 percent of the attorneys relied upon a cooperative style, 24 percent relied upon a competitive style, and 11 percent could not be placed in one of the two categories. Clearly, the cooperative style predominates. If a major indicator of this style is making offers or demands that approximate what is actually sought, then the pattern in the data described in chapter 2 suggests that the cooperative style predominates in negotiating settlements in ordinary litigation.

What are the implications of choosing one style over another? Williams (ibid.: 19) found that those negotiators who adopted a cooperative style or strategy[24] were more likely to be effective than those utilizing a competitive approach. Of the cooperators 58 percent were effective and only 3 percent were ineffective,[25] compared with the competitors, who were 25 percent effective and 33 percent ineffective. Despite the apparently greater likelihood of effectiveness with the cooperative style, Williams noted that ". . . neither pattern has an exclusive claim on effectiveness. Use of the cooperative pattern does not guarantee effectiveness, any more than does the use of the competitive pattern. An attorney can be very effective or very ineffective within the constraints of either" (1983: 18–19).

Although there may be a clear distinction in favor of the cooperative approach with regard to effectiveness, the impact of cooperation versus that of competition is less clear with regard to the "success" of the negotiation (i.e., the result achieved) vis-à-vis what was initially sought, particularly in the kinds of zero-sum situations that characterize ordinary litigation. If cooperation can lead to quick settlements with relatively little expense, the net outcome for both parties would be better than if the *same* settlement terms were achieved through a more competitive, time-consuming process. However, from the viewpoint of at least one party, a competitive approach may improve the settlement more than enough to offset any additional processing costs.[26] Furthermore, to the extent that a competitive approach is distinguished by demanding high or offering low, the data presented in chapter 2 do indicate that competitive negotiators in ordinary litigation do better than cooperative negotiators.

Assuming that the lawyers on both sides take the same approach (i.e., both seek to be competitive or both seek to be cooperative), and there is no systematic differential in processing costs, there is no theoretical reason that one approach or the other should lead to consistently better outcomes. However, as Williams acknowledged (1983: 54; see also Lowenthal, 1982: 82–83, 109–110; and Gifford, 1985: 60–62), there is reason to believe that where one side seeks to be competitive and the other sees the process in more cooperative terms, the competitive side (particularly if that negotiator can mask his or her competitive stance) will be at an advantage over the cooperative side. This is particularly true in the case of cooperative attorneys who fail to recognize a tough, competitive opponent.

This "disparate style" effect, where competitive negotiators are advantaged when confronting cooperative negotiators, comes out clearly in Genn's recent study (1988) of bargaining over personal injury claims in England. The insurance officials whom Genn spoke to were quite open in acknowledging that their goals were to achieve the best outcome that they possibly could for their companies. More important, the insurance officials also acknowledged that they were less able to get "good deals" when the plaintiff's solicitor was clearly prepared and willing to take the case to trial if the company's offer was not satisfactory. In the words of one claims inspector: "'Well if it was me and I was on the other side of the fence I would adopt the aggressive approach, without a doubt, because insurance companies then come running'" (ibid.: 48).

The idea that an aggressive approach to negotiation leads to a better outcome is supported by the pattern I reported in chapter 2. As I noted above, plaintiffs' lawyers who made initial demands that were high relative to what they felt were appropriate settlements tended to be able to get larger portions of those amounts for their clients; in actual fact, given that so many plaintiffs' lawyers initially demanded amounts equal to or less than what they felt were appropriate settlements, it is not surprising that those who demanded more got more. The pattern for defendants was even stronger; those defendants that offered substantially less than what the plaintiffs' lawyers felt were appropriate outcomes tended to achieve results that saved money in the end. In my data, it is not possible to compare the styles of the two attorneys. However, the pattern described here is consistent with a disparate style effect.

But what are the kinds of bargaining attributes that led some attorneys to "play hardball" while most seem to be unwilling to engage in this kind of negotiation?[27] In Genn's study in England, the solicitors who were clearly recognized as the toughest players in the game were those retained by trade unions to represent union members. Those solicitors had a reputation for not hesitating to take a case to trial and for making tough, exacting demands for settlement. This reputation, Genn suggests, may be the crucial attribute in the power game of zero-sum negotiations:

. . . [T]he solicitor may be in the business of creating a reputation for himself, either as a hard, uncompromising litigator or as a reasonable, realistic negotiator, and this may have implications for plaintiffs since individual litigation decisions may be influenced. Thus although the solicitor's decisions as to whether to settle or litigate are clearly dependent on the individual facts of the case before him, they may also have to be viewed within a more general context related to the creation and maintenance of the negotiator's own reputation *vis-à-vis* defendants. (Genn, 1988: 48)

But this idea of the importance of reputation may beg the question, What constitutes the crucial bargaining resources? Is it simply that some attorneys are aggressive while others shy away from this style? Or is there something about the attorney's situation that makes it desirable or possible for her to take an aggressive stance in negotiation?[28] In the next chapter, I will suggest that the economic constraints and incentives that the lawyer lives with help to account for whether she wants or is able to be a competitive bargainer. It may also be that disparities in "power," particularly disparities attributable to differences in risk preference and information, allow one side to be more competitive. This leads to the third major approach to negotiation that I want to consider in this chapter: game theory.

Game-Theoretic Approaches to Bargaining

AN INTRODUCTION TO GAME THEORY

Game theory as an approach to understanding conflict began with the work of von Neumann and Morgenstern (1944). The goal of game theory is to model a conflict situation in a way that both captures and simplifies the fundamental elements of that situation. Game theory is an important tool in the study of bargaining, because many of the games involve implicit or explicit bargaining.

Probably the best-known game is the Prisoner's Dilemma. This game derives from the problem of two persons taken into custody in connection with a crime. They are separated for purposes of interrogation, and each must decide whether to cooperate with the police:

—If neither cooperates, they both will be convicted of a minor offense with a minimal penalty (e.g., a brief jail term).

—If one cooperates and the other does not (i.e., one turns state's evidence and the other pleads not guilty), the former will be released and the latter will go to jail for a long time.

—If both cooperate (i.e., plead guilty so that there is no need for one to turn state's evidence), both will got to jail, but will receive reduced sentences in return for pleading guilty.

Given the lack of communication between the two players, the incentives tend to pressure both into confessing. Neither wants to be the "sucker" who insists on innocence while the other has confessed and turned state's evidence, even though both are better off if neither confesses than if both confess. That is, as stated by Axelrod (1984: 7), "the pursuit of self-interest leads to a poor outcome for all."

In the formal game-theoretic analysis, a specific set of relationships are established among the "payoffs." Typically, these payoffs are represented in the form of a game matrix such as that shown in Figure 4.1. The game is played by one player (R) selecting one row (cooperate or defect) and the other player (C) selecting one column (cooperate or defect); the moves can be simultaneous or sequential, so long as each player knows nothing about any

Column Player

		Cooperate	Defect
Row Player	Cooperate	$R_C = 3, R_R = 3$ Reward for mutual cooperation	$S_C = 0, T_R = 5$ Sucker's payoff and Temptation to defect
	Defect	$T_C = 5, S_R = 0$ Temptation to defect and Sucker's payoff	$P_C = 1, P_R = 1$ Punishment for mutual defection

Figure 4.1. The Prisoner's Dilemma Game Matrix. The subscript C represents the column player, and the subscript R represents the row player. Adapted from Axelrod (1984: 8).

of her partner's moves. For each player there are four possible payoffs:

Reward (R), if there is mutual cooperation;

Temptation (T) to defect;

Sucker (S), if the partner defects;

Punishment (P), if both defect.

The formal Prisoner's Dilemma game requires two conditions:[29]

$$T > R > P > S$$

and

$$R > (T + S)/2$$

The latter condition states that the Reward for cooperation must be greater than the average of the Temptation and Sucker. This means that "the interests of the two players are not in total conflict" (Axelrod, 1984: 14), and that the two players cannot expect to do better *over the long run* by taking turns exploiting each other than by cooperating.[30]

The *repeated* Prisoner's Dilemma game has formed the basis of extensive analysis, both theoretical and empirical; that is, most research examines what happens over a series of plays of the game between two players. There is an extensive literature in social psychology that uses this game (see Rubin and Brown, 1975), and variants of it, to examine the implications of characteristics such as those of the players, differences in the magnitude of the payoffs, and the like for their impact on bargaining and negotiations.

Another approach to analyzing the implications of the Prisoner's Dilemma employs a form of simulation. Axelrod (1984: 27–54) reports in detail the results of two computer tournaments in which professional and amateur game-theorists submitted computer programs to compete against one another in repeated plays of the Prisoner's Dilemma. The results demonstrated that no one strategy always does better than other strategies, but that certain types of strategies *tend* to lead to better outcomes. The more successful strategies rely upon three principles or rules:

1. They are *nice;* nice rules never defect first.
2. They are *forgiving;* forgiving rules are willing to cooperate in the subsequent moves even after the opponent defected. A totally unforgiving rule always defects after the opponent has defected once.
3. They are *retaliatory;* retaliatory rules defect immediately after the opponent defects.[31]

Interestingly, the most successful approach overall was the simplest rule, Tit for Tat. This rule starts out cooperating, and thereafter always moves in the way that the opponent did on the previous move; thus, it combines niceness, retaliation, and forgiveness. The rule does not succeed by necessarily defeating many other rules, but rather by inspiring other rules to be relatively cooperative; thus, in Axelrod's tournaments, Tit for Tat's average score across the competition was high, and the variation in its score was relatively narrow.[32] Despite this success, one can imagine specific environments where Tit for Tat would not do well, and this reinforces one of the key propositions of game-theoretic analyses: there is no absolutely best rule or strategy independent of the environment (i.e., independent of what the other player or players are doing).

This long excursion into the Prisoner's Dilemma is useful primarily for purposes of illustrating what game theory is about.[33] It may be useful for understanding certain types of bargaining contexts (Axelrod goes on to examine a number of real-world examples of implicit and explicit bargaining that are illuminated by the principles derived from the computer tournament), but it sheds relatively little light on the kinds of bargaining that occur in the context of civil litigation generally and ordinary civil litigation more particularly. Results based on the Prisoner's Dilemma are difficult to apply to bargaining in civil litigation because of several features of the game:

—the very specific restrictions on the payoff structure,
—the repeated nature of the game,[34]
—the restriction or exclusion of explicit negotiations from the actual game,
—the lack of opportunity for third-party decisions, and
—the players' limitation in choosing between only two strategies—cooperating and defecting.

As Kahan (1983: 3–4) notes, many of these problems are not unique to the Prisoner's Dilemma; two other games commonly used to study bargaining-type situations, the Pachisi coalition-formation game and the Acme-Bolt Trucking game, suffer from some of these same defects.

APPLYING GAME THEORY TO BARGAINING IN CIVIL LITIGATION

Another game may be more relevant to the civil litigation context: the bilateral monopoly game.[35] As the name suggests, this game is set in the context of a market in which there is a single seller and a single buyer; the two players *must* agree to a trade in order for either to profit. In order for a trade to occur, the two players must agree on a price and a quantity. As classic supply-demand theory posits, the lower the price the more the buyer will want to purchase (i.e., the buyer's profit is inversely related to price), and the higher the price, the more the seller will want to make available for purchase (i.e., the seller's profit is directly related to price). For each player there is a "profit table" known to that player; it shows the profit for a given quantity traded. The two players' tables are related in that for a given quantity there is a fixed total profit to be shared regardless of the price, though the total profit varies with quantity (not necessarily as a linear function of the quantity). For example, for a quantity of 10, the total profit might be 1,000; at a price of 100, there could be a profit of 500 each for the seller and the buyer, whereas at a price of 200, the profit might be 900 for the seller and only 100 for the buyer. For a quantity of 15, the total profit could be 1,200; at a price of 100, the profit might be 400 for the seller versus 800 for the buyer, compared with 800 for the seller and 400 for the buyer if the price were 15.

Thus, this game represents a mixture of cooperative and conflictual motives: both players tend to increase quantity (at least up to a certain level) while each wants to manipulate the price in his or her own favor (maximizing it for the seller and minimizing for the buyer). Most important, neither player can make any profit unless some agreement is reached. This game is useful for studying negotiation, because many factors can be readily manipulated, and those factors have important analogies to the civil litigation context:

—the amount of time pressure each side is faced with (pressures can be either equal or different);

—the type of communication that is permitted between the two sides;

—the use of agents in the negotiating process (i.e., is the negotiation direct or through representatives?), and what incentives those agents have;

—whether third parties may intervene, and what kinds of interventions are permitted (mediation, arbitration, etc.);

—the number of "commodities" being negotiated, and whether multiple negotiations occur simultaneously or serially;

—the type of information (i.e., degree of uncertainty) each side has concerning the other: what each side knows about the other's profit table—nothing, everything, something, or a probability distribution;

—bargainer characteristics (e.g., gender, race, age, personality, experience, etc.).

The relevance of this game for studying certain types of bargaining situations (e.g., bargaining between labor and management, one of the classic situations of bilateral monopoly) is very clear. It has certain commonalities with civil litigation: the negotiation involves two parties, each of whom has no alternative negotiating partner if an agreement cannot be reached. However, even though many of the manipulable variables are highly relevant, there is at least one important discontinuity between the bilateral monopoly context and civil litigation: the *integrative* nature of the bilateral monopoly situation. That is, the game is positive sum in nature (i.e., the total profit tends to increase as the quantity exchanged increases); in chapter 3, I argued that ordinary civil litigation tends to be more akin to a zero- or negative-sum game, leading to bargaining that is essentially *distributive*.[36]

Several other differences between litigation and the bilateral monopoly game can be manipulated *theoretically* in the game-theoretic context, but it is unlikely that those manipulations can be approximated in a laboratory context in a way that will come close to resembling the realities of litigation First, ordinary litigation typically involves a risk-averse one-shot player confronting a risk-neutral repeat player; although risk preference can be controlled or manipulated to some degree, it is hard to see how a game can approximate the *reality* of having to choose between a real payment of some thousands of dollars and a chance of winning substantially more by going to trial. Second, the uncertainty in litigation extends not only to the opponent's preferences and payoffs but to the bargainer's own position as well; again this can be dealt with theoretically, however, it is difficult to design experimental situations that capture the type of uncertainties that exist for those actually engaged in litigation.

Thus, although game theory can be extremely useful as a device to clarify conceptual and theoretical issues, it has many problems as a paradigm for the empirical study of the bargaining situations that occur in the litigation context. In a general review of the classic works on game theory applied to bargaining, Young (1975: 36–37) enumerated a number of limitations, all of which are directly relevant to the application of game theory to litigation:

The assumptions upon which the models of game theory are founded . . . have the effect of abstracting away a number of problems that are widely regarded as

Table 4.1. Litigant Strategies in P'ng's Litigation Game

Plaintiff's Strategies	Defendant's Strategies
"Do not sue"	
"Sue" and:	
"Settle, try"	"Settle, settle"
Settle if defendant offers to settle, otherwise go to trial	Offer to settle whether or not liable
"Try, try"	"Try, try"
Go to trial regardless of the defendant's move	Do not offer to settle whether or not liable
"Try, drop"	Settle, try"
Go to trial if defendant offers to settle, otherwise drop the action	Offer to settle if liable, otherwise do not
"Settle, drop"	"Try, settle"
Settle if the defendant offers to settle, otherwise drop the action	Do not offer to settle if liable, otherwise offer to settle

Source: Adapted from P'ng, 1983: 542.

important in the context of bargaining [e.g., the problematic nature of rationality, the unfixed nature of potential payoffs, etc.]. . . .

. . . [T]he models of game theory are fundamentally static models in the sense that they focus on outcomes in contrast to processes. . . .

. . . [T]he models of game theory have not produced good predictions in empirical terms. That is, the outcomes predicted by these logical models do not correspond well with the actual outcomes that occur in related real-world situations even though a number of the models are logically and mathematically elegant. In fact, the descriptive accuracy of the models is poor even in carefully controlled experiments specifically designed to test the extent to which the predictions of the models correspond to actual outcomes.

These limitations can be seen in one of the first direct applications of game-theoretic models to bargaining in the context of litigation. P'ng (1983) applied the theory of two-person games of incomplete information. In this model, the defendant is assumed to know whether or not he is liable, but the plaintiff can only estimate the probability (q) that the defendant is liable.[37] Based on this assumption, P'ng posits a game involving a series of decisions: the plaintiff's decision whether or not to sue, the defendant's decision whether or not to make an offer, the plaintiff's decision to go to trial if no offer is made or if the offer is inadequate.[38] For this game there are two sets of strategies, one for the plaintiff and one for the defendant; these are outlined in Table 4.1. For each strategy P'ng deduced the payoffs for the two litigants (see P'ng, 1983: 543, table 1), and examined which strategies are suggested by those payoffs by assuming that the following are all fixed and known: the amount that would be awarded if the case were to go to trial and the plaintiff prevailed (W), the amount of a settlement (S), and the costs of going to trial for the plaintiff (P) and the defendant(D).[39]

Clearly, this is not so much a theory of bargaining as it is a theory of settlement. In fact, P'ng himself recognizes this in discussing his assumption that the amount of the settlement is fixed ("exogenous" in his terminology): "We recognize that this is a very restrictive assumption. Our justification is that a realistic model of the process of settlement must rely on a theory of bargaining. Such a theory is still in gestation" (ibid.: 542).[40] However, even accepting this, the assumptions made in this model are so far from the reality of litigation that the model offers little beyond its heuristic value.[41] This is particularly true with regard to ordinary litigation where the values associated with the key parameters P (the plaintiff's costs) and D (the defendant's costs) can easily approach W (the potential award).[42] P'ng in fact notes that "the theory is ambiguous" when $S < D$, and/or when $qW - P < S$ (ibid.: 546); in ordinary litigation, there is a substantial probability that either or both of these conditions will be met.

RECENT DEVELOPMENTS IN THE APPLICATION
OF GAME THEORY TO LITIGATION

Over the last several years the theories of bargaining based on game theory and the application of those bargaining theories to litigation have made a number of major advances. These theories with their recent changes overcome some of the limitations spelled out by Young (1975) (e.g., the newly evolved models, which encompass games with an "extensive" or tree-like form, begin to focus on processes as well as outcomes). In general the models have not been applied to data drawn from actual examples of litigation (I will describe some interesting exceptions to this below), and this in part reflects the inherent "trade-off between complexity (and hence realism) of a model and the scope and strength of [mathematically derived] results that can be obtained" (Chatterjee and Samuelson, 1987: 176). In fact, the emphasis in most of the analyses drawing upon these models is on what *should* happen. In effect, these models are largely prescriptive (suggesting how players in the game should behave) rather than descriptive (comparing actual behavior with that suggested by the game).[43] Although the models typically yield useful predictions, those predictions primarily relate to what one would expect to happen in the bargaining arena if the rules governing the game were to be changed (e.g., allocation of transaction costs, rules governing liability, etc.). Such predictions, if robust (in the sense that they do not depend too directly on the more unrealistic assumptions built into the game), are extremely valuable for those considering reforming the litigation system. The models are less valuable when it comes to accounting for the patterns described in chapter 2.

It is not possible for me to summarize in any kind of comprehensive fashion this recent literature as applied to bargaining in litigation. The heuristic value of these models, along with their limitations, can be seen in a brief treatment. Game-theoretic models of bargaining have generally been classified (see Roth, 1985: 2–3; Sutton, 1986) as either cooperative ("axiomatic") or noncooperative ("strategic"). In cooperative games, the parties have a shared interest, whereas in noncooperative games they have distinctly opposing interests. For purposes of understanding bargaining in the litigation context, noncooperative, or strategic, games are clearly the most appropriate,[44] particularly noncooperative games under conditions of uncertainty. In fact, as shown in Table 4.2 (which summarizes a number of models), it is the assumptions about the nature and locus of the uncertainty that serve to distinguish among the various models. A key difference between bargaining in the litigation context and most other forms of noncooperative bargaining under conditions of uncertainty is that in litigation one side has the option of obtaining a definitive resolution from a third party;[45] thus the bargaining is not only noncooperative but also, for at least one party, nonvoluntary in the sense that that party has not chosen to enter the relationship that leads to the bargaining.

The obvious problem with most of the models summarized in Table 4.2 is that they presume only a single round of bargaining, but there is nothing that fundamentally limits the amount of bargaining that takes place (see Chatterjee and Samuelson, 1987, for a model without this limitation), particularly in the litigation context. Still, what these models suggest is that the function of bargaining under conditions of uncertainty is to provide a means of coping with and reducing some of that uncertainty and, as I will discuss below, a means of manipulating uncertainty to advantage one side or the other. When stated this way, the game-theoretic models can be seen to be not unlike the learning-theory model described by Cross (1969).

A good illustration of the role of uncertainty and the imminent presence of the shadow of adjudication can be illustrated by adapting a game-theoretic model presented by Grossman and Perry (1986) to the litigation context. In this model, both sides are seen as preferring settlement to trial, and the acceptable range of settlement for each party in the bargaining arena is a function of the party's expected value of going to trial (as defined in chapter 2). For purposes of the bargaining model, it is the expected value itself that is important, not the combination of probabilities, damage evaluations, and

Table 4.2. Summary of Game-Theoretic Models of Bargaining in Litigation

Author	Information	Rounds	Liability/damages	Strategies
P'ng (1983)	D knows whether or not he is liable P knows the proportion of defendants who are liable Both sides know amount of damages (quantum)	P makes demands; D accepts or rejects If rejected, P must decide whether to go to trial or drop suit (One round only)	Amount of damages fixed and known	D can take advantage of fact that Ds who are not liable will always reject offer ("pure pooling"—all Ds act as if they will win) P can use D's rejection as a guide whether to go to trial
Ordover and Rubinstein (1983)	Side A knows whether or not he will win Side B does not know whether A will win but knows that A does know; B has a prior estimate of probability that A will win	First move by B; A must decide whether to accept B's proposal After each move by A, B updates his prior estimate of the probability that A will win (i.e., whether A is strong) (Multiple rounds)	(Not discussed)	Weak informed players (those that will lose) may try to take advantage of fact that strong informed litigants (those that will win) do not win by "pretending" to be strong Uninformed Player B must try to infer from A's behavior whether A is strong or weak
Bebchuk (1984)	D has private information on chance of P winning at trial Both sides know size of judgment that would be awarded ("quantum exogenous")	P makes single take-it-or-leave-it demand If D rejects demand case goes to trial (One round only)	P either liable or not; P knows his liability, D does not	P knows chance of D settling is function of amount demanded

(*continued on the following page*)

Table 4.2. Summary of Game-Theoretic Models of Bargaining in Litigation (*continued*)

Author	Information	Rounds	Liability/damages	Strategies
Salant (1984)	P knows whether he has large or small damages; D does not know magnitude of P's damages	P makes demand; D either accepts or rejects; rejections always lead to trial, outcome of which is determined solely by actual damages (One round only)	All Ds are liable (liability assumed); some Ps have large damages, and some have small damages	Three strategies: All Ps demand high damages (pure pooling) Some Ps with low damages Demand high and some demand low (semipooling) All Ps demand according to actual damages (separating)
Reinganum and Wilde (1986)	P knows damages; D knows only that damages lie in an interval with a strictly increasing frequency distribution	P makes demand; if D rejects demand, case goes to trial (if P wins, he receives his damages)	P knows damages; D does not. There is a known probability that P will win at trial	P's demand is a function of damages D's decision to accept is a function of demand (D can use demand to assist in estimating damages
Spulber (1985)	P has information about his degree of contributory negligence D has information about his negligence level Both are represented as a probability	1. P and D determine their own levels of negligence 2. P and D decide whether to settle 3. If no settlement, P decides whether to go to trial	Damages are an increasing function of probability that P was not contributory and D was negligent	D's settlement amount increases as his negligence increases P's settlement amount decreases as his negligence increases Example: P informs D of his probability of acceptance of each level of offer; D must then decide what offer to make given his level of negligence
Banks (1986)	Each side knows its own negligence but not the other side's	(Unclear)	(Unclear)	(Unclear)

D = defendant
P = plaintiff

costs that make up that expected value. The crucial assumption here is that neither side knows what the other side's evaluation is, but each side has an estimation of that evaluation expressed as a probability distribution. In fact, in the adaptation of Grossman and Perry that I present below, each side has an estimation of several points in the other side's settlement distribution. The problem for the bargainers is to make an offer or a demand that prompts the desired response from the opposing party and avoids undesirable responses (in effect there are three kinds of responses: desirable, tolerable, and undesirable). There are four possible responses:

1. acceptance of the offer or demand;
2. rejection with an acceptable responding offer or demand;
3. rejection with an unacceptable responding offer or demand;
4. rejection, with a break-off of negotiations, leading to trial.

As illustrated in Figure 4.2A, each of these is represented by a distinct range along a continuum, with the order of each range differing for the two sides. An "extensive" form of the game (involving multiple exchanges of offers and demands[46]) can be specified in a treelike form (see Figure 4.2B), with each node having three branches, two branches that terminate the game (acceptance or termination through trial) and one branch that continues the game (rejection with either an acceptable or an unacceptable counter).[47] It is important to note that the desirable, tolerable, and undesirable responses are not necessarily fixed across rounds.

One can easily imagine that players in the initial round would not want to make offers or demands that are immediately accepted by the other side because, given the uncertainty, they might view such responses as indicating that the initial demand was too low or the initial offer was too high; thus in the first round, an acceptance might be tolerable, but the desired response might be an acceptable or an unacceptable counter. At some point, particularly if there are costs in continuing the game (and even more so if those costs escalate in later rounds—for example, as it becomes necessary to get ready for a trial because the trial date is approaching), the desired response will become an acceptance or an acceptable counter.

Two kinds of analyses are typically undertaken with a game-theoretic model of this type. First, one or more "equilibria" are derived mathematically; these represent theoretically expected outcomes based upon the assumptions built into the game, normally expressed in terms of the unspecific (i.e., symbolic) utilities and probability distributions. In principle, if actual values could be assigned to these utilities and probability distributions, predictions could be made about what should happen if the game were to approximate the real world of bargaining. Although there have been some

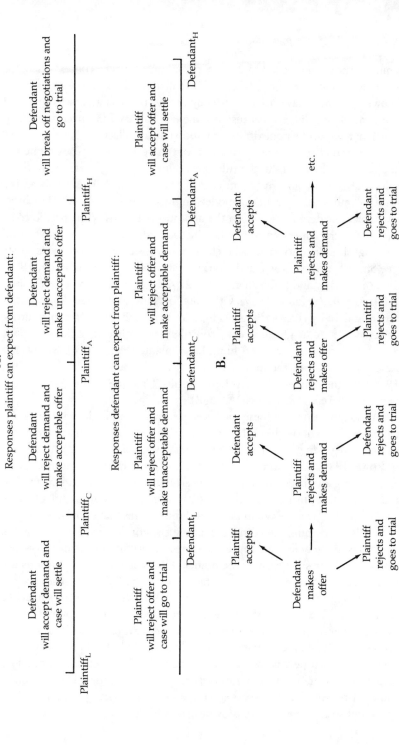

Figure 4.2. A Multistage Litigation Game. Part A. Expected Responses from Each Litigant. The subscript L represents low offer, subscript C represents counter offer, subscript A represents acceptable offer, and subscript H represents high offer. Part B. The Form of the Game.

simulations that have tried to do this in nonlitigation-type contexts (see, for example, Chatterjee and Ulvila, 1982; and Raiffa, 1982: 44–65), to my knowledge, there have been no attempts to do this using data from actual cases (no doubt, largely because no one has collected the necessary data, which may in fact be nonexistent or impossible to collect.)

The second type of analysis, mentioned previously, is to examine the implications of changes in the rules governing the game, particularly those rules that actually govern litigation in the real world.[48] This has been the primary import of most of the models summarized in Table 4.2. The most common consideration has been the allocation of costs, with specific comparisons of the American rule, whereby each side pays its own lawyer, and the English indemnity rule, whereby the losing side pays both sides' costs (see Shavell, 1982; Cooter and Marks, 1982: 244–246; Samuelson, 1983: 23–26; Ordover and Rubinstein, 1983: 22–27; Spulber, 1985: 18; Bebchuk, 1984: 412–413; Hause, 1989). Other authors have considered the impact of differing liability rules such as negligence, strict liability with contributory negligence, and "negligence with contributory negligence" (Banks, 1986: 5–34), the effect of increased filing fees (Salant, 1984: 25–30; Salant and Rest, 1982: 12–14), the impact of who bears the burden of proof (Sobel, 1985), and the frequency of frivolous lawsuits (P'ng, 1983: 548–549; Rosenberg and Shavell, 1985; Bebchuk, 1988).

Although results of these analyses are interesting and useful, most of them have been derived in other ways outside the game theory context (for example, regarding allocation of litigation costs, see Tullock, 1980: 64–69; or Rowe, 1984). The more important value of the game-theoretic model is in emphasizing the need to consider uncertainty in a distributional fashion rather than just positing a probability associated with a given outcome. As applied to the game shown in Figure 4.2, this means that each side has a set of beliefs concerning the points delimiting each of the other side's possible responses; these beliefs are represented by a subjective probability distribution of the values for each of the points. The probability distributions are successively narrowed based on the opposing party's responses as the exchanges are made. Each side's strategy is a function of these subjective distributions, the history of prior exchanges, and what is acceptable to that player. One criticism of this type of work, to put it bluntly, is that it often represents a "painful elaboration of the obvious." In fact, what appears to be obvious in retrospect is frequently less clear before the elaboration. More important, the game theoretic models serve to systematize what are often rather disparate bits and pieces of common wisdom (and perhaps wisdom that is not so common) and to provide a useful, albeit perhaps only heuristic, framework for thinking about bargaining. Such models also point to the basic fact that negotiations do involve a substantial component of gamesmanship. The gamelike quality of actual negotiation can be seen in some recent efforts to apply game-theoretic approaches in analyzing data derived from actual cases of litigation.

One study (Swanson, 1988) focuses on the impact of the repeat player in litigation in the English context, drawing upon 220 case histories of civil tort disputes filed with the High Courts of England.[49] The "game" that is examined is derived from the work of Flemming (1976; see also Phillips, Hawkins, and Flemming, 1975), and is built on the idea that a repeat player who is risk neutral can use this position to take advantage of the likely risk aversion of the typical one-shot player. The game described by Swanson is predicated upon several specific features of litigation in England:

—For relatively routine injuries, the magnitude of damages is more certain than in the United States because quantum is set by a small cadre of decision-makers (judges of the High Court and circuit judges sitting in the county courts), who rely upon a standard reference work, *Kemp and Kemp* (Kemp, 1986), for guidance.

—The transaction costs of going to trial (and to various other stages of the litigation process) are set by standards enforced by court officials (called taxing masters).

—The English rule mandating that the loser pay both sides' costs is in fact less general than the law suggests, particularly as regards plaintiffs; some plaintiffs are fully at risk for the other side's costs (these cases are "privately funded") some are only partly at risk (these cases are usually "legally aided"),[50] and some are effectively fully insured against the risk of those costs ("union supported").[51]

—There is no contingent fee in England, so there is no procedure for the plaintiff's lawyer to assume the primary burden of risk as happens in the United States.

—The normal bargaining procedure in English injury cases is for the defendant to make offers to the plaintiff (usually in response to a request for such an offer by the plaintiff), and for the plaintiff to accept or reject the offer or offers that are made.[52]

The result of these factors is that tort litigation in England almost always pits a repeat player (i.e., an insurance company) against a one-shot player (the injured party). The level of risk facing the one-shot player depends upon the degree to which he or she is "insured" against the possibility of having to pay the repeat player's costs and his or her own costs if the opponent should win at trial. Thus, the one-shot players are differentiated from one another by their willingness to risk having a judge decide the question of liability, and this differentiation takes the form of a probability distribution of risk preferences. The repeat player is assumed to know (from experience with large numbers of cases) this probability distribution, but not the particular preference of the current opponent.

Swanson shows that in these circumstances the optimal strategy for the repeat player (who will be making the offers to which the one-shot player will be responding) is a mixed strategy in which the repeat player refuses to make an offer in some proportion of cases.[53] This serves to create uncertainty in the one-shot players and to enhance the advantages that accrue to the risk-neutral repeat player from the one-shot player's risk aversion. The implications of this particular game are that the specifics of the strategy employed by the repeat player should vary depending upon the distribution of risk preferences associated with the current opponent.

The game then is multistaged, with each node represented by the defendant deciding whether to make an offer, followed by the plaintiff's decision whether to accept the offer if one is made or to go to trial if no offer is made; if the plaintiff rejects the defendant's offer, the game advances to the next stage, with the defendant again deciding whether or not to make an offer (see Figure 4.3). Swanson (1988: 38) shows that the likelihood that the defendant will make an initial offer decreases as the level of risk facing the plaintiff increases; that is, the likelihood of an offer being made is greatest when the plaintiff is union supported against the costs of losing (offers in 90 percent of such cases) and smallest when the plaintiff privately funds the litigation and is thus fully at risk for those costs (offers in 53 percent of such cases), and somewhere in between when the plaintiff is legally aided and thus often partly at risk (offers in 66 percent of such cases). Even stronger support for Swanson's model comes from the fact that the figures are more or less unchanged in subsequent stages of the bargaining game. That is, if the plaintiff refuses the first offer, the likelihood of receiving a second offer is very close to the likelihood of having received a first offer, and this holds regarding third offers for those that refuse second offers.

Applying this specific model to the United States is not straightforward, because many of the conditions that make it applicable to England do not hold here. Particularly, with the American jury system, there is often substantial uncertainty concerning the magnitude of damages that will be awarded if the case goes to trial (see Priest, 1985; Wittman, 1985, 1988). Also, because the vast majority of tort plaintiffs are represented by contingent-fee lawyers,[54] there is a single risk-preference distribution rather than the multiple distributions found in England. Furthermore, there is an argument to be made that,

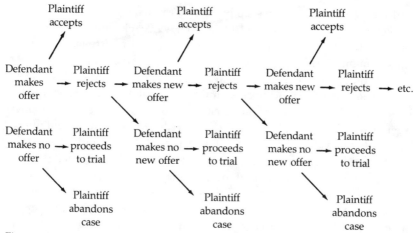

Figure 4.3. Swanson's Litigation Game

to the degree that it is the plaintiff's lawyer who is the decision-maker (reflected by the fact that the lawyer generally makes recommendations to his or her client concerning whether or not an offer should be accepted), most American tort litigation involves two repeat players.[55]

Interestingly, the image of the repeat-player contingent-fee attorney facing the repeat-player defendant leads back to the kind of analysis represented by Axelrod's replicated Prisoner's Dilemma, a game that is played a number of times between a given pair of players, so that each player learns to anticipate the actions of the other. Such a model could be applied to negotiations between insurers and personal injury plaintiffs' lawyers, where there are repeated dyadic negotiations between a lawyer and an insurance adjuster or between a plaintiffs' lawyer and an insurance defense lawyer (see Ross, 1980; Carlin, 1962; Genn, 1988). To what degree does the anticipation of future negotiations influence the resolution of any given case? To my knowledge, there has been no attempt by game-theorists working specifically in the litigation-bargaining context to explore the implications of this particular aspect of bargaining in personal injury disputes.[56] The implications of Axelrod's analysis demonstrating the benefits of cooperation over competition in a repeated game structured around the Prisoner's Dilemma could be read as suggesting that negotiation in routine tort litigation should be more cooperative than in other areas of ordinary litigation; however, the data in chapter 2 indicate that,[57] if anything, negotiation in tort cases is *less* cooperative than in other areas.[58]

The second recent study, by Fenn (1988), is also based on English data and complements Swanson's study. Fenn starts from the same antecedent studies (Phillips, Hawkins, and Flemming, 1975; Flemming, 1976). The problem for the repeat-player insurance company is to estimate the plaintiff's "minimum ask" (i.e., the minimum amount that the plaintiff will accept to settle the case).[59] The obvious way of doing this is to start out with a low offer, then increase by increments until the plaintiff accepts. However, this undermines the credibility of the defendant's threat to go to court if an offer is rejected.[60] The strategic problem then is to determine a finite set of offers, each with a particular probability of acceptance by the plaintiff. Once that set of offers has been exhausted, no further offers will be made and the case will go to trial (unless the plaintiff drops the action).

As a solution to this problem, Fenn posits that the defendant relies upon an *estimate* of the subjective probability distribution of the plaintiff's minimum ask, which can be revised in light of the plaintiff's response to any offers of settlement that are made. According to Fenn's models, a first offer will be made if the mean of the estimated probability distribution is less than the defendant's "maximum offer" (i.e., the maximum amount the defendant is prepared to offer to settle the case); the offer will equal this mean; if the mean of this probability distribution exceeds the defendant's maximum offer, the defendant will prefer to go to trial. If the plaintiff refuses the first offer, the defendant can presume that the plaintiff's minimum ask lies in the upper half of the original subjective probability distribution,[61] and can accordingly revise his or her estimate of the subjective probability distribution of the plaintiff's minimum ask.

Note that the revision process will effectively halve the range of the subjective probability distribution after each rejected offer, assuming that the upper limit of the distribution remains constant. As a result, Fenn argues, it will take only a small number of rejections to push the mean of the distribution (which is the defendant's potential offer) beyond the defendant's maximum offer. This serves to create a finite set of possible offers, and thus creates a credible threat of forcing the plaintiff to trial.

Based on this model, Fenn carries out a number of statistical analyses using data collected as part of a large study of compensation for injury in England (see Harris et al., 1984). In this injury study 224 respondents reported seeking compensation from the parties they believed to have been responsible for the injuries. Using these cases, Fenn employs probit analysis to examine the effect of a number of variables on the probability that an offer will be made (i.e., the likelihood that the defendant's maximum offer will exceed the defendant's estimate of the plaintiff's minimum ask). He also looks at the factors affecting the plaintiff's decision to reject that offer (which Fenn presumes is indicative of the offer falling below the plaintiff's minimum ask).

Perhaps what is most interesting about the results of the first of these probit models concerns the way the plaintiff's solicitor is to be paid. Controlling for damages, it appears least likely that a settlement offer will be made if the plaintiff is unrepresented (.88).[62] The likelihood then goes up in increments: first, if the plaintiff has retained a solicitor at his or her own expense (.96); next, if the solicitor is retained by a trade union (.98); and finally, if the solicitor has obtained legal aid on behalf of the plaintiff (.99).[63] This is generally consistent with Swanson's analysis described above, though the last two categories are reversed. On major difference between Fenn's and Swanson's findings, however, is that offers of settlement appear to be more frequent in Fenn's data set than in Swanson's; this probably reflects the fact that Swanson's analysis included only those cases where a formal legal action had been filed and had led to substantial conflict.[64]

These results raise some intriguing questions for both Swanson's and Fenn's models of the bargaining and settlement process. If one presumes that the plaintiff's risk-preference discount is inversely related to the fear of having to pay the costs of the litigation if the claim is unsuccessful, and that other factors are equal, the union-supported plaintiff should have the lowest risk-preference discount and thus the highest minimum ask. If this is an accurate analysis, the probability that the defendant's estimate of the plaintiff's minimum ask exceeds the defendant's maximum offer should be highest for the union-supported plaintiff, and fewer offers should be made to such plaintiffs. However, this does not appear to be the case, either in Fenn's data or in Swanson's data.

Swanson's model—where the repeat-player defendant seeks to maintain some set level of uncertainty among plaintiffs, and that level is a function of the expected willingness of each type of plaintiff to go to trial—is more consistent with the pattern in Fenn's data. Clearly, Fenn's model needs to incorporate some factor to control for variation in the plaintiff's willingness to go to trial. Apparently, assuming that Fenn's general model is on the right track, this aspect of risk preference does function simply as a discount on the plaintiff's minimum ask. Although the thrust of Swanson's model suggests an explanation for the observed ordering of the likelihood of offers, the relatively small differences raise doubts about whether the kind of manipulation suggested by Swanson is actually occurring. The pattern in the likelihood of offers is more consistent with a blunter calculation of the impact of risk preference on the willingness of a claimant to proceed to trial. In the next chapter I will discuss in some detail another recent English study

(Genn, 1988) that suggests that insurer defendants are directly responsive to the willingness of claimants' solicitors to start and pursue formal legal actions.

Conclusions

The various approaches to bargaining found in the game-theory literature are of limited value in brining into clear focus what actually occurs in ordinary litigation in the United States. Analysts such as Axelrod have obtained results that are interesting and important for the understanding of bargaining in general.[65] Some of these analyses have relied upon simulations devised to represent a particular game; others involve elegant mathematical representations. However, the assumptions that are *essential* to most of these analyses differ so much from the reality of day-to-day ordinary litigation that the results drawn from them must be viewed with a healthy skepticism.

In some ways, the analyses and frameworks discussed in this chapter raise more questions than they answer (some of which have already been considered in previous chapters). Why are there so few exchanges when it would seem that those exchanges are one of the primary ways by which the two sides share information about their goals and expectations? Why do so few attorneys engage in tactical bargaining (demanding very high or offering very low)? What is the impact of the way in which the costs of litigation are actually distributed (i.e., what is the importance of the fact that the potential costs of going to trial are frequently borne not by the plaintiff but by the plaintiff's attorney)? In the next two chapters I will consider factors that relate directly to these questions: agent (i.e., lawyer) incentives and shared goals among the regular players.

CHAPTER 5

The Structure of Economic Incentives for the Lawyer

Introduction

One central aspect of litigation in the United States, compared with most other countries, is the direct economic stake that lawyers frequently have in the *outcome* of litigation. This is dramatically illustrated in the fee reportedly received by Joseph Jamail, the attorney representing Pennzoil in its lawsuit against Texaco; one account reported that, for the eventual settlement of approximately $3 billion, Jamail earned $300 million (*National Law Journal,* September 26, 1988, p. 2). Although this particular fee obviously represents an extreme of an extreme, a small number of lawyers working on a percentage basis (see Grady, 1976)—what is misnamed a contingent fee in the United States—regularly earn multimillion-dollar fees (see Jenkins, 1989). It is also true that in big-time cases, lawyers can invest a large number of hours and earn nothing. For example, in a major case in which it was unsuccessfully alleged that the morning-sickness drug Bendectin caused birth defects in the children whose mothers used the drug during pregnancy, the firm of one of the lead plaintiffs' lawyers, Stanley Chesley, invested 19,000 hours for zero return.[1]

One of the traditional criticisms of the contingent fee is that, by having an interest in the outcome of the cases, lawyers are hindered in providing the kind of dispassionate professional advice they should be rendering to their clients (MacKinnon, 1964; Benson Commission, 1979: 176–177). With the kinds of huge fees and losses described above, it is hard to see how someone could remain objective and dispassionate.[2] But what about the kind of ordinary litigation that is the subject of this book? Recall that the median state case in the sample involved stakes of approximately $4,500; it would be hard to get passionate about the typical $1,500 (a third of $4,500) contingent fee such a case would earn. However, in such cases, rather than

99

there being a problem with the lawyers' inability to look dispassionately at the clients' causes, there can be a problem of direct conflict of financial interests. That is, frequently it is more beneficial financially for the lawyer to secure a quick settlement, even if the amount paid is much lower than what could be achieved by going to trial.

Some of the many theories of negotiation and settlement that I discussed in the previous two chapters consider the economic incentives that can influence the *litigants'* decisions regarding negotiation and settlement. Interestingly, those theoretical approaches seldom consider the separate economic incentives of "agents," such as lawyers. Actually, it is not surprising that the element of lawyer incentives is missing, because one typically thinks of the *professional* lawyer as the client's *alter ego* (see Johnson, 1980–81), and persons acting in this kind of role do not consider their own economic interests ahead of those of their clients'.

There is, however, a growing acceptance of the fact that professionals cannot help but be influenced by the same kinds of mundane financial concerns that affect all members of society:

The way doctors (and hospitals) are paid affects how medicine is practiced. . . . For doctors and hospitals [the fee-for-service] payment system means that the more services and procedures they perform, the more they're paid. Naturally, the line between what is appropriate medicine and what is rewarding has blurred. . . . It is not that doctors or hospital officials are venal. They're human and respond to economic signals. (Samuelson, 1986: 78–79)

Although this quotation discusses the practice of medicine, it is actually taken from a consideration of the "litigation explosion." In thinking about the work of lawyers in general, and bargaining and settlement in ordinary litigation in particular, one must take into account the fact that lawyers are engaged in their practice for remuneration.[3] The importance of this simple fact can be seen in several different ways.

Contingent Fees and the Content of Negotiation

In chapter 2, I observed that contingent-fee lawyers are more likely to restrict their demands to money, and are extremely unlikely to make demands that do not involve money (see Table 2.13). This is not at all surprising.

In her analysis of legal negotiation, Menkel-Meadow (1984) points out that in many cases it is possible to find solutions that may serve more of a "problem-solving" function than what she refers to as "adversary negotiation." She uses a hypothetical example involving the purchase of a defective car to illustrate what a problem-solving solution might look like (ibid.: 772):

Ms. Brown buys a car from Mr. Snead, a used car salesman. After a short time the car ceases to function, despite repeated attempts by Ms. Brown to have the car repaired. Ms. Brown, therefore, sues Mr. Snead for rescission of the sales contract, claiming misrepresentation in the sale of the car, or, in the alternative, breach of warranty, with consequential damages, including lost income from the loss of a job due to repeated latenesses and absences as a result of the malfunctioning car. Mr. Snead counterclaims for the balance due on the car [plus attorneys' fees as permitted under the sales contract], claiming that the warranty period has ended and the dealership was given insufficient time in which to cure any possible defects.

As Menkel-Meadow points out, although the lawsuit is over money, both parties have concerns that go beyond simple dollars and cents:[4]
—Mrs. Brown wants a reliable form of transportation (and her job);
—Mr. Snead wants both to retain his profit on this sale and to sell Ms. Brown (and her friends) cars in the future.
Given these goals, there are outcomes which allow both parties to go away relatively happily, outcomes that differ from those of the typical damages-oriented lawsuit. For example, Mr. Snead could provide Ms. Brown with another car from his inventory, including with it an extended warranty to compensate her for her difficulties; he could also then repair the car originally sold to Ms. Brown before selling it to another customer.

However, this kind of alternative solution becomes problematic as soon as a contingent-fee lawyer enters the picture. Although a lawyer might recognize the possibility of resolutions that do not involve a direct exchange of money, he or she is in the law business to make a living; it is unlikely that a client in a situation like that of Ms. Brown would have the funds to pay a lawyer on an hourly basis, and there is no way that the lawyer can take a third of a car.[5] Contingent-fee lawyers who seek nonmonetary resolutions for their clients, even if those resolutions are better from the clients' perspectives, would soon go out of business unless there were some alternate-payment method available for such settlements.[6]

This is not to say that contingent-fee lawyers will never consider the possibility of some kind of creative resolution for a case. Recall the class-action case involving claims by former employees of a meat packer (mentioned in chapter 3) in which a quarter of the settlement was to be paid to the plaintiffs in the form of coupons for products made by the defendant.[7] There are clear problems with this settlement when it comes to paying the lawyers representing the plaintiffs. Given that the lawyers were to be paid 25

Table 5.1. Percentage Distribution of Negotiation Contents, by Fee Arrangement, for Monetized Cases Only[a]

	Monetary	Nonmonetary	Mixed	N
Hourly	63	5	32	370
Contingent	78	1	21	300
Other	62	8	30	60

$\chi^2 = 27.04$
$p < .001$

[a]This table excludes cases in which lawyers were unable or unwilling to express stakes in wholly monetized terms.

percent of the settlement, and that fee payment would be in money and not in coupons, the effective percentage of the cash component of the settlement that would be received by the plaintiffs would be substantially less than 75 percent. This point was not lost on at least some of the plaintiffs, one of whom suggested that the lawyers should in fact accept a quarter of their fee in coupons (*National Law Journal,* March 9, 1987, p. 8).[8]

There is a certain element of self-fulfilling prophecy to the argument that contingent-fee lawyers want to achieve monetary settlements. It is no doubt true that this is the case, but this also means that there is a high probability that a lawyer will refuse to work on a contingent-fee basis if a nonmonetary resolution were likely. Yet, as shown in Table 5.1, even in those cases in which stakes could be expressed wholly in monetary terms, contingent-fee lawyers were more likely to concentrate on money than were hourly fee lawyers or lawyers paid on some basis other than a contingent or hourly fee; the difference between the contingent- and noncontingent-fee lawyers is smaller than that shown in Table 2.13 (which includes both monetized and nonmonetized cases), but the gap is still clearly present.

There are several other pieces of evidence regarding ways in which the settlement-related behavior of lawyers is affected by fee considerations. The *National Law Journal* (August 19, 1985, p. 3) reported on a problem arising from modifications in the schedule of fees paid to court-appointed counsel in criminal cases before courts in Detroit and elsewhere in Wayne County (these modifications were ordered by the chief judges of the courts involved). The changes simultaneously resulted in a reduction from $300 to $150 in the daily fee for trial work and an increase from $100 to $150 in the fee paid to a lawyer for appearing in court with a client who enters a guilty plea. One of the judges was reported to have said prior to the changes that he was concerned about a significant increase in the number of bench trials in his court, which he attributed to lawyers foregoing guilty pleas in favor of unnecessary trials that brought an easy $300 fee. A spokesperson for one of the bar groups opposed to the new fee schedule conceded that some lawyers did "go to trial when a guilty plea might be more appropriate," but attributed this, at least in part, to the county prosecutor's policy vis-à-vis plea bargaining.

Another example of a problem related to fee considerations is to be found in cases where it is the judge who sets the fees to be paid to the lawyers representing the plaintiffs (e.g., class-actions where the judge serves as the guardian of the interests of the class members not represented in court, or cases where the law authorizes fee awards to successful plaintiffs [see Zemans, 1984]). In such cases, there are a number of alternative ways in which the judge could, at least in theory, fix that fee.[9] One possible approach would be a simple extension of the contingent fee used in most cases involving individual plaintiffs: the lawyer is paid some percentage of the recovery. Percentage fees provide an incentive for the lawyers to seek the best settlements possible, because the resulting increase in their fees is likely to more than offset the time spent obtaining the better results.[10] The problem with this approach in large class actions is that fees computed on a percentage basis could yield windfall payments to lawyers (see Cavanagh, 1988: 76).[11] The alternate method of fee calculation, which is the accepted practice, at least in cases under federal statutes authorizing fee awards (see *Pennsylvania v. Delaware Valley Citizens' Council,* 483 US 711 [1987]), is the "lodestar" method, in which lawyers are compensated for their time at an appropriate hourly rate, sometimes adjusted by a multiplier to reflect the quality of the work or the element of risk involved (see Leubsdorf, 1981: 477–488). The problem that has been identified with the lodestar-fee calculation is that it may create an incentive for plaintiffs' lawyers to delay settlement and to pad their time by engaging in "unnecessary" pretrial maneuvering, because the more time they put in, the more they will be paid, even where there is little chance that the additional effort will materially affect the outcome (see Cavanagh, 1988: 80–81; Coffee, 1986: 675n16). This is particularly a problem in class-action cases or mass tort cases (e.g., Agent Orange), where there is no real possibility of significant client input in the decisions of the plaintiffs' lawyers (see Cavanagh, 1988: 81–83; Feinberg and Gomperts, 1986).[12]

Tactical Bargaining and Fee Arrangement

In chapter 2, I presented a variety of statistics related to the tactical nature of bargaining. Of particular interest here is the apparent asymmetry between plaintiffs and defendants. Sixty-five percent of defendants' lowest offers were less than or equal to what they felt to be appropriate resolutions of the cases, and 37 percent of defendants' lowest offers were half of or less than what they were in fact prepared to settle for. On the other hand, fewer than half (48 percent) of the highest plaintiffs' demands were greater than what they felt was at stake, and only 15 percent of the highest demands were at least twice what the lawyers felt the cases were actually worth. Thus, defendants appear to be significantly more likely than plaintiffs to engage in tactical bargaining.

To what degree is this because a large proportion of plaintiffs' lawyers are retained on a contingency basis, and it is to those lawyers' economic advantage to achieve quick resolutions (see Johnson, 1980–81; Kritzer et al., 1985; Kritzer, 1990: 137–143; Miller, 1987: 198–202) by coming directly to what they believe to be fair resolutions rather than beating around the bush? One way to evaluate this consideration might be to compare the de-mands made by hourly fee plaintiffs' lawyers with those made by contingent-fee plaintiffs' lawyers; everything else held constant, one would expect to find that hourly fee lawyers making demands are more likely to be tactical than contingent-fee lawyers. In fact, without introducing controls, the reverse appears to be the case: only 38 percent of the hourly fee lawyers' highest demands were greater than the stakes, compared with 54 percent of the contingent-fee lawyers' highest demands. In actuality, the validity of this comparison is dubious, because tort cases are handled almost exclusively by contingent-fee plaintiffs' lawyers, whereas other cases (contracts, discrimi-nation, property, etc.) are handled by both contingent- and hourly fee law-yers. Given that the amounts in dispute in contracts cases can often be calculated with relatively more precision, hourly fee plaintiffs' lawyers are probably less likely to be in a position to engage in tactical bargaining than are contingent-fee lawyers, whose caseloads are oriented more toward tort cases.

If it is not possible to evaluate the argument that fee arrangement influ-ences bargaining tactics by directly comparing hourly and contingent-fee lawyers, what evidence is there that contingent-fee lawyers have incentives not to engage in tactical bargaining? In chapter 2, I considered the rela-tionship between the ratio of highest demand to stakes (or lowest offer to stakes) and the success achieved by the plaintiff, the defendant, and the contingent-fee lawyer (with the lawyer's success measured in terms of effec-tive hourly rate). I found that there was a very strong relationship between tactical bargaining and defendant success, a modest relationship for plaintiff success, and *no relationship at all* between tactical bargaining and the effec-tive hourly rate for the contingent-fee lawyer.[13] What this indicates is that it is not in the contingent-fee lawyer's own financial interest, at least in ordinary litigation, to engage in tactical bargaining.

Two factors probably account for the contingent-fee lawyer's desire to avoid tactical bargaining. First, speed is of the essence for the contingent-fee lawyer; the best effective hourly rates are achieved by a rapid turnover of cases, with relatively little effort devoted to those cases.[14] This rapid turnover means that the plaintiff's lawyer must arrive at a quick evaluation of what the case is worth, and present that evaluation to the other side in a form that will produce an immediate acceptance or elicit an acceptable counteroffer.[15] Second, and closely related to the first point, if the lawyer is engaged in a series of cases with an opposing party, it is advantageous to establish a relationship with that opponent that allows cases to be resolved with minimum effort; a reputation for making reasonable demands is most likely to further such a relationship.

With regard to both of these points, it is crucial to keep in mind that I am concerned with the modest cases that make up the bulk of ordinary litigation; in big cases (i.e., those involving $50,000 or more), the structure of incentives for the contingent-fee lawyer changes greatly.[16] As suggested in the discussion of fee awards at the end of the last section, even a modest percentage in a very large case creates an incentive to devote more time to that case. For example, if 1,000 additional hours increases a settlement by $1 million, a 10 percent contingent fee yields $100 per hour, and a 33 percent contingent fee yields $333 per hour.

A Comparative Perspective: The Impact of Fees and Costs on Bargaining in England

Hazel Genn's (1988) recent study of bargaining over personal injury claims in England provides further support for the argument that lawyers are influenced by their own financial situation when they enter into negotiations in a litigation or dispute context. The English system of litigation differs in several important respects from civil litigation in the United States, and these differences highlight the impact of the method of lawyer compensation on the negotiation and settlement process.

Formally, in the English system there is a prohibition on American-style contingent fees;[17] solicitors and barristers customarily expect to be paid regardless of the outcome of a case. The second major difference is the indemnity rule whereby the loser in a case pays both sides' costs, which in the English system are taken to include legal fees[18] (although there are some specific provisions for fee shifting in the American system, it is relatively rare here[19]). Thus, the accepted wisdom of the English system is that lawyers are not in the business of what might be thought of as subsidizing or financing litigation,[20] and the litigants have to consider the risk of losing and having to pay *both* sides' costs.[21]

If this were all there is to the English system, there would be relatively little that it might tell us about the role of the lawyer's incentives in bargaining and settlement behavior. In fact, as noted in chapter 4, there are significant variations in the system which create important differences in the incentives that lawyers in England must take into account. There are, in reality, at least three different cost/fee systems in operation in England: privately funded litigation, legally aided litigation, and union litigation.[22]

The one that most clearly parallels the formally acknowledged system is what is termed *privately funded* litigation. When litigation is privately funded, both parties are "actually" at risk for the costs of the litigation; I qualify the word "actually" with quotation marks because, in reality, solicitors representing a private individual of modest means may have difficulty collecting fees (other than those that have been paid "on account" as the case progresses) if the client's case is unsuccessful.[23] Moreover, Genn found evidence of what amounts to an informal contingent fee. That is, there are numbers of solicitors who take cases knowing that they will, in all probability, be unable to collect their fees from their clients if they are not successful (Genn, 1988: 109–110).[24] Regardless of whether solicitors assume they will not be paid if they lose the cases or they simply recognize the difficulties, both practical and interpersonal, that will be encountered in collecting what is due, there is a substantial incentive for solicitors to achieve settlements (thus having their fees paid by the defendants[25]), so that any problems that might arise with regard to being paid can be avoided.[26]

Genn's analysis suggests that solicitors, particularly those who are not litigation specialists, working on a privately funded basis are not aggressive negotiators. They tend to view the settlement process as a cooperative enterprise rather than as a conflictual one. She also found that claims inspectors for the insurance company are ready and willing to take advantage of this kind of solicitor when the opportunity presents itself. Genn argues that, given the insurance company's natural desire to maximize profits by minimizing amounts paid in settlement, a solicitor who approaches negotiations expecting a cooperative attitude by the claims inspector is asking to be "taken" (ibid.: 132).

There are two pieces of evidence that tend to support the view that cases that are privately funded settle without a lot of give and take, or without getting particularly close to the door of the courthouse. First, a study carried out by the Oxford Centre for Socio-Legal Studies (Harris et al., (1984: 94) found that almost two-thirds of the claimants who settle out of court (and virtually all claims that are pursued are settled rather than tried) accept the very first offer that is made, typically on the advice of their solicitors. Unfortunately, the Oxford data are not broken down by the manner in which the litigation is funded, but Genn (1988: 110) estimates that over half the litigation is privately funded, so it must be the case that a large proportion of the privately funded cases are settling on the first offers. Second, and more specific to the question of private funding, Genn (ibid.) found that the barristers she interviewed "were of the opinion that it was very rare for a plaintiff to be privately-funded." This suggests that, even though half the personal injury claimants are privately funded, only a small faction of their claims progress to the point that barristers are briefed by the solicitors.[27] This can mean only that privately funded claimants have a high likelihood of either settling relatively early or abandoning their claims.

The evidence that "sticking it out" yields better results is less certain. Comments that insurance claims inspectors made to Genn suggest that the tougher plaintiffs' lawyers achieved better results. The only statistical evidence in support of the view that holding out for a better offer in fact yields better offers is that, in most cases, second (and subsequent) offers are better than the offers that preceded them (Harris et al., 1984: 97–101). However, what is unclear from this is whether better offers were made because earlier offers were refused or early offers were refused because they were too low.

The incentives for the solicitor in the legally-aided case are very different. Solicitors are under an ethical obligation to alert clients to their possible eligibility for government-funded legal aid, but once a client is receiving assistance from legal aid, costs are imposed on the solicitor. The first cost is in terms of delay and administrative overhead; at various junctures in a case, it is necessary for the solicitor to obtain the approval of those responsible for the legal aid before proceeding, and the solicitor is required to make a full report of the case to the legal aid authorities when the case has concluded (Genn, 1988: 88). The second cost is in terms of reduced fees. Although a defendant is still obligated to pay the legal fees of a prevailing plaintiff, if the plaintiff is legally aided those fees are paid into the legal aid fund, and the plaintiff's solicitor is paid directly by legal aid. The fees paid by legal aid tend to be lower than those that the solicitor might expect if the case were funded privately: solicitors are expected to give the legal aid fund what amounts to a 10 percent discount,[28] and for some (perhaps many) solicitors the schedule of fees paid by the fund is somewhat lower that they can expect to charge to a private client (see ibid.: 89).[29]

There is one very significant exception to the expectation that the solicitor of the legally aided client will accept payment from the legal aid fund with the required 10 percent reduction: if the case is settled before a court action is initiated, the 10 percent reduction is not made, but the solicitor must still be paid by the fund rather than directly by the opposing party.[30] Clearly, assuming that a solicitor has other work demands that pay more than the reduced legal aid fees, it is to his or her advantage to try to settle a legally aided case without initiating a formal legal action. There is another aspect of the rules regarding legal aid that can put pressure on the other side (i.e., the defendant) to settle where it might otherwise be prepared to fight a relatively small case: when a legally aided litigant loses a case against an opponent with substantial financial resources (e.g., an insurance company), the prevailing party is not permitted to recover its costs either from the losing party or from the legal aid fund.[31] This effectively removes threats vis-à-vis costs that a defendant can use as a bargaining endowment (see ibid.: 90–91).

A number of the solicitors Genn interviewed were particularly concerned about the delays and administrative burdens associated with legally aided cases. One solution to this problem is to handle the case on a *de facto* contingent-fee basis rather than to apply for legal aid,[32] particularly if the solicitor sees the case as a sure winner: "'Some very odd things go on with solicitors taking on cases and not really discussing the question of costs and somehow if they win then there's no problem and if they lose then they just write it off'" (a plaintiff's barrister quoted, ibid.: 110). This situation creates significant inducements on the plaintiff's solicitor to settle the case, preferably without initiating court proceedings (which most likely means accepting the first offer made by the insurance company). This reflects not only the solicitor's concerns about being paid but also the problems that might arise if the case were ultimately to go to trial and the opposing party were to win. The solicitor would be in the very difficult position of explaining to the client (who would be expected to pay the winning side's costs regardless of expectation of payment to the solicitor) why he, the solicitor, had not sought legal aid funding for the litigation; the solicitor would in fact be in breach of the rules of practice.

Although the reduced legal aid fees create an incentive to settle for solicitors who have other, more remunerative work available, solicitors in marginal practices might be very happy to accept the level of fees that legal aid offers. Moreover, those solicitors need have no concerns about being paid if the case is ultimately unsuccessful. Thus, if a settlement is not arrived at easily, a solicitor in this position has little to lose by pursuing it as far as necessary.[33] Hence, it is not surprising that barristers handling personal injury work find that legally aided clients compose a larger proportion of their caseload than is true for solicitors.

The last form of financing of personal injury litigation is through the trade unions. Historically, one benefit offered by trade unions in England has been the assurance that, if a member were injured on the job, the union would fight to see that he or she received compensation for that injury.[34] What this has meant is that for a workplace injury, the trade union retains a solicitor on behalf of the member and covers any costs associated with the case (e.g., if the member's case were unsuccessful, the union would pay both the fees of the member's solicitor and the other side's costs). Thus a solicitor retained by a trade union need not have any concern about being paid and need not worry about the client having fears about losing and having to pay the fees of the other side's solicitor. The result is that offers acceptable to others can be refused by union solicitors[35] without too much concern about the costs and risks of having to go to trial if necessary. In Genn's (1988) analysis of bargaining over personal injury claims, it is the union solicitor, well insulated both from concerns about being paid and from client fears about losing and having to pay costs, who is consistently the most successful advocate.

A fourth form of financing is beginning to evolve in England, and that is "legal insurance." A variety of plans are now available, particularly with regard to injuries arising from motor vehicle accidents, where for as little as £5 a year[36] motorists can receive coverage of up to £25,000 both for their own legal fees and for costs they might have to pay if they lose a court action. This serves to remove the disincentives associated with fee shifting (i.e., the potential plaintiff no longer needs to worry about the downside risk of losing and having to pay both lawyers), and may make potential litigants much more willing to contact solicitors in the first place. A conversation that I had with a solicitor who handles cases for one of these insurance plans made it very clear that the presence of the insurance affects the way that he handles cases:

I do a lot of motor claims, and the DAS [legal insurance program] makes a difference in how I pursue them. Because insurance companies are very, very slow to handle claims, and where I have a client who is privately paying, I will write half a dozen letters to the insurance company virtually begging them to get on with it and threatening to sue, but not doing it because I need to say to the client, "Bring me in £45 for the plaint fee," and he doesn't want to. Whereas when I've got the DAS, I give the insurers 14 days in which to get going, and if they don't I'll just put it straight into court. It's a lot faster procedure, and it's all because of finance. Clients are happy to go ahead when they are not looking at the bill.

This solicitor went on to illustrate the impact of the insurance by referring to a specific case he was handling at the time of the interview:

> This man has instructed me to pursue it. I've actually written to [the legal insurance plan] to get their authority to pursue it, because we are under instruction to do so. And they wrote back to me and sort of said, "Well, if you think there is a good chance of success then go ahead." I wrote back again and said, "I've already told you I don't think there's a good chance. Please confirm." And I fully expect them coming back and refusing it, because this bloke has nothing to lose, really, other than that cost [other side's expenses], which I don't think he'd get stuck with.
>
> If he was privately paying, it wouldn't have got this far. No way. Because I would have said, "Right, you've got less than a 50–50 chance, and it's going to cost you X pounds to try it," and he wouldn't pursue it.

This specific example does not explicitly illustrate the impact of the legal insurance plan upon the willingness of solicitors to advise clients to reject initial, unsatisfactory offers, however, it certainly does suggest that solicitors need not worry about either their own fees or clients' fears about costs.

Conclusion

Although the comparative perspective provided by Genn's study does not explain any of the specifics of bargaining in the American context, it does serve to reiterate the importance of the economic incentives for the key bargaining participants in litigation. Clearly, one must take into account the perspectives of all the participants, not just the litigants themselves.[37] This is particularly important given the variations that exist within the legal profession and the way those variations may relate to the manner in which lawyers conduct their litigation work. As I have suggested here and elsewhere (see Kritzer et al., 1985; Kritzer, 1990), one very important aspect of those variations is how the lawyer is to be paid.

This does not necessarily mean that lawyers knowingly engage in actions of questionable propriety with the intention of improving their financial position to the detriment of their clients. The argument is more subtle. Lawyers, like all of us, see the world through green-tinted glasses; that is, when confronted by a choice for which there is no definitive answer, they will tend to select the option that is in their own interest. The financial incentives of the lawyer's work situation will often produce the nudge in one direction or the other, and it is not coincidental that the decision-maker will benefit personally from the choices made. Thus, the strident defense of the contingent fee by the plaintiffs' bar reflects a belief that the contingent fee *is* the poor person's key to the courthouse door. However, that belief is shaped by the fact that plaintiffs' lawyers are not hurt when that same key also brings clients to their doors, and thus brings them a professional livelihood.

In this chapter, I have concentrated my attention on the behavior of contingent-fee plaintiffs' lawyers, but these issues are not peculiar to that particular form of payment for legal services. I can think of at least one other specific group that merits attention, one that I am not able to examine with the data I have available: lawyers who repeatedly represent a specific insurance company. These lawyers have a continuing relationship with a very sophisticated client, a client that may have exacting expectations that could serve to shape and control the behavior of the lawyers they retain. It is likely that insurance companies vary in their approaches to settling claims, and the differences among companies may be reflected in the styles of the lawyers the companies retain for representation. Given that lawyers who work repeatedly for insurance companies—particularly those lawyers that derive large proportions of their caseloads from concentrated sets of clients—have a rather particular set of interests of their own, it would be useful to explore the nature of those interests and their impact on the lawyers' bargaining behavior.

Finally, the discussion above should make clear that the influence of the financial incentives of the lawyers involved in civil litigation is not limited to ordinary litigation, though the nature of the influences may differ depending on the scale of the case. For example, in big-time litigation, the repeat-player lawyer may tend toward preferring to take a risk (i.e., by rejecting a settlement offer and going to trial) when the client would be better off accepting a settlement that was only a fraction of what might be gained by trial. Or, in a multiclient case, particularly something like a class action, the plaintiffs' lawyer might prefer to settle for an amount that yields a reasonable fee but nets relatively small payments to individual clients, whereas the clients would prefer to try for a substantially greater individual return by running the risk of losing at trial. Thus, although the calculations of how the lawyer's interest can influence settlement negotiations depend greatly on the specific case situation, that interest is something that must be taken into account in understanding bargaining in civil litigation across the full range of cases.

CHAPTER 6

The Forms of Negotiation: A "Sociological" Approach

Introduction

The various theoretical approaches covered in the preceding chapters provide a variety of useful insights into the patterns of negotiation in ordinary litigation. By contrasting the situation of ordinary litigation to that of big-time litigation, we have seen that the incentive structures of the bargaining participants, both principals (litigants) and agents (lawyers) encourage a process that limits uncertainty and reduces actual and potential costs. In this chapter, I move beyond the simple distinction between ordinary and big-time litigation to consider other contextual issues involved in the settlement process. This contextual focus suggests more of a descriptive orientation to understanding negotiation.

Menkel-Meadow's efforts (1984) to lead lawyers in the direction of problem solving and away from the adversarial stance in legal negotiations represent one of a number of sociological analyses of the negotiation context. As discussed in the previous chapter, she argues that lawyers need to consider the kinds of outcomes that can serve both the interests and desires of their own clients and those of the opposing parties. These outcomes in turn reflect a combination of characteristics of the negotiation participants and the subjects of the bargaining itself.

The study of bargaining has a long tradition of sociological analysis focused on descriptive categories. For example, one recent analysis of negotiation in litigation was a study of the patterns of argumentation that occurs in the negotiation sessions. Condlin (1985) drew upon theories of rhetoric to set out six dimensions that can be used to define "good" argument: detail, multidimensionality, balance, subtlety, emphasis, and emotionality. These six dimensions served as a framework for analyzing simulated negotiations in a case raising a prisoners'-rights issue; from the efforts of approximately

100 teams of law student negotiators, Condlin (ibid.: 123) reached the conclusion that the negotiations he observed generally exhibited "few of the qualities" that define "good argument." Obviously, this analysis has very limited scope, and is not applicable to the data I have in hand. It does, however, suggest the way that category frameworks might be used to analyze negotiation in ordinary litigation.

A more comprehensive example of this kind of sociological approach to negotiation can be found in Gulliver's book *Disputes and Negotiations: A Cross Cultural Approach* (1979). Based upon his research on dispute processing in several different cultural settings,[1] Gulliver offers two complementary descriptions of negotiation within the dispute context. The *cyclical model* focuses on the offer-counteroffer image of negotiation, and the *developmental model* focuses on the process of getting from initial contact to final outcome.[2] Both models provide sets of categories for use in observing and interpreting an actual set of negotiations. These categories could be used to analyze negotiations in ordinary litigation, though the cyclical model may be of marginal use, given the apparent lack of substantial give and take. However, the level of detail necessary for using Gulliver's categories is not available in my data.

The general approach of sociological analysis—defining and applying categories and typologies—can provide substantial insights into the negotiation process. In this chapter, I will review some of the major sets of categories and typologies that have been proposed, and then suggest my own typology, which, I will argue, helps to account for the prevalence of the low-intensity pattern in negotiations in ordinary litigation.

Categories and Typologies for Analyzing Negotiation

In the preceding chapters, we have already seen a number of typologies relevant for the study of negotiation in ordinary litigation. Two of these focus on the ends that the negotiations are intended to serve:
—integrative versus distributive bargaining (Raiffa, 1982);[3]
—adversarial versus problem-solving negotiation (Menkel-Meadow, 1984).[4]
Two others, which are very similar, focus on the means used in the negotiation process:
—cooperative versus competitive negotiators (Williams, 1983);[5]
—collaborative versus competitive negotiators (Lowenthal, 1982).
Figure 6.1, adapted from Menkel-Meadow's discussion of problem-solving negotiations, illustrates how the dimensions of ends and means might be combined to produce a typology of what could be labeled negotiation styles (as distinct from negotiat*or* styles). The two dichotomies, when crossed, suggest four different styles:

ENDS

		Adversarial	Problem Solving
MEANS	Competitive	hard bargaining	limited problem solving
	Cooperative	compromise	open problem solving

Figure 6.1. Negotiation Styles. Adapted from Menkel-Meadow (1984a: 818). Originally published in 31 *UCLA L. Rev.* 754. Copyright 1984, The Regents of the University of California. All Rights Reserved.

—hard bargaining: seeking greatest individual gain, using whatever competitive tactics best serve that end;

—compromise: seeking individual gain, but willing to consider the needs and desires of the opposing party;

—limited problem solving: considering common solutions while looking out for "number one"; and

—open problem solving: seeking common solutions through a joint endeavor.

Three of these four categories roughly correspond to the three "strategies" of negotiation described by Gifford (1985): *competitive* (hard bargaining), *cooperative* (compromise), and *integrative* (open problem solving).[6] The omission of one combination suggests that ends and means, although conceptually distinct, are not necessarily unrelated, a point that I will return to later in this chapter.

What is not recognized by these typologies is that negotiations, including those aimed at settling civil disputes, involve at least two sets of goals and two sets of negotiators. That is, one side might use a competitive means to achieve an adversarial goal while the other side uses a cooperative approach to achieve a problem-solving goal. The problem described by Hazel Genn in *Hard Bargaining* (1988) is that much of the negotiation over personal injury claims in England involves precisely this type of context: cooperative, non-specialist solicitors seeking compensation from highly experienced, competitively oriented claims inspectors.[7] The most successful plaintiffs' solicitors, those who customarily are retained by trade unions on behalf of members of the unions, engage in negotiations that might be described as combining an adversarial approach with a problem-solving goal. I describe the goal as problem-solving rather than adversarial because the worth of

Means:	Ends:	DEFENDANT			
		Competitive		Cooperative	
		Adversarial	Problem Solving	Adversarial	Problem Solving
Competitive	Adversarial				
Competitive	Problem Solving				
Cooperative	Adversarial				
Cooperative	Problem Solving				

(PLAINTIFF, left margin)

Figure 6.2. Negotiation Contexts

injury cases in England is defined with more precision than is true for tort cases in the United States. Experienced solicitors can handle injury cases with more confidence that they have evaluated damages properly, and thus seek compensation based upon a relatively easily determined "going rate."[8]

As Figure 6.2 shows, when the ends-means categories of two sides are combined, the result is a 16-cell figure. If one presumes that the two sides are equal, this could be reduced to 10 unique combinations because of the symmetry in the table. There might be some danger in such a reduction, however; van Koppen (1988) has found fundamental asymmetries between claimants and respondents in risk preferences, *independent of any resource differences*. Regardless of whether I collapse Figure 6.2 into 10 cells or retain the original 16, I could attempt to insert labels in each cell. It is doubtful that the combined categories would be very useful for analysis. Many combinations are likely to be rare, and most of the actual negotiations in the civil litigation context are likely to fall into a small subset of the possible combinations.

One need not limit the categories used to define the negotiation situation to factors concerning ends and means. In recent years a number of researchers have identified lists of categories or factors that can be used to differentiate among negotiations. Table 6.1 shows categories or factors suggested by Raiffa (1982), Strauss (1978), Menkel-Meadow (1983), and Lowenthal (1982). More extensive sets of categories like these can be powerful tools for analyzing and understanding specific aspects of negotiation if used carefully and appropriately. However, for purposes of understanding the patterns of negotiation in ordinary litigation, ideas following from the two key dimensions of ends and means may be most productive.

For example, Lowenthal (1982), Williams (1983), and Genn (1988), all argue that the approach of the negotia*tor* (described as competitive or cooperative by Williams, and competitive and collaborative by Lowenthal) has important implications for the outcome. The three authors reach somewhat different conclusions regarding the importance of negotiator style:

—Genn argues that the hard-bargaining, competitive negotiator will do best: negotiators approaching the resolution of tort claims in a cooperative spirit are likely to be disadvantaged.

—Williams leans toward the cooperative approach (he finds that cooperative negotiators are much more likely to be effective than are competitive negotiators; and competitive negotiators are much more likely to be ineffective than are cooperative negotiators), though he recognizes that a cooperative negotiator can be disadvantaged if the opponent takes a competitive stance.

—Lowenthal (see also Gifford, 1985) suggests that negotiators need to choose between competitive and collaborative styles, depending upon situation-specific factors.

How might these different sets of findings be reconciled, particularly the apparently conflicting results reported by Genn and Williams? One of the factors that comes up in several of the lists of categories in Table 6.1 relates to the continuing relationships involved in the negotiating context. In the criminal justice setting, Eisenstein, Flemming, and Nardulli (1988) have described the continuing relationships that flow from the presence of "sponsoring organizations" (i.e., the district attorney's office and the public defender's office). The general question presented by sponsoring organizations is, To whom do the negotiators owe their loyalties? In Genn's study, the key negotiators on the defendants' side were insurance company claims inspectors, direct employees of the profit-oriented insurance companies. In contrast, in Williams' study both negotiators were attorneys representing private clients; thus, for Williams the loyalties to the individual clients would be mitigated by other types of professional commitments, including profes-

Table 6.1. Dimensions of the Negotiation Situation/Context

Categories according to:			
Raiffa (1982: 11–19)	Strauss (1978: 237–238)	Menkel-Meadow (1983: 927–928)	Lowenthal (1982)
Are there more than two parties?	The number of negotiators, their relative experience in negotiations	Subject matter	Process-related:
Is the game repetitive?		Content	Rigidity with which negotiators hold to positions
Are the parties monolithic?	Whether the negotiations are one-shot, repeated, sequential, serial, multiple, or linked	Voluntariness—do parties have a choice about negotiating?	Flow of information between negotiators
Are there linkage effects?		Visibility of the negotiation process	Modes of communication employed by the parties
Is there more than one issue?	The relative balance of power exhibited by the respective parties in the negotiation	Relationships among parties and negotiators	How negotiators perceive one another
Is an agreement required?		Accountability of negotiators	Size of the negotiation agenda
Is ratification required?	The nature of the respective stakes in the negotiation	What's at stake in the negotiations? Who stands to win and lose the most?	Payoff structure of the negotiation (zero sum, nonzero sum, etc.)
Are threats possible?			
Are the contracts binding?	The visibility of the transactions to others; that is their overt or covert character	Routineness of the negotiations—the problems, the issues	Personality and values of the negotiators
Are there time constraints or time-related costs?		Relative power possessed by the parties	Continuing relationships apart from the negotiations (both principals and agents)
Are the negotiations private or public?	The number and complexity of the issues negotiated	Personal characteristics of the negotiators	
What are the group norms?	The clarity of legitimacy boundaries of the issues negotiated	Medium of negotiations (face-to-face, written, telephonic)	
Is third-party intervention possible?	The options for avoiding or discontinuing negotiation; that is, the alternative modes of action perceived as available	Alternatives to negotiation	

sional reputation and ongoing relationships with the negotiating partner. It may be that the kinds of sponsoring organizations standing behind the negotiators influence the approaches that negotiators take and their abilities to pursue their chosen approaches with vigor.

In the next section, I will suggest a typology of negotiations in the litigation context that places the patterns described in chapter 2 in perspective. The distinctions I will draw build upon those suggested by the categories shown in Figures 6.1 and 6.2, though the typology does not fit simply with either the ends or the means dimensions. The image that I will draw flows from work on negotiation in the criminal justice setting. The typology joins ends and means (or, goal and style) to capture a sense of the *function* that is to be served by the negotiation that takes place. Note that I am not using the term "function" here in a strict technical sense, but rather to capture that element of the negotiations that includes both the goal that is sought and the approach that is taken to achieve that goal.

Three Modes of Negotiation

What is the function of the negotiation process? In almost tautological terms, one might say that it is to achieve a settlement of the dispute without turning to the formal adjudicatory mechanisms that are available. Within this general statement of the function of negotiation, one can distinguish between those negotiation situations where the negotiator has in mind some particular kind of resolution and those situations where little thought has been given to what might be specifically achieved (here the emphasis is on simply achieving some resolution, *period*). More specifically, is the goal of the negotiations

—to extract concessions from the opposing party in order to achieve the best result possible?
—to reach some consensus with that party to achieve what is judged to be an appropriate result?
—to dispose of the problem or case by getting something (perhaps anything) from the other party?

MAXIMAL-RESULT, CONCESSIONS-ORIENTED AND
APPROPRIATE-RESULT, CONSENSUS-ORIENTED NEGOTIATION

In explicating the three modes of negotiation associated with the goals listed above, let me begin by concentrating on situations where the negotiator has some result-oriented goal in mind. The two types of "ends" suggested in Figures 6.1 and 6.2 and the accompanying discussion were labeled adversary and problem-solving or, alternatively, distributive and integrative.

In the mode associated with the first of these goals (adversary/distributive), the negotiator seeks to obtain the *best result* possible under the circumstances. This represents the traditional image of the negotiation process that one typically associates with the bargaining between buyer and seller at a flea market or bazaar: each side seeks a *maximal result* from its perspective (i.e., the "best" result) by extracting *concessions* from the other side. Each side keys its behavior, in terms of initial position and concession patterns, to its ultimate goal and to the expected behavior of the other side.

Although the combinations shown in Figures 6.1 and 6.2 make it clear that ends and means are distinct, common sense would suggest that concessions-oriented negotiation will be strongly associated with a competitive negotiating style. Thus, one might expect maximal-result, concessions-oriented negotiation to be characterized by a series of exchanges of offers and counteroffers in which each side seeks to position itself initially in such a way as to force the opposing side to make the first concession. Typically, in the litigation context, this means that plaintiffs would make initial demands substantially above the minimum they are willing to accept and defendants would make initial offers substantially below the maximum they are willing to pay (i.e., the ratios of the plaintiffs' initial demands to stakes are high and the ratios of the defendants' initial offers to stakes are low). As suggested by analysts like Ross (1980) and Cross (1969), the exchange of information in this kind of negotiation can be seen as a tool to further the goal of achieving a maximal result (i.e., each side will husband its information, sharing only that which will further its position).

Much of the early research on plea bargaining viewed criminal case dispositions in this kind of maximization framework. Each side in the plea bargaining arena has a set of resources that it can marshal to apply pressure on the other side in order to achieve its goal; the two sides try to wear each other down by drawing upon "tools" such as delay, caseload, quality of evidence, and the like (see, for example, Landes, 1971; Posner, 1972; Matheny, 1980). Analyses like these are heuristically valuable in helping us to think systematically about the criminal justice system, but they introduce distortions that can be avoided by applying frameworks that do not presume that maximal results are being sought by the negotiators. The data presented in chapter 2 indicate some of the key weaknesses of the maximal-result, concessions-oriented mode with regard to civil litigation; in particular, the lack of more than two exchanges of demands and offers in most ordinary cases casts substantial doubt on the "information exchange" functions of the bargaining, and thus raises questions about the frequency of this mode of negotiation in the world of ordinary litigation.

I label an alternative mode *appropriate-result, consensus-oriented* negotiation. Here the goal of the negotiator is geared not toward achieving the
best outcome possible but toward achieving an *appropriate* outcome by
arriving at some consensus with the opposing party concerning the parameters of the case.[9] Although there is nothing that precludes a connection
between appropriate-result, consensus-oriented negotiation and distributive/
adversary bargaining, the idea of seeking an appropriate result by arriving at
a consensus seems more closely connected to Menkel-Meadow's image of
problem-solving negotiation. As for negotiator style (competitive versus
collaborative), the contrast between maximal-result, concessions-oriented
negotiation and appropriate-results, consensus-oriented negotiation seems
somewhat sharper. One obvious expectation is that seeking a consensus
would be linked to a more collaborative or cooperative style, in contrast with
the competitive style which seems more geared to extracting concessions.
Still, the English example of plaintiffs' solicitors retained by trade unions
shows that appropriate-result, consensus-oriented negotiations can be conducted in a hard-nosed competitive fashion. Thus, although the maximal-
result, concessions-oriented negotiation and appropriate-result, consensus-
oriented negotiation are *associated* with contrasting ends and means, the
distinction I am drawing differs in important respects from the standard
ends and means dichotomies that one finds in the bargaining literature.

One can clearly see the usefulness of this alternative perspective in the
criminal area. In an analysis of criminal case disposition, Utz (1978: 10)
characterized that process as one of "settling the facts": "In most criminal
cases, the issue of guilt has been effectively resolved by police and prosecutor
screening practices that tend to eliminate the doubtful cases early. Guilt or
innocence of the defendant is not under serious dispute in most cases. Rather
the issue is: of what is he guilty, and what should be done with him."[10]
Either competitive or cooperative bargaining can be used to pursue the
search for the answers to the questions: Of what is the defendant guilty? and
What sanctions should be imposed? However, once the basic assumption of
guilt is accepted, the nature of the negotiation changes substantially to one
of trying to come to, first, an understanding of the specifics of the case by
sharing information and, next, a common interpretation of that information
(cf. Sudnow, 1965). The issue is no longer who is going to win and who is
going to lose, at least in the absolute sense. The shift in focus suggested by
Utz cannot be expressed simply in terms of the goals of the negotiation or in
terms of the means used by the negotiators to reach their goals. The focus on
settling the facts represents a specific combination of means and ends that
reflects the function served by the negotiation.

Recent extensive work reported by Nardulli, Flemming, and Eisenstein (1985; Eisenstein, Flemming, and Nardulli, 1988; Nardulli, Eisenstein, and Flemming, 1988) develops in rich detail the evidence supporting a consensus-oriented view of the guilty-plea process in routine criminal cases: ". . . [G]uilty pleas do not always result from explicit give-and-take bargaining. Rather, some result from the defense's accepting the standard disposition, the 'going rate.' They take the sentence that forms part of the consensus on how defendants with given criminal records should be sentenced for a given offense" (Eisenstein, Flemming, and Nardulli, 1988: 119–120). Based on their analysis of data from a large-scale study of felony cases sampled from nine different courts in three states, Eisenstein, Flemming, and Nardulli found relatively little evidence of concession-oriented bargaining. Of the 5,600 defendants entering guilty pleas, 60 percent pled guilty to the exact charges entered at the time of their arrests, and 80 percent received sentences falling into one of three narrow categories. Almost two-thirds of the defendants who did not plead guilty to *all* the original charges did plead guilty to the original primary charge; only subsidiary charges were dropped. Overall about 30 percent of the defendants pleading guilty obtained reductions in the number of charges they faced, but 23 percent of those convicted at trial also had reductions in the number of charges; 15 percent of guilty-plea defendants saw the primary charges reduced, but so did 11 percent of those convicted at trial (ibid.: 247–248). In summary, across the nine communities where the research was carried out, relatively few defendants appear to have used the guilty-plea process to extract concessions;[11] rather, the process appears to have relied upon perceptions of "going rates."[12]

Likewise in civil cases, once the basic question of liability is settled—and in a very large proportion of civil cases (particularly ordinary, everyday cases) the disputes are over damages, not liability[13]—the discussions concerning damages may be less a series of offers and counteroffers and more a process of exchange of information intended to place the instant cases in the context of the presumed going rates. The style of the players may again be either competitive or cooperative, but the goal is not necessarily one of maximizing the resulting outcome for each party. With the movement away from an emphasis on maximization, it seems likely that appropriate-result, consensus-oriented negotiations will be characterized by a freer flow of information and fewer actual exchanges of offers and counteroffers than will maximal-result, concessions-oriented negotiations. In fact, more actual time may be spent in consensus-oriented negotiations than in concessions-oriented negotiations, because it may take longer to exchange and interpret information than it does to exchange relatively explicit demands and offers.

Furthermore, in appropriate-result, consensus-oriented negotiations, one would expect the actual demands and offers to correspond relatively closely to the players' perceptions of what is at stake (where stakes are defined in terms of what the party is in fact willing to pay or accept to settle the case), because there is no reason (assuming neither player is seeking to maximize the outcome from his or her perspective) to engage in tactical bargaining by demanding high or offering low. In fact, as I showed in chapter 2, when one looks at the initial demands and offers reported by lawyers in the CLRP survey, there is close correspondence to stakes for a large proportion of respondents. For purposes of discussion, let us presume that offers of 75 percent or more of defendant's view of stakes and demands of 133 percent or less of the plaintiff's view of stakes indicate an effort to make an initial demand or offer in the "appropriate" range. In contrast, presume that demands of 200 percent or more and offers of 50 percent or less indicate initial moves in the "tactical" range[14] aimed at result maximization. Approximately 52 percent of the initial offers reported by the lawyers in the CLRP survey fell in the appropriate range, and 69 percent of the reported initial demands fell into the reciprocal appropriate range. In contrast, only 32 percent of the offers and 13 percent of the demands fell into the tactical range. Furthermore, as one would expect, a greater proportion of initial demands and offers fell into the tactical range when there were three or more exchanges of demands and offers as compared with when there were only one or two exchanges (16 percent versus 11 percent for demands, and 43 percent versus 26 percent for offers).

The greater likelihood that offers as opposed to demands will be tactical points up the dilemma mentioned above: that a competitive bargainer is at an advantage when dealing with a cooperative bargainer. Figure 6.3 shows the combinations of negotiation face-offs that can occur, based upon the two modes of negotiation detailed in this section. Apparently, defendants have a somewhat greater inclination to take advantage of plaintiffs who are prepared to "give away the store"; this may reflect advantages accruing to repeat players or to fundamental asymmetries in risk preference associated with being a claimant or respondent (see van Koppen, 1990). Nonetheless, over half of the defendants' initial offers were in the "appropriate" range. This suggests that there are important incentives for defendants to seek appropriate rather than maximal results. No doubt this reflects that the vast majority of claims leading to litigation have a strong basis in fact and that the marginal improvements which might be reflected in a maximal (or perhaps better termed *minimal* in the case of defendants) result do not warrant the costs that would have to be incurred.[15] Overall, it appears that the most

DEFENDANT

	Concessions Oriented, Maximal Result	Consensus Oriented, Appropriate Result
Concessions Oriented, Maximal Result	potential stalemate	moving the business
Consensus Oriented, Appropriate Result	giving away the store	settling the facts

Figure 6.3. Negotiation Face-Offs

dominant form of negotiation in the American civil litigation context is probably to be found in the "settling the facts" cell of Figure 6.3.

There is, however, an alternate explanation for apparent asymmetry between defendants and plaintiffs which serves to blur the distinction between maximal-result and appropriate-result negotiations: one or both of the negotiators are agents rather than principals. Agents often have interests that are not necessarily consistent with the goals their principals might be presumed to have (see Miller, 1987; Schelling, 1960: 29). This point was the basis of much of the discussion in chapter 5. As applied to the two modes of negotiation described here, the inconsistency of interests may reflect that the lawyer's own interest might be best served if a "satisficing" result is achieved for the client (i.e., one that the client is willing to accept) even if that result does not maximize the client's interest. This might well account for the apparent asymmetry between plaintiffs and defendants, because the potential conflict between the contingent-fee lawyer and her client is so clear, and because the individual client of the contingent-fee lawyer exercises so little control over his lawyer (see Kritzer, 1990; Rosenthal, 1974).[16]

One interpretation this suggests is that, although negotiations are not maximizing from the litigant's viewpoint, they may be maximizing from the lawyer's viewpoint, and the analysis suggested in chapter 5, where the emphasis is on the lawyer's interest, is the correct approach. However, I am not convinced that the answer is this simple. First, it presumes that lawyers are motivated solely by self-interest; although there is evidence that lawyers are affected by their self-interest, it is clear that this motivation accounts for only a portion of what lawyers do (see Kritzer, 1990). Second, on the criminal side, the notion that lawyers maximize their own interests by satisficing their clients' interests is difficult to sustain, particularly for the public defenders who do the bulk of criminal defense work. There are organizational pressures that serve to limit public defenders' options of taking large numbers of cases to trial; however, the young lawyers who typically work as public defenders are likely to have a strong interest in obtaining the kind of trial experience that will benefit them in private practice. One could build an argument that, all things considered, these defenders are still self-maximizing by defining everything they do as maximizing, but this is obviously tautological. Third, the conflict that does exist between contingent-fee lawyers and their clients in large part is an artifact of the fee arrangement; if the individual clients involved in ordinary litigation were actually paying their lawyers on an hourly fee basis, they would most likely want the lawyer to get a quick, appropriate result rather than hold out for the maximal gross result. The point here is simply that the appropriate result may in fact be something of a "maximal" result when the real transaction costs are figured in, and the effect is to alter substantially the way negotiations are approached.

The two modes of maximal-result, concessions-oriented negotiations and appropriate-result, consensus-oriented negotiations sketched above do correspond with many aspects of negotiation in ordinary litigation; nonetheless, they are abstractions. There are likely to be few cases where there is not at least some concern over the potential that the cases will have to be adjudicated, and there are likely to be many cases where, because of differing valuations by the two sides in a dispute, the outcome will be perceived as somewhere between maximal and appropriate. The line between the two modes is further clouded by the fact that, given high case-by-case transaction costs, appropriate results in individual cases may well lead to maximal results over a set of cases; that is, when the cost of things like information is high, a rapid turnover of the "inventory" of cases is probably better from a financial viewpoint than is the return associated with any specific case in the inventory. Although this discussion of transaction costs is couched in terms that one would most likely associate with repeat players (particularly insurance companies), if one considers the high probability that most one-shot players will be risk averse, that risk aversion is likely to push such players in the direction of appropriate result rather than maximal result. Furthermore, most individual litigants have effectively sold a share of their claims to their contingent-fee attorneys, and although the individual may be a one-shot player, the lawyer is most certainly a repeat player. This would further propel the litigant toward what I referred to above as a satisficing orientation, because he would be almost entirely dependent upon his lawyer for evaluating the adequacy of any offer of settlement.

The above discussion suggests some of the ambiguities inherent in the distinction I am drawing between the maximal-result, concessions-oriented and appropriate-result, consensus-oriented modes of negotiations. Nonetheless, when one considers them in the context of ordinary litigation, the data on the level of intensity presented in chapter 2 come clearly into perspective: if a lot of the negotiations are oriented to obtaining an appropriate result by reaching a consensus rather than a maximal result by extracting concessions, one should not be surprised by either the relatively small proportion of cases that involve more than two exchanges of demands and offers or the large proportion of cases where offers and demands closely approximate the stakes.

There are negotiations that clearly deviate from the two patterns I have concentrated on above. As I have noted several times, the trade union solicitor in England uses a competitive stance to obtain an appropriate outcome. In his study of attorneys who defend individuals suspected of committing white-collar crimes, Kenneth Mann (1985) shows how those attorneys use a competitive process to create an image for the prosecutor. The goal of the defense attorney is not to extract concessions after charges have been filed but to control information aggressively so that the prosecutor concludes that no charges are warranted or that a prosecution would not be successful. The defense attorney uses a competitive approach to *create* a consensus concerning the appropriate resolution of the matter. These two situations do not fit clearly with the patterns shown in Figure 6.3, but neither appears to be particularly common in the context of ordinary civil litigation in the United States.

PRO FORMA NEGOTIATIONS

I suggested above that the concern about transaction costs would push repeat players in the direction of appropriate-result negotiations. At the extreme, where likely (as opposed to simply potential) transaction costs are very high relative to probable return, there may be little concern about either maximal or appropriate results in individual cases. The concern might be simply turning over the "low end" inventory rapidly. That is, the emphasis is on disposing of cases rather than on the results that are achieved, and the dispositional emphasis dominates the negotiation and bargaining that takes place.

In this kind of situation, the parties may never get to negotiation in anything other than a *pro forma* sense. That is, the parties go through the motions of negotiations, but there is neither a series of offers and counteroffers of the kind associated with maximal-result, concessions-oriented negotiations nor an exchange of facts and information that would be associated with appropriate-result, consensus-oriented negotiations. The image that I want to associate with the *pro forma* mode of negotiation is one that sees the process as little more than a set form or procedure that the parties go through in *disposing* of a case. This form or procedure has little impact on the actual outcome; it is simply "the way things are done," a kind of "ritual."[17] Where negotiations are *pro forma,* they are also minimal, in terms of both the time involved and the numbers of exchanges of offers and counteroffers.

Some analyses of plea bargaining in misdemeanor cases are quite consistent with this image of *pro forma* bargaining. Based on transcripts of 52 plea-bargaining sessions, Maynard (1984a: 98–99) reports that over half the cases examined involved "bargaining" of the form where "one party takes up a position which the other accepts" or where "each party advances a position [and] one gives up his position and accepts the other's." In only 3 of the 52 cases were compromise positions arrived at. Maynard also reports that the typical plea-bargaining session was very short, with an average session length of about 12 minutes (ibid.: 77). This figure is based on Maynard's report of having a total of "nearly ten hours of recordings" (ibid.); 600 minutes across 52 cases yields an average of about 12.

Similarly, in another study of plea bargaining, Heumann (1978: 35) observes: "Generally, only a few words have to be exchanged before agreement is reached. The defense attorney mutters something about the defendant, the prosecutor reads the police report, and concurrence on 'what to do' generally, but not always, emerges." The reason that such dispositions are arrived at so perfunctorily is suggested by Eisenstein, Flemming, and Nardulli's (1988: 121) discussion of Erie County, Pennsylvania. There the going rate for many lesser offenses was a form of probation. This was clearly known to the regular participants in the process, and in cases involving those lesser offenses "little doubt ever arose about how the case[s] would end." Because of the existing consensus on how the cases should be handled, "next to no bargaining in the normal sense took place." The defendants either accepted the standard penalties or went to trial to seek outright acquittals.[18]

In the civil arena, the situation in which *pro forma* negotiations are likely to take place is one involving a modest case where a one-shot plaintiff (or claimant) faces a repeat-player defendant (see Galanter, 1974). The typical discussion of differing valuations presumes that the plaintiff sees the worth of the case as being greater than the defendant does; in such situations, if the gap is too great, no settlement will occur. However, it is likely that in a substantial number of cases, particularly with an unrepresented one-shot plaintiff and an experienced defendant, the plaintiff may see the case as being worth less than the defendant does (particularly when the defendant has in mind the potential transaction costs if the case is not quickly resolved). What might negotiations look like in such a situation?

Take as an example a situation where Party A has a claim that she feels is worth $1,000, but Party B feels that the most he will pay is $1,500. If A makes an initial demand of $1,400, B might immediately accept the offer, though he is probably more likely to try to lower the amount by responding with something like $1,200. Because this is still above A's floor (and below B's ceiling), it is probable that A will accept B's offer of $1,200. In this type of situation, the parties never get to negotiation in anything other than a ritualistic sense. That is, the parties go through the motions of negotiation— they make demands and/or present offers—but there is neither a series of offers and counteroffers (as associated with maximal-result, concessions-oriented negotiations) nor an exchange of facts and information (as one would expect in appropriate-result, consensus-oriented negotiations).[19]

The smaller the stakes, the more likely negotiations are to be *pro forma*. Consider as an example a simple property-damage case: A driver pulls into a neighbor's driveway and runs over a child's bicycle that was left lying in the car's path. Assuming the damaged or destroyed bike is in the same condition that most children's bikes rapidly fall into, it might be worth $10 or $15 at a garage sale. The adjuster for the driver's insurance company, after viewing the damaged bike, might offer $25 or even $50; the likely response would be an immediate acceptance.[20] The adjuster's goal in such a case would be simply to get rid of the case as quickly as possible; the transaction costs would probably exceed the amount in question.[21] This would be *pro forma* negotiation in its most extreme form.

Conclusion

What I have suggested in this chapter is that in thinking about negotiation and bargaining in ordinary litigation, it is helpful to distinguish among what might be thought of as three different functions or modes: maximal-result, concession-oriented negotiation; appropriate-result, consensus-oriented negotiation; and *pro forma* negotiation. Each type of negotiation creates its own set of expectations about the content and intensity of the negotiation process; a full analysis relying upon this typology would require substantially greater detail about specific negotiations than I have available from the data collected by the Civil Litigation Research Project.

Even though a detailed analysis cannot be carried out using the data in hand, it is striking that the kinds of patterns described in chapter 2, based upon analyses of those data, do make more sense when viewed in light of this framework. With both *pro forma* and appropriate-result, consensus-oriented negotiation in mind, it is not at all surprising that negotiation in ordinary litigation is low in intensity. Similarly, it is not surprising that only a minority of the negotiators report engaging in strategic or tactical bargaining. It is also easy to understand why repeat players might choose to approach negotiation with intentions other than obtaining the best result for the instant case, particularly in the kinds of modest cases that dominate the world of ordinary litigation.

At the same time, as with the various frameworks considered in the previous chapters, identifying the function to be served by the negotiation is only part of the explanation for what transpires in the negotiation process. A fuller explanation can be achieved only by bringing in a variety of perspectives, as I have sought to do. It is also necessary to acknowledge that negotiation in certain types of contexts, or negotiation involving particular types of participants, may not conform to any of the three function-related modes I have described. One can think of the four patterns illustrated in Figure 6.3 as representing the "standard," most frequent subset of the 16 patterns suggested by Figure 6.2. There is nothing that precludes other specific combinations from occurring, as the example of trade union solicitors in England described by Genn (1988) illustrates. One avenue for future research might be to develop theoretical expectations concerning the conditions under which "nonstandard" patterns might appear.

The typology I have proposed bears some similarity to the distinction drawn in criminal justice literature between the adversarial/due process model and the dispositional/crime control model (see Packer, 1964). The linkage lies primarily in the members of each typology that emphasize moving cases through the justice system. Both of the typologies seek to move beyond the theories of how systems of justice should operate to try to describe how the actors in the system learn to cope with the day-to-day realities of working in that system, whether it is the overwhelming guilt of defendants in the criminal courts or the economics of processing modest disputes in the civil courts.

Finally, it is worth speculating on the factors that would account for the mode of negotiation that occurs in individual civil cases. My description of *pro forma* negotiation suggests that a primary differentiating variable is size of the case. In small cases, transaction costs should lead to standardized dispositional guidelines (either explicit or implicit) that leave little room for "real" negotiation. This should be most likely where both sides have strong concerns about transaction costs; in ordinary litigation, this would include the situation of a contingent-fee plaintiff's lawyer and an insurance adjuster.

Identifying the factors accounting for the choice between *concessions-oriented, maximal-result* negotiations and *consensus-oriented, appropriate-result* negotiations is more difficult. Intuition suggests that it may relate in part to the personalities of the negotiators, but efforts to link negotiator personality to negotiator style in real-life negotiations (as opposed to laboratory settings—see Rubin and Brown, 1975) have not shown strong connections. The thrust of chapter 4 suggests the hypothesis that negotiators are influenced by their own self-interest, which implies that cases that can be handled profitably only on a high-volume basis should lead toward resolutions that can be achieved with relatively little difficulty. To the extent that consensus can be achieved more readily through routinized interaction than concessions can, stakes should predict the choice between consensus-oriented, appropriate-result and concessions-oriented, maximal result negotiations. However, the options for alternative resolutions may be greater in larger, more complex cases; consequently, the relationship is probably curvilinear, with consensus-oriented, appropriate-result negotiation most likely both for very simple, very small cases and for very complex, very large cases (i.e., nonordinary litigation).

The mode of negotiation may also be a function of the "community of negotiators." In settings where negotiators have frequent regularized contact, the need to sustain positive ongoing relationships may encourage the consensus-oriented pattern. This is quite common in the criminal justice system, even in large cities (see Eisenstein and Jacob, 1977); in the civil arena it is most likely to occur in smaller communities (see Landon, 1985). Similarly, the presence of strong sponsoring organizations (e.g., the dependence of a lawyer on work provided by a small number of insurance companies) may allow those organizations to dictate the style adopted by their agents; the sponsoring organizations may or may not establish policies favoring one mode of negotiation over another.

All the hypotheses above are highly speculative. However, they suggest questions that future research might seek to answer. Knowing the factors that influence the modes of negotiations that occur will allow for systematic consideration of the impact of changes in the civil justice system that affect the context of bargaining and settlement.

CHAPTER 7

Conclusions: The Need to Keep Negotiation in Perspective

In the United States, courts are an important forum for the redress of grievances arising from injuries, unfulfilled agreements, and unfair treatment. The coercive power of the state can be used to force a party in a dispute to respond to claims that have been asserted against it, and ultimately to extract some form of redress from a party found to have acted improperly or to have been responsible for an injury. The image of the impartial judge and the jury of citizens delivering justice is a powerful one in a country where the most fundamental legal document—the Constitution—lists the "establish[ment of] justice" as one of its first goals and where the Pledge of Allegiance learned by young school children concludes with the words "with . . . justice for all."

However, in the everyday world of processing cases, the image of judge and jury is more symbolic than real. Most cases brought to court are disposed of, not by an impartial adjudicatory process, but by the consent of the parties: pleas of guilt in criminal cases and out-of-court settlements in civil cases. This reality does not mean that the judge and jury are insignificant. The standards that guide the reaching of agreements anticipate the implications of having the case at hand proceed through the complete adjudicatory process. Partly this condition arises from what Mnookin and Kornhauser (1979) describe as the "shadow of the law": agreements may be framed to anticipate specific adjudicatory outcomes. Elsewhere, I have noted that the shadow of adjudication not only affects the substance of agreements that occur but also provides the environment in which agreements *can* occur; that is, without the threat of adjudication, it is unlikely that most of what we think of as civil disputes would lead to *any* agreements (Kritzer, 1990: 146–155; see also Galanter,, 1988: 61–62).[1] The discussion in chapter 3 adds a third element that influences the disposition of cases: the costs of the

130

adjudicatory process, notwithstanding the specifics of the judgments that might be reached. For ordinary litigation these costs can often overwhelm the substance of the dispute, and settlement processes are strongly influenced by the potential costs of going through the full adjudicatory process. Thus, by setting standards, coercing parties, and imposing costs, threatened and actual adjudication is a central part of the agreements that are reached in both civil and criminal cases.[2]

Even acknowledging the importance of the adjudicatory process, the vast majority of cases are in some sense "settled." On the criminal side of the American justice system we have a rich literature that describes and analyzes what is best labeled the guilty-plea process. Research (Eisenstein, Flemming, and Nardulli, 1988; Nardulli, Eisenstein, and Flemming, 1988; Heumann, 1977; Utz, 1978) has made it clear that the image of a "justice bazaar" reflected in the idea of plea bargaining does not accurately describe what occurs in *most* cases in *most* communities. The dominance of guilty pleas in the American criminal justice system cannot be explained by simple references to heavy caseloads (Feeley, 1979b; Heumann, 1975); likewise, guilty pleas are not necessarily the overwhelmingly dominant mode of termination, even in a large urban criminal court system (Schulhofer, 1984, 1985).

The description and analysis in the preceding pages extend the kind of analyses that have been done regarding the disposition of criminal cases to the civil arena. With the exception of the divorce area, most discussions and analyses of negotiation and settlement of civil cases have been theoretical and prescriptive, with few attempts to assess the theories against large numbers of actual cases. In terms of the overall image provided by my analysis, the similarity to the guilty-plea process is striking. The give and take of the bazaarlike setting is absent. Concessions, either those that are sought or those that are offered, do not appear to be the driving force of the negotiation and settlement process. This is not to say that concessions do not occur or are not important in some cases; rather, they are not the dominant element in settling ordinary civil disputes. Negotiations in civil cases are marked more heavily by either an orientation toward finding a consensus or a *pro forma* style of exchange.

The explanation for this pattern lies substantially in the realm of money. This book was not intended as an economic analysis of settlement and negotiation. Yet, if one things of *economics* in the terms that a noneconomist might—the analysis of that part of the social world concerned with dollars and cents (or any other monetary unit)—it is not surprising that so much of my discussion has been oriented toward economics: *most civil litigation is about money,* at least at some level.[3] The realities of stakes and costs in ordinary litigation provide a set of incentives that strongly *discourages* a process aimed at extracting concessions through competitive bargaining if that bargaining process itself will require substantial expenditures of time and money. The repeat players in the process, lawyers and routine litigants for whom use of the court process is an institutionalized part of their working world, need to regularize the process of disposing of cases so that livelihoods can be earned and business can be conducted.

In his seminal study of insurance adjusters, Ross (1980) showed how the need to move cases is a strong force mitigating against the insurance company's profit motive. The balance between moving cases and making profits, combined with the institutional need to evaluate employee performance, contributes to a process with a heavy emphasis on adjuster productivity. Similarly, for lawyers representing defendants that routinely use the courts, a balance must be struck between the results that are obtained and the costs of obtaining those results. For most types of ordinary litigation, it is very easy for the costs of defense, primarily made up of fees paid to lawyers on an hourly basis (see Kritzer, Sarat, Trubek, et al., 1984, Kritzer et al., 1987), to exceed any savings the defense might achieve, at least when considered on a case-by-case basis. A defendant might express the intention to fight every case through the complete litigation process, but the cost realities of such a policy force most defendants in ordinary litigation to seek to avoid either standing by such a policy or extracting every last possible concession from the opposing side. Finally, the opportunity cost structure for the contingent-fee lawyer substantially limits the lawyer's ability to pursue a large proportion of ordinary cases with the kind of zeal the American adversary system implies should be the norm. The potential fees that can be earned from ordinary cases in the American system are modest, and it is not in the lawyer's own interest to seek substantial concessions when such a strategy would require major investments of valuable time. The contingent-fee lawyer must establish a settlement mode that either entails minimal *pro forma* negotiations or quickly arrives at a consensus about the appropriate resolution of a case.

When this set of economic realities is taken together, the pattern of negotiations described in detail in chapter 2 makes a lot of sense:

—Most cases are settled with one or two exchanges of offers and/or demands.

—Most lawyers devote relatively small amounts of time to actual negotiation.

—A large portion of initial offers and demands are very close to the acceptable settlement.

—Relatively few cases involve substantial shifts in offers and demands in the course of the bargaining.

—Plaintiffs are less likely to engage in tactical bargaining (i.e., making demands that are substantially different from the acceptable outcome) than are defendants.

—Contingent-fee lawyers do not obtain higher effective hourly rates by engaging in tactical bargaining.

The process appears to be relatively cut and dried, with relatively little in the way of subtle bargaining strategy and tactics. One might argue that this portrait is an artifact of data that do not allow for the kind of subtleties that might exist. However, other studies that have examined negotiations in ordinary litigation (e.g., Genn, 1988) also find little evidence of a subtle, finely grained process. Moreover, the theoretical analyses in the preceding chapters clearly provide an account for why negotiation in ordinary litigation cannot involve a richer, more complex style of interaction than is indicated by the patterns discussed in chapter 2.

Given that ordinary civil litigation, including divorce litigation if one considers the perspective of the attorneys representing the divorcing spouses, is in some way connected to conducting business, it is extremely difficult to justify in a business sense a process that *routinely* involves complex and time-consuming interaction. Processing of disputes, particularly when that processing involves the use of agents (i.e., lawyers), is nothing more than a particular kind of service, and the dilemma of service costs relative to value is the type of trade-off people deal with day in and day out. The problem of costs relative to benefits is one that we inevitably face in a service economy where the hourly labor rate for services we buy seldom drops under $20 (and is more typically in the $40–$60 range—$75–$100 for services of a professional like a lawyer), and the value of many of the goods we want serviced is often not much more than the cost of a couple hours of the service.[4] When considering ordinary litigation, one has to keep in mind the inherent problems associated with disputes over relatively modest amounts of money, and one must add to these problems the fact that for most individuals *any* cost is likely to be seen as too great, because, unlike expenses associated with health care, people do not think about legal expenses as an inevitable part of day-to-day life.[5]

Although much of the discussion in the preceding chapters suggests that rigorous applications of the economic analyses of the settlement process are difficult to make for many individual cases, and they are seldom definitive in the sense of predicting actual outcomes with any kind of specificity, there are undoubtedly strong truths underlying these analyses. People may not be strictly rational, and they may have substantial disagreements over what a particular case is "worth" (see Rosenthal, 1974: 204–205), yet they are sensitive to what they will get and/or lose in a case, and they make decisions with that in mind. In situations where the potential costs in pursuing a claim are large relative to the amount at issue, even a minimal level of rationality will push parties toward quick, relatively modest settlements. One might argue that this will tend to encourage nuisance suits or claims, because players, like insurance companies, should find it economically advantageous to get rid of such cases before significant transaction costs are incurred. However, it typically will not be in the interest of someone in the situation of contingent-fee lawyers, who think of their time in terms of opportunity cost, to pursue marginal cases including those that might be labeled nuisance suits; even minimal transaction costs (where those costs include the alternative uses of the lawyer's time) in a small case or a case with some minimal nuisance value can quickly exceed any possible return.

Despite the above point concerning the underlying truth of some of the key insights of economic analyses of settlement and negotiation in cases of ordinary civil litigation, analysts and observers should be cautious in attempting to generalize about negotiation and settlement in such cases. Money is a dominant concern in the negotiations represented in the sample we are considering, and economics help us to understand a lot of what happens in negotiations (at least in the aggregate), however, there is no dominant image of the actual bargaining that occurs, except that there does not appear to be a lot to it. In a substantial proportion of cases, the offers and demands that are made do not reflect a clear bargaining strategy, but rather they represent attempts to resolve the case for what is believed to be at stake; this is less true of tort cases, where tactical bargaining appears to be more in evidence. Thus, there is substantial variation in the way this settlement process proceeds, even given cases of similar magnitude and complexity.

The three modes of negotiation I described in the last chapter—maximal-result concessions-oriented, appropriate-result consensus-oriented, and *pro forma*—provide one portrait of bargaining variations that accounts for the small number of exchanges of offers and demands in the vast majority of everyday, ordinary cases. To assess further the validity of the distinctions I have drawn, it will be necessary to go substantially beyond the kinds of data that I have available and look in some detail at the content of the negotiation that takes place, both the negotiation that occurs in a face-to-face context and that which occurs over the telephone or through written correspondence. To what degree are the exchanges aimed specifically at coming to a common agreement over the "facts" of a case, and to what degree is the focus on explication and justification of specific offers and demands? My data do not provide information on this kind of content.

There are many other important questions raised by my analysis: When cases do not appear to involve monetary issues, to what degree are they transformed into monetary claims either because courts are better able to deal with monetary issues or because lawyers are more at ease in dealing with monetary compensation (see Menkel-Meadow, 1985a: 33)? To what degree does the lack of tactical bargaining in many cases reflect naïvety on the part of the bargainers (see Genn, 1988)? Or does it indicate that there is no rigorous way to value cases in many situations, so lawyers simply make a wild stab at what they think the other side might be willing to pay (see ibid.; Williams, 1983; Rosenthal, 1974)? In pursuing these kinds of questions, future research on negotiations in the civil justice system must keep sight of the day-to-day realities that face that system: most cases are not "big," most plaintiffs rely on contingent-fee arrangements to secure representation, and those lawyers must secure monetary resolutions in order to be paid. These realities shape the nature of the process that goes on in negotiations between parties through their lawyers, and in the civil justice system as a whole.

Negotiation and Civil Justice Reform

Reforming the civil justice system has been a much-discussed issue in recent years, reflecting perceptions that:

—the United States is in the midst of a litigation explosion;

—unscrupulous litigants and lawyers regularly and frequently abuse the litigation process;

—there is widespread lack of access to the justice system by those with legitimate grievances;

—the system is suffering from excessive costs and rampant delays;

—runaway juries hand down outlandish verdicts; and

—there is a crisis in the availability of liability insurance resulting from one or more of the above problems.

Many of the claims about the problems and crisis are supported by specific reference to examples of the problem. Even though many, if not most, of these examples did in fact occur,[6] frequently they represent what might best be called horror stories—extreme experiences that dominate news coverage of the courts and that stand out in the memories of participants in the court process. When such discussions lead to calls for reform, a phenomenon that might be characterized as "court reform by anecdote,"[7] they are dangerous. Reforms designed to deal with extreme, atypical cases may make the day-to-day operation of the civil justice system worse, not better.

Calls for reform must take into account the fact that the scale of activity in most ordinary court cases is relatively modest, as are the amounts at stake (see Trubek, Sarat, et al., 1983; Trubek, Grossman, et al., 1983; Kritzer, 1990); this can readily be seen in the analyses of the negotiation and settlement process presented throughout this book. Proposals for change must also be sensitive to the economic realities confronting the litigants and attorneys involved in day-to-day litigation. The failure to consider the way that the system *routinely* operates can readily be seen in several proposals for change that relate directly to negotiation and settlement: calls for modifying the way that lawyers negotiate settlement, and proposals for methods of "alternative dispute resolution" (ADR).

The role of economic incentives has important implications for efforts to improve negotiations in legal contexts including litigation (e.g., Menkel-Meadow, 1984; Raiffa, 1982; Fisher and Ury, 1981). Most clearly it suggests that prescriptive considerations of negotiation must take into account the transaction costs involved in the proposals that are advanced. Proposals that are likely to increase substantially the costs of arriving at a settlement are not likely to have much impact if one of the crucial factors pushing parties toward settlement is the concern about potential transaction costs. In chapter 5, I suggested that proposals calling for lawyers to play down the emphasis on financial settlements (i.e., moving away from distributive to integrative negotiation) are likely to have little impact where the lawyers' livelihood depends directly on the dollar base of the settlement (e.g., in the case of the contingent-fee lawyer). The generalization of that point is that costs and potential costs and returns and potential returns are the driving force of much of what goes on in the arena of civil litigation,[8] and this is particularly true of settlement and negotiation. If one is going to talk about that process, one must be sure both to understand the economic realities that the day-to-day players live with and to try to see the process in light of those realities.

Discussions of the currently popular world of alternative dispute resolution have included the observation that "most of what goes on in adjudication [*sic*] is negotiation and settlement" (Green, 1986: 284).[9] Although this is correct, analysts must recognize that negotiation and settlement in the context of litigation has to take into account the shadows of law and adjudication, because these shadows make negotiation in the litigation context fundamentally different from the negotiations that might occur over the purchase of a house or in the context of developing a political agreement (whether international or intranational). It is certainly true that many more cases in our courts are settled than are adjudicated,[10] however, focusing on simple indicators of adjudication, such as the trial rate, misses much of the role of adjudication in the resolution of cases brought into the civil justice system. *The settlement of many (if not most) cases relies upon the adjudication of others;*[11] to separate those that settle from those that are adjudicated misses the fundamental reality underlying the working of the system (see Alschuler, 1986; Danzon and Lillard, 1982; Engel and Steele, 1979; Galanter, 1988). Thus, one of the fundamental aspects of negotiation and settlement in civil litigation is anticipating the *adjudicatory alternative.* This comes to the heart of what Marc Galanter referred to as litigotiation ("the strategic pursuit of a settlement through mobilizing the court process"). The expectation in most cases may be that a resolution will be arrived at by settlement rather than by adjudication (Melli, Erlanger, Chambliss, 1988: 1143), but the availability of the nonvoluntary and adjudicatory alternative is a *very* important aspect of the settlement process.

In a real sense, as others have previously said, much of the discussion of alternative dispute resolution may have the world upside down. Drawing again from Galanter's (1984: 268) discussion of litigotiation:

On the contemporary American legal scene the negotiation of disputes is not an alternative to litigation. It is only a slight exaggeration to say that it is litigation. There are not two distinct processes, negotiation and litigation. . . . [A]djudication remains a compelling presence even when it does not occur. . . . *Full-blown adjudication of the dispute—running the whole course—might be thought of as an infrequently-pursued alternative to the ordinary course of litigation* [emphasis added].

Finding alternatives to litigation or adjudication is not the problem of our civil justice system; rather, we need to understand the impact of adjudication as the alternative to settlement,[12] whether that settlement is reached through simple negotiations, mediation, or what might be called quasi adjudication (minitrials, summary trials, etc.).

Finally, is settlement (and, by implication, negotiation) of civil cases, in contrast with adjudication, good or bad (Alschuler, 1986; see also, Fiss, 1984; McThenia and Shaffer, 1985)?[13] There is a very important distinction to be drawn between settlement for the right reasons and settlement for the wrong reasons. Cases that leave the courts through settlement may in fact exit because adjudication has resolved some or all the key questions in dispute, even if the case did not go all the way to trial (see Kritzer, 1986). Even where no adjudication takes place, settlement may occur for the "right" reasons:

—the parties are able to agree upon the valuation appropriate for the case when there is no real dispute over liability;

—after a thorough examination of the evidence, the parties come to a consensus about what happened; or

—the two parties realize that the needs of both are best served by compromising their differences.

Certainly, some settlements do occur for the "wrong" reasons:
—one party can no longer afford the costs of litigation;
—the delay until trial forces a party to take a lower settlement now than could be achieved through a jury trial; or
—one party's lawyer has misadvised a client to accept a low settlement because the lawyer either has incorrectly valued the case or is anxious to finish it with a minimum of effort.

One cannot presume that all settlements are wrong or all adjudicated outcomes are wrong; the world is not black and white. Thus, in order to advance the discussion of adjudication, negotiation, and alternative dispute resolution, researchers and reformers must come to grips with the problem of assessing when particular modes of resolution are good or bad, and when one mode of resolution is better than another.[14]

Negotiation *is* the primary method of resolving disputes in the United States, and perhaps throughout modern society. The way that negotiation is conducted reflects the alternatives available to aggrieved parties (e.g., adjudication) and the financial incentives that define the context in which the negotiations take place. Rules and procedures can greatly shape the way negotiation is carried out, but the end result will reflect the way that those factors intervene in the operation of incentives. If rule and procedural changes do not modify the incentives of litigants and lawyers, the system will probably continue operating with relatively little change. Moreover, changes that fail to take into account the current nature of incentives, or the way that these incentives reflect the existing context, will have little of the desired effect; the system may change, but probably in unpredictable and counterproductive ways. Understanding the system as it actually is, not as it stands out in the minds of participants and observers, is crucial for any process of change and improvement. I hope that this volume has contributed to that understanding.

NOTES

REFERENCES

INDEX

Notes

Chapter 1. Adjudication, Bargaining, and Settlement

1. One of the most often quoted statements about the role of the legal system in the United States comes from the nineteenth-century writings of the French observer of American democracy, Alexis de Tocqueville (1945: 280): "Scarcely any political question arises in the United States that is not resolved, sooner or later, into a judicial question."

2. If anything, this 90 percent figure may be low. During the period July 1, 1984, through June 30, 1985, fewer than 5 percent of federal civil cases terminated reached trial (Administrative Office of the United States Courts, 1985: Table C-4).

3. The 90 percent figure applies, in approximate terms, to both civil and criminal cases; the 99 percent figure is applicable only to civil cases. It is based on the fact that only about 10 percent of disputes lead to court cases (see Miller and Sarat, 1980–81: 544), and only about 10 percent of court cases ever come to trial.

4. The civil courts perform other functions besides "doing justice"; for example, one function of the courts is to establish norms and expectations (see Engel and Steele, 1979; Engel, 1980).

5. In Galanter's words, ". . . [A]djudication remains a compelling presence even when it does not occur" (1984: 268). Furthermore, there is much more to adjudication itself than the resolution of cases through a formal trial before a judge or jury, and a very sizable proportion of cases involve some actual adjudication (see Kritzer, 1986).

6. Compare with Green (1986: 284): ". . . [M]ost of what goes on in adjudication is negotiation and settlement. . . ."

7. This perception was neatly phrased by Lenny Bruce: "'In the halls of justice, the only justice is in the halls'" (quoted in Green,1982: 311).

8. A recent study of negotiation and settlement in divorce cases suggests the important distinction between settlement as resolution and settlement as disposition, arguing that in many (if not most) "settled" divorce cases, at least one of the parties has agreed to the settlement in what can be characterized only as an "unwilling" fashion (Erlanger, Chambliss, and Melli, 1987).

9. See Shannon, 1988, for a juror's description of the case and the trial.

10. The third special master, Leonard Garment, worked primarily on the issue of what the federal government would be willing to contribute to the settlement.

11. In fact, by the time the first distributions to claimants occurred in 1989, the

fund had grown to $240 million (*Capital Times,* Madison, Wisconsin, January 3, 1989, p. 3).

12. Exceptions to this statement include Danzon and Lillard's (1982, 1983) analysis of medical malpractice cases, Viscusi's (1986, 1988) studies of product liability, and Eisenberg and Schab's study (1987; Schwab and Eisenberg, 1988) of "constitutional" tort litigation (e.g., civil rights and discrimination cases in the federal courts); Swanson (1988) has carried out such analyses using data drawn from English courts, and Fenn (1988) analyzed negotiations using a set of English cases, many of which never led to actual filings in court.

13. Trubek, Sarat, and their colleagues (1983) have used the term "ordinary litigation" for the routine dispute-processing activities of civil courts (cf. Eisenberg and Yeazell's "The Ordinary and Extraordinary in Institutional Litigation" [1980]). Even after excluding uncontested collections cases and "small" cases (involving claims of less than $1,000), the median case in state courts of general jurisdiction (and most cases are filed in state, not federal, courts) involves stakes of about $4,500 (as of 1978). Reinforcing this finding, Peterson and Priest (1982: 23) report that the median jury verdict for the plaintiff (i.e., excluding cases where the verdict was for the defendant) in Cook County, Illinois, was $7,000 in 1979; this figure goes up to $15,000 if cases processed by the Municipal Division, which handles claims involving $15,000 or less, are excluded (Shanley and Peterson, 1983). According to the data reported by Trubek, Sarat, and their colleagues (1983), only 36 percent of federal cases and only 11 percent of state cases come up to the $25,000 level that Brazil (1980) characterized as a small case in his study of discovery problems. There is some evidence of increase in the *median* stakes in recent years, particularly in courts with a significant jurisdictional minimum (see Peterson, 1987).

14. There was also some property damage to Michael's rusty bicycle and his glasses.

15. This anecdote also raises the interesting question of negotiator ethics: Was Michael behaving unethically by asking for $1,700 when he was hoping to get $700? The potential ethical issue here is completely obscured by the absence of any systematic way of valuing injuries of the type Michael had suffered (but see Bovbjerg, Sloan, and Blumstein, 1989). No effort was made to conceal actual financial losses (e.g., medical costs or repair costs to his glasses and bicycle), which were relatively small. Most of what was involved was compensation for discomfort and inconvenience, as well as the potential cost to the insurance company of any formal legal action that Michael might have started. The one possible ethical issue that one might identify in Michael's actions was the wearing of the wrist brace during the discussions with the insurance adjuster. For more on negotiator ethics, see White, 1980; Bellow and Moulton, 1981: 253–273; Peters, 1987; or Dahl, 1989.

16. Beginning with chapter 3, I will explore a number of theoretical perspectives on negotiation and bargaining. As will be clear from my discussion, I do not find most of the theories I discuss to be very helpful in accounting for the patterns described in chapter 2. Consequently, I do not try to build a confirmatory analysis of negotiation in ordinary litigation employing one or more of the existing frameworks,

and I do not propose any specific hypotheses or model, because I do not believe that any single theoretical framework can adequately account for the patterns that will be described in chapter 2. At the same time, the discussion and analysis is not simply exploratory in nature, because some components of the rich theoretical materials do provide useful insights into the patterns reflected in the data I use. Thus, the analytic style in the following chapters falls somewhere between a confirmatory analysis (which would test a proposed theory) and an exploratory analysis (which would develop a new theory for future testing).

17. The Civil Litigation Research Project arose out of the desire of the Office for Improvements in the Administration of Justice in the Carter Justice Department to create a data base that would be useful for understanding the civil justice system in order that improvements in that system could be rationally considered (see Rosenberg, 1980–81; Sarat, 1981). The specific focus that was of immediate concern when the project was being set up in 1978–79 was on the costs of litigation. Many of the design decisions were dictated by the requirements imposed by the department.

18. This number does not include the federal judicial districts that serve Puerto Rico, the Virgin Islands, and Guam.

19. Two federal judicial districts, the Southern District of New York and Washington, D.C., are probably noteworthy exceptions to this statement. The kinds of cases appearing on the dockets of those courts are likely to be quite different from other districts around the country because of New York's prominence as a financial center and Washington's prominence as a center of government.

20. The overall study also included cases from alternative third-party dispute-processing institutions and from cases that were handled bilaterally without third-party involvement, but those cases are not included in the analysis presented in this book. For information on those cases, see Kritzer and Anderson, 1983; Trubek et al., 1984; and Miller and Sarat, 1980–81.

21. The specific courts were:
—Richland County (Columbia, South Carolina, and the surrounding area) Court of Common Pleas
—District Court for the Second Judicial District (Albuquerque, New Mexico, and the surrounding area)
—Los Angeles County Superior Court (downtown branch).

22. In Eastern Pennsylvania the two courts were the Philadelphia Court of Common Pleas and the Chester County Court of Common Pleas; in Eastern Wisconsin the two courts were the Milwaukee County Circuit Court and the Dodge County Circuit Court.

23. Where possible a simple random sample was drawn based upon a list of terminated cases; in some courts it was necessary to resort to a cluster sampling procedure, which is described in Kritzer, 1980–81: 515–516. The only bias in the latter sampling procedure that became evident was that "old" cases (i.e., those filed in 1974 or before) were not represented in the sample.

24. All four of the state cases excluded as being too large were from the Los Angeles County Superior Court.

25. See Melli, Erlanger, and Chambliss, 1985, 1988, and Erlanger, Chambliss, and Melli, 1987, for a discussion of the realities of the negotiation process in the divorce context. Seltzer and Garfinkel (1990) and Maccoby, Depner, and Mnookin (1988) describe the outcomes of divorce bargaining. See Mnookin, 1985, and Mnookin and Kornhauser, 1979, for a discussion of some of the theoretical issues involved in divorce-related bargaining.

26. Cases were omitted from the interview sample for any of three reasons:
—After examination the case was found to fall into one of the categories that had been excluded.
—It was unclear whether or not the case had in fact terminated.
—Funds for conducting interviews had been exhausted.

27. Lawyers directly employed by governmental agencies or departments were not included in this survey.

28. A list of individual categories, showing how the broad categories were formed can be found in Kritzer, 1990: 38–39.

29. I have excluded domestic relations from Table 1.2, because the sampling design is such that it cannot provide an accurate representation of the relative role of such cases in the courts' caseloads.

30. I have endeavored to use male and female pronouns in a random fashion throughout this book.

31. This image of stakes contains an important dynamic element: the stakes may change over the life of a case, either going up or down (or both). Moreover, the perception of stakes may depend upon which party one is talking to; the plaintiff and defendant are likely to see the stakes somewhat differently. This definition of stakes also incorporates attitudes toward risk (a risk-averse party may be willing to settle for less than the actual damages in order to be certain of obtaining something), uncertainty (a party involved in multiple cases will be willing to settle cases at something around an average value even if that is more or less than the specific case is thought to be worth), and the time value of money (a party may be prepared to settle a case for a lesser amount than could be obtained at some point in the future, because that amount constitutes the "current value" of what could be obtained by waiting). I believe that this conceptualization of stakes captures the notion of "case worth" as that idea is commonly used by lawyers.

32. Where the response was monetary but was expressed in terms of a periodic payment, it was converted into a single lump sum by figuring the present value of those payment streams using the average prime interest rate in 1978 (9.06 percent) as a discount factor and establishing a duration based on case type. Case types were determined by visual inspection of the court record coding form. Duration was then figured by applying the following rules of thumb:
—divorce: 9 years (median of 0–18) unless only alimony, in which case 2 years was used
—social security, retirement, or black lung benefits: life expectancy (by sex) at age 65
—disability payments: life expectancy (by sex) based on actual age (if known) or 43 (median of 21 and 65)

—mortgage payments: 10 years (median of 0 and 20)
—consumer credit: 2 years
—unemployment benefits: 1 year
—tenant debt: 2 years

33. There was one case that settled for $10 million in which the lawyer replied that he had not formed an opinion of the stakes according to the terms in which the question was asked.

34. These figures can be compared with those reported by Peterson and Priest in their study of jury verdicts in Cook County, Illinois. That study drew upon the Cook County Jury Verdict Reporter, which reports virtually every jury verdict handed down in Cook County. One should note that the universe of cases in that study is quite different from the universe in the study at hand: civil cases resulting in jury verdicts versus "all" civil cases, respectively. The median jury verdict in Cook County, in 1979 dollars, was $7,900, and this figure excludes those cases where the jury found for the defendant (Peterson and Priest, 1982: 8–9).

35. All these figures are based on cases terminated in 1978, and it is likely that they would be somewhat higher today; however, I doubt that the rise would fully reflect increases in the cost of living since 1978.

36. I should point out here, as I noted previously, that only four of the cases that were excluded from the sample because they were too complex to code came from state courts.

37. Although accurate figures exist on the number of federal court cases, comparable figures for state courts are difficult to acquire (but see National Center for State Courts, 1978; and Flango, Roper, and Elsner, 1983). Lieberman (1982: 12–18) suggests that there may be as many as 350–500 times as many state court cases filed as federal court cases. This figure includes courts of both general and limited jurisdiction. He estimates that about 20 percent of state cases are in courts of general jurisdiction. This would mean, then, that about 70–100 times as many state general jurisdiction cases as federal cases are filed each year. In one of Galanter's articles on the supposed litigation explosion, he cites a figure of 98 percent for civil litigation taking place in the state courts (Galanter, 1986a: 6).

38. What kinds of systematic variations are there in stakes? There is very little variation by judicial district for federal cases (the ratio of the largest median to smallest median for federal cases is 1.66). This should not be particularly surprising, because the jurisdictional rules governing the federal courts are uniform throughout the country. There is somewhat more variation in the state cases (the ratio of the largest to smallest median is almost 2.00). At least part of this variation is probably attributable to the presence of courts of limited jurisdiction that process moderate-sized cases involving claims under a specified amount (e.g., $5,000 or $3,000); however, Eastern Wisconsin, where there is no such limited jurisdiction court, was only slightly smaller in its median case than was Central California or New Mexico, where limited jurisdiction courts do exist (LEAA, 1973, 1982), and was slightly larger than South Carolina, where there is also a limited jurisdiction court.

Areas of law are closely related to the kind of court that hears the case, with state courts hearing domestic-relations cases, federal courts hearing most of the business regulation, civil rights/discrimination, government benefits, and government action cases, and both types of courts hearing substantial numbers of cases involving torts, contracts, and property. Given the jurisdictional rules of the federal court, it should not be surprising that there is a large gap between the stakes in state and federal cases. There is relatively little variation within state courts by area of law (i.e., the amount at issue in a typical state contract case is not all that different from the amount at stake in a typical state tort case). There is more variation in the federal courts by area of law, because some areas were affected by the $10,000 jurisdictional minimum (now $50,000) for diversity cases (contracts, torts, property), whereas other areas come into the federal court by specific statutes that do not place a floor on the amount at stake (e.g., discrimination suits).

39. Some of the cases in the sample raised questions which, like those suggested by Merry and Silbey (ibid.), do not readily lend themselves to resolution by one side making a monetary payment to the other side. Examples of the goals sought in those cases include:

—Finding the respondent a place to live with rent comparable to the previous lodging.
—Revoking the license of opposing party permanently and take him off the road; he should be punished and made to pay in some way for the life he took.
—Stopping manufacture of those guns.
—Compelling opposing party to take back the house that was sold to respondent because information was withheld on structural deficiencies that made the house unsound.
—Giving respondent citizenship.
—Compelling government agency to release all information sought by respondent.
—Vindicating respondent's professional integrity.

However, these cases represent a small minority of what comes into courts of general jurisdiction.

40. If litigants are asked in a close-ended format to indicate how important are goals like:

—proving that you were right
—protecting your reputation
—making sure that others know you can't be pushed around
—making sure that the other party won't do it again

substantial numbers of them will respond, "very important." However, this kind of *post hoc* prompting provides little indication of whether or not such concerns are reflected in demands and/or offers that are made.

41. When respondents were asked to describe what was at stake in terms of what they wanted from the other side, about 25 percent mentioned something other than the exchange of a specific sum of money. Not surprisingly, individuals were more likely to mention something other than a specific sum (39 percent) than were organizations (13 percent). However, these figures substantially overstate the role of non-monetary stakes, because when one looks at the specific responses of what was

sought, 43 percent of the individual responses are actually unspecified amounts of money, and perhaps 33 percent of the other responses could reasonably be labeled as essentially monetary. This leaves only about 10 percent of individual respondents having nonmonetary stakes. For organizations, about the same proportion of the stakes reported in terms other than specific sums of money were nonmonetary, leaving only about 3 percent of organizations having nonmonetary goals.

It is probably worth noting that, when asked what was at stake in terms of what the other side should do or pay, many fewer individual respondents (14 percent) described the stakes in terms other than specific sums of money; the percentage of such responses for organizational respondents declined somewhat less (to 10 percent), but the percentage of nonmonetary stakes was, as noted above, quite low even for what organizations sought from the opposing sides.

42. Several authors (e.g., Jacob, 1979; Zemans, 1980) have noted that the line between civil and criminal cases is often vague and/or arbitrary. Although many of the kinds of cases referred to by Merry and Silbey could have been approached as civil matters, casting them in a criminal context may seem to shift burdens of cost from the complainants to governmental institutions charged with maintaining order (the police and the courts). However, many of the kinds of interpersonal disputes of interest to Merry and Silbey may be viewed as "garbage" by those same authorities (see Yngvesson, 1988: 414).

43. It is worth noting that individuals involved in significant disputes not handled through the courts are much more likely to describe the stakes in terms not involving specific monetary sums. As noted above, 39 percent of individual respondents from the CLRP courts sample described what they sought from the other side in terms of something other than specified sums of money; the comparable figures for respondents from samples drawn from alternative dispute-processing institution cases (see Kritzer and Anderson, 1983; Trubek et al., 1984) and from a household-screening survey (see Miller and Sarat, 1980–81) are 62 percent and 63 percent, respectively!

44. In fact, as I will argue in chapter 5, the realities of ordinary litigation make it difficult to pursue cases that cannot be translated into simple dollars and cents, and arguments for changing negotiating styles (see, in particular, Menkel-Meadow, 1984; Fisher and Ury, 1981; or Raiffa, 1982) in litigation contexts must take into account these realities.

45. There is a variety of other dimensions that I might consider but for reasons of space have omitted. Three, in particular, may seem conspicuous by their absence, so let me at least mention them briefly in passing. First, almost all the lawyers in the sample were men. The lawyer survey did not explicitly ask the gender of the respondents, but from the first names, I estimate that at most 10 percent, and probably closer to 5 percent, of the lawyers handling the cases were women.

The lawyers in this sample did not stand out in terms of income or in terms of working in either large firm settings or solo practices. The median income from legal practice was $45,000 (these figures were collected in1980). Only 3 percent of the lawyers reported marginal incomes (less than $15,000), and only 8 percent reported incomes over $100,000. Ordinary litigators make a comfortable living, but they are not getting rich from their legal work. Although few ordinary litigators have to worry about where their next meal (or client) is coming from, the lawyers in this sample probably had more in common with the solo practitioners or small-city lawyers described by Carlin (1962) and Handler (1967) than with the elite lawyer described by Smigel (1964) and Nelson (1988).

Most of the lawyers (95 percent) in the sample were in private practice. The exceptions were those who worked as direct employees of organizations that are not law firms (i.e., house counsel), for some sort of prepaid legal-services plan (including legal aid), or in some other kind of situation (e.g., as a volunteer). Of those lawyers in private practice, only 18 percent were working solo (i.e., outside of a multimember law firm). This differs strikingly from the situation for all lawyers working in private practice in the United States, which involves, according to Curran (1986: 28), 48.6 percent of those lawyers in private practice (Curran's figures, in turn, are quite similar to those reported by Carlin nearly 30 years ago: "[H]alf the lawyers in Chicago, as in practically all the other cities of the United States, are individual practitioners" [1962: 17]). Another 30 percent of the lawyers handling ordinary litigation were in firms with two, three, or four lawyers. Large firms with 50 or more lawyers were also underrepresented among lawyers handling ordinary litigation, which is not surprising, because it simply indicates that ordinary cases are not the typical work of the larger law firms. The low percentage of solo practitioners suggests that ordinary civil litigation does not usually go to the most marginal practitioners (typically found in solo practice). This is less surprising than it might first appear, because it probably means that institutional defendants (e.g., insurance companies) turn to established firms for their representation, and that individual plaintiffs, particularly those seeking to hire lawyers on a contingency basis, need not seek out the lowest-cost alternatives, as might be the case for those individuals seeking divorce counsel or counsel to handle probate or property-related matters.

46. This classification of law schools is based in part on the Carter Report (1977) rankings. I have followed the convention (see Zemans and Rosenblum, 1981: 232) of labeling the top six schools as elite and the next nine as prestige. I have not attempted to distinguish between "regional" and "local" schools but have simply divided the remaining schools among "public," "private," and "proprietary and other."

47. As one might expect from the literature on the elite law firms (e.g., Smigel, 1964; Nelson, 1981, 1985, 1988; Slovak, 1979, 1980, 1981a,b), the formal educational background of the lawyers is clearly related to the size of the firms in which they practice. Only 6 percent of the lawyers in small firms (or not working in firms at all) attended an elite law school (11 percent prestige) compared with 15 percent elite (20 percent prestige) in medium firms and 23 percent elite (35 percent prestige) in large firms. There is less of a relationship between income and formal legal education: 19 percent of the typical-income lawyers went to elite or prestige schools compared with 28 percent of the high-income lawyers and 36 percent of the very-high-income lawyers.

48. At first glance, this high level of performance may seem a bit suspicious. Did

the respondents puff up their backgrounds for the benefit of the interviewers? The performance that this group of lawyers claimed is very similar to the overall group performance reported in a study of the impact of legal training; Zemans and Rosenblum (1981: 24) found that over half the lawyers in their survey, all of whom were practicing in Chicago during the late 1970s, reported being in the top 20 percent of their classes and over three-quarters reported being in the top 40 percent. In addition, 24 percent of the Chicago lawyers reported participation in the law review (ibid.: 108). This comparison suggests that lawyers doing ordinary litigation do not differ appreciably from practicing lawyers as a whole in terms of how well they did in law school. It would appear that for whatever reasons (see ibid.: 24–25) law students in the lower half of their classes have a notably smaller chance of developing a career practicing law than do those in the upper half, or that lawyers systematically misreport their law school performance when asked by survey researchers how they did in school.

49. This is broadly similar to the findings of a recent national study which reported that 42.3 percent of lawyers in practice in 1980 had been admitted to the bar after 1970 (see Curran, 1986: 37). Overall, the lawyers handling ordinary litigation bring substantial numbers of years of experience to their work; however, there are also substantial numbers of younger, less experienced lawyers handling these cases. Interestingly, in terms of background, it is experience that distinguishes lawyers in the high- and very-high-income groups: 37 percent of lawyers in the high-income group and 34 percent of lawyers in the very-high-income group had been in practice for 20 years or more compared with only 15 percent of lawyers with equal experience in the typical-income group (under $75,000). Forty-two percent of the lower-income lawyers had been practicing five years or less versus only 7 percent of the higher-income lawyers.

50. Higher-income lawyers bring not only years of experience to their cases but also case-specific experience. Two-thirds of the very-high-income group reported having handled 100 or more similar cases previously, and over a third reported 500 or more prior similar cases. The lawyers in the high-income group ($75,000–$100,000) also reported substantial amounts of case-specific experience: slightly fewer than two-thirds had reached the 100-case plateau, but only 22 percent had handled 500 or more similar cases. Fewer than 50 percent in the lower-income group reported 100 or more prior cases, and only 12 percent reported 500 or more.

51. The level of self-perceived expertise is much higher for the high-income lawyers. Seventy-nine percent of the very-high-income group and 61 percent of the high-income group rated themselves as experts; this compares with only 36 percent for the lawyers outside these income groups. The higher expertise is also reflected in the numbers of outside activities related to the fields which the various groups of lawyers reported. Only 23 percent of the typical-income lawyers reported involvement in three or more of the various activities compared with 50 percent for the two higher-income groups taken together.

52. One way to look at the relationship among these 11 items is to employ a statistical technique called factor analysis. Factor analysis shows how the items are

related by suggesting broad dimensions that can be seen as underlying the individual items. For these 11 items, such an analysis does not suggest an easily interpretable set of dimensions.

53. There were some modest but interesting variations in attitudes related to firm size or income: large-firm lawyers were more likely to rate "intellectual challenge" and "working with pleasant and interesting people" as very important. Small-firm and solo lawyers were substantially more likely to rate "being your own boss" as very important. Small-firm and solo lawyers also appeared to be more "service oriented," rating both "serving the community" and "helping individuals" as very important substantially more often than did the large-firm lawyers.

As for income-related variations, the two items that stand out are "making a lot of money" and "having a high standing in the community." High-income lawyers viewed both of these as more important than did lawyers with more typical incomes. All these variations are more or less what common sense would lead one to expect. The lower importance placed on "being your own boss" by big-firm lawyers and the lower importance of "making a lot of money" or having "high standing" by lower-income lawyers may simply reflect rationalizations of the lawyers' situations. That is, rather than leading the lawyers in particular career directions (i.e., attitudes causing behavior), the attitudes toward legal practice may largely represent accommodations to the situations the lawyers find themselves in. This explanation is consistent with the greater weight put on service by the small-firm lawyers; because they are less likely to obtain satisfaction from the intellectual aspects of their work, they derive their satisfaction from a sense that they are helping people.

54. There are some interesting variations in likes and dislikes related to income and amount of litigation a lawyer does. As income goes up, lawyers seem to be slightly more inclined toward arguing and trying (52 percent for typical income to 59 percent for high income to 66 percent for very high income) at the expense of planning and research (20 percent to 14 percent to 10 percent). More striking, however, is the sharp increase in preference for arguing and trying that is associated with the proportion of practice composed of litigation: 27 percent of those spending a quarter or less of their time on litigation most liked arguing and trying compared with 63 percent of those who spent more than half their time on litigation.

55. This suggests an intriguing contradiction in the lawyers' attitudes. The lawyers were almost unanimous in their belief that being thorough was very important in order to be a successful litigator; at the same time very few of the lawyers said that the part of their work that they liked the most was the planning and research that go into being thorough. Typically, the lawyers said that what they liked best about their work was the more glamorous aspect of arguing and trying cases. This tension between what is important and what is liked does not necessarily mean that lawyers shortchange their efforts regarding planning and research (very few lawyers reported spending more than 25 percent of their time actually trying cases), but it does suggest something of the reality of the workday world of the ordinary litigator.

56. There were some slight variations in attitudes about what makes a good

litigator related to firm size. The lawyers in the large firms were less likely (by 10–15 percentage points) to rate all factors except thoroughness as being "very important."

Chapter 2. A Portrait of Negotiation and Bargaining in Ordinary Litigation

1. As I discussed in the last chapter, I am not saying that ordinary litigation is only about money, but rather that, by the time lawyers start talking about settlement, the conversation focuses on how much money is to be paid. In later chapters, I will argue that this reflects, at least in part, the need for lawyers to denominate cases in monetary terms.

2. The mean percentage of time is 12.0.

3. In fact, one might wonder how settlement discussions in a relatively routine case could take as long as three hours. If the "discussions" take the form of correspondence, it might easily take three hours to plan and compose the text of the letters conveying the demands or offers.

4. Recall that up to four areas of law were coded for each case. Consequently, any given case may be counted in more than one area of law in Table 2.2. I repeated the analysis shown in Table 2.2 for those cases involving only a single area of law, and found no differences.

5. Because of the skew in the *number* of hours, I report medians in connection with this variable; since skew is not a problem for the *percentage* of time variable, I use arithmetic means in describing its patterns.

6. This may mean that cases involving government are not appropriate for negotiation or are past the negotiation stage by the time a lawsuit is filed. It may also reflect the fact that government lawyers do not work under the same kinds of economic constraints that fee-for-service lawyers confront, and are freer to push a case to final adjudication or simply to wait until the opposing party backs down. This latter explanation may be combined with a government litigator's concerns about the potential precedents (not necessarily of the legal variety) that may arise from settling a case; the nature of the economic constraints (or lack thereof) makes it possible for government lawyers to act upon beliefs about the importance of principle and a concern about "precedent." The CLRP data base includes a survey of a small number of government lawyers. The negotiation patterns found in that data are consistent with what is reported above.

7. Recall that stakes are measured not by the demand contained in the pleadings but by asking the lawyer what an appropriate outcome would be.

8. A one-way analysis of variance indicates that this relationship is significant ($F = 3.17$, d.f. $= 4,822$, $p = .013$), but a Scheffe range test indicates that only the two most extreme groups differ significantly from one another at the .05 level of statistical significance. Also, if one looks at the medians rather than the means, those medians are constant across the stakes range.

9. The exact wording of the question was, "On a scale of 1–5, if 1 is simple and 5 is very complex, how would you rate this case as to its complexity of fact and law?"

10. For the percentage of time, there appears to be a strong break between the two least-complex ratings and the three higher ratings; no similar pattern exists for the number of hours.

11. All three of these relationships, both percentage of time and number of hours with subjective complexity and percentage of time with docket entries, are statistically significant at least at the .01 level.

12. Recall that the lawyers were asked which of the following they liked most and which they liked least: negotiating, planning and research, and arguing and trying.

13. The four questions were:
— How much enjoyment do you get out of gambling for money?
— How likely are you to put all your money in one business opportunity if the chances are good that you would make a big profit?
— Which would you be more likely to do with the money you have been able to save—be very careful about what you do with it, or put it in a new business in the hope of making a lot more?
— If you had a choice, which kind of job would you be more likely to accept—a job you knew you could keep but didn't pay as much as you would like, or a job that paid what you want but that you would less likely be able to keep?

14. The overall relationship is strongly significant in statistical terms (F = 12.47, d.f. = 4,1303, p < .001), though district accounts for only 3.7 percent of the variation in the percentage of time devoted to settlement discussions. Using range tests, Central California differs significantly from all the other districts; of the remaining four, the only two that are significantly different from one another are South Carolina and Eastern Pennsylvania.

15. Separate one-way analyses of variance and range tests of the effect of district for state and federal cases indicate that California differs significantly from the other districts (the only exception being Eastern Pennsylvania for federal cases); none of the other districts differ significantly from one another.

16. The ambiguous nature of this sentence reflects the ambiguity of the analyses. A one-way analysis of variance for all federal cases does indicate statistically significant differences; multiple range tests indicate that California differs only from South Carolina. Because the one-way analysis of variance is based on means which are sensitive to skew, the analysis was repeated excluding outliers (cases where more than 50 hours were devoted to negotiation); this analysis indicated no significant differences among the five districts.

17. It is worth noting that another settlement-related study, this time in the Northern District in California, reported that lawyers litigating federal cases there were more interested in having judges be active in the settlement process than were lawyers in three other federal districts (see Brazil, 1985). Perhaps there is something about the legal culture of California as a whole that affects the settlement/negotiation behavior and attitudes of attorneys.

18. The significant geographic variations that I was able to find were in relation

to contact intensity, and it is worth speculating on why it is only contact intensity appears to have a possible connection to local legal culture. One possible explanation is that this is the one negotiation-related variable that is least affected by the nationalizing forces involved in the civil litigation process. That is, given that most cases involve at least one organizational litigant (either explicitly or, in tort cases, implicitly), and a very large proportion of those organizations operate beyond the confines of a single judicial district, that organizational presence may have a homogenizing effect on those aspects of the process over which a knowledgeable client has substantial control. An organizational client that is experienced in litigation is probably going to have a lot of control over the specific offers and/or demands that its lawyer makes on its behalf; this control would probably extend to both the number and content of such offers/demands. The conduct of the settlement discussions themselves will lie more in the hands of the lawyers; if the local culture emphasizes a more extended style of discussion, the client is likely to have little control over that aspect of the process. In summary, the geographic pattern described here suggests the potential role of "sponsoring" organizations (see Eisenstein, Flemming, and Nardulli, 1988) in determining the impact of local legal culture on the conduct of court-centered activities. Where sponsoring organizations are largely local, as is true in criminal cases, local legal culture may exert a greater influence on the process (ibid.) than if those organizations were broader in geographic scope.

19. One might wonder whether these figures accurately represent the number of bargaining exchanges that occur, or whether the lawyers are "forgetting" intermediate exchanges. In fact, a study of injury compensation cases in England (many of which did not get to the point of a lawsuit being commenced) found that in 63 percent of the cases the *first* offer made by the "defendant" was accepted (Harris et al., 1984: 95). In the U.S. data, focusing solely on plaintiff-respondents in cases where the opposing party made a payment in settlement, 46 percent of the plaintiffs accepted the first offer made, 42 percent the second, and only 12 percent went to three or more offers.

20. Unfortunately, no information is available in the CLRP data set on who made the initial move. In an unpublished survey of Wisconsin attorneys undertaken by the editors of the *Wisconsin Law Review,* lawyers were asked about their most recently concluded civil cases. Among the questions asked was, Which side "made the first offer of settlement"? The survey, which focused on the valuation of cases, was conducted by mail (a response rate of 52 percent was obtained from a sample of 853 attorneys selected from the membership lists of the Wisconsin State Bar Association, the American Trial Lawyers Association, and the Civil Trial Council). Attorneys were asked to focus on their most recently resolved cases (whether settled or tried) that involved a significant amount of money. Approximately 61 percent of the respondents had represented plaintiffs in the cases. In personal injury cases, 74 percent of the respondents reported that the plaintiffs had made the first moves; this includes a generic personal injury category, plus separate product liability and medical malpractice categories (the percentage for the generic personal injury category was 75 [N = 209], for product liability 65 [N = 46], and for medical malpractice 76

[N = 17]. In business corporate cases, plaintiffs made the first offers in 57 percent of the cases (N = 51).

21. The survey of lawyers asked about discussions aimed at settlement; the idea (and implication) that these "discussions" might in fact be correspondence was not considered when the questionnaire was written.

22. The lawyer's degree of specialization was measured by an index that combined responses to questions about the lawyer's experience and expertise in the area of law into which the case fell. This measure of specialization was created by combining the number of similar cases the lawyer had previously handled (using weights derived from factor analysis), the lawyer's own rating of her expertise in the area of law, the percentage of the lawyer's practice in that area, and outside activities related to that area (e.g., continuing legal education [CLE] courses taken or taught, articles or books written, committee/commission service); see Kritzer, Sarat, et al. 1984: 599, for more detail.

23. See Maynard, 1984a, for an analysis of the content of negotiations in minor criminal cases. Maynard finds little evidence of concessions by the prosecution; most offers are presented on a take-it-or-leave-it basis (and most are taken). Nardulli, Flemming, and Eisenstein (1985; see also, Eisenstein, Flemming, and Nardulli, 1988; Nardulli, Eisenstein, and Flemming, 1988) report very similar patterns for felonies in nine diverse, medium-sized counties in three states.

24. In Table 2.10, I have counted cases involving multiple areas of law in *each* of the categories in which they appeared. I also computed the statistics relegating cases involving multiple areas to a residual "mixed" category (so that each case was counted in only a single category); the pattern remained essentially unchanged.

25. One of the nonmonetized stakes most frequently mentioned by individual litigants related to discrimination, particularly discrimination on the job (hiring, salary, promotion, etc.).

26. I participated in a focus group discussion with lawyers representing persons with discrimination claims. The biggest concern expressed was the inadequacy of the *monetary* remedies that were available; there was no dissatisfaction with the availability of remedies such as orders that a discrimination victim be given a job. Essentially, the lawyers said that many cases were not worth pursuing because the potential for monetary damages was inadequate—there was nothing tangible that they could obtain for their clients (or, not incidentally, for themselves).

27. Although small cases may be less complex than big cases, there is no necessary correlation between size and complexity (see Yngvesson and Hennessey, 1975).

28. I should note that there may be some link between negotiation content and location. Initial gross tabulations indicated that negotiations in New Mexico tended to be the most monetary in nature of the five districts surveyed. However, introducing controls for case type suggests that this is primarily a result of variations in case mix. Negotiations in contract cases in New Mexico do seem to be more monetary, but this may reflect very aggressive use of the courts in that state to collect defaulted student loans and for other kinds of collections cases that did not end with simple default judgments.

29. For purposes of this analysis, the specialization scale was broken into four

levels, ranging from low to high expertise.See note 22 above for more detail about the scale.

30. Interestingly, the only relationship between the monetary content of negotiation and lawyers' attitudes concerned the attitudes toward the work involved in litigation. Those who said they most liked arguing and trying cases were more likely to be involved in cases in which the negotiations were entirely monetary, though the difference between these lawyers and those who most liked either negotiating or planning and researching was not great (77 percent versus 67 percent reporting entirely monetary negotiations).

31. In part this no doubt reflects what might be called a selection bias; that is, contingent-fee lawyers will tend to avoid cases in which nonmonetary outcomes (and hence nonmonetary demands or offers) are likely. However, as I will show in chapter 5, even with the exclusion of cases in which stakes cannot be expressed in monetary terms, contingent-fee lawyers tend to concentrate more on monetary concerns in the negotiations.

32. As I reported above, very few tort cases involved nonmonetary offers or demands. Where there were such demands, they were most often procedural in nature (only one respondent reported an offer/demand dealing with liability).

33. In addition to the lawyer attitudes discussed earlier in this chapter, I looked at indicators of the lawyer's contentiousness and personal efficacy (i.e., self-confidence), which, along with risk preference, are characteristics that some studies have found to be related to whether or not a negotiator will adopt a competitive (i.e., tactical) approach to negotiations (see Lowenthal, 1982: 110–111). However, I could find no evidence of a relationship between tactical bargaining and these psychological characteristics.

34. The table does not show statistics for the location variable; none of the statistical tests between location and these ratios was significant.

35. Expenses, as the term is used here, include only those that are paid to or through the lawyer. They do not include any direct expenses incurred by the plaintiff or defendant, nor do they take into account the value of the time devoted to the case by the plaintiff or the defendant. This omission introduces relatively minor distortions because many of these expenses would be incurred regardless of whether or not a lawsuit had been filed and these expenses tend to represent a very small fraction of the total cost of litigation (see Kritzer, Sarat, et al., 1984: 562–563).

36. A net loss is most likely to occur when the plaintiff has retained his lawyer on an hourly fee basis. But it can also occur when the lawyer is paid on a contingency basis, because the out-of-pocket expenses (such as filing fees, witness fees, and the like) are typically deducted from the payment before the lawyer takes her percentage (and often have to be paid even if no settlement or award is obtained).

37. The relationship between the two measures is:

$$ds = 1 - \frac{1}{DS}$$

38. Although professional and legal norms are intended to protect clients from

this conflict (see Perschbacher, 1985), there is little doubt that the conflict is real (see Miller, 1987; Rosenthal, 1974; Johnson, 1980–81). This will be considered in more detail in chapter 5.

39. For a more extensive discussion of the issues involved here, see chapter 5, and Kritzer et al., 1987, or Kritzer, 1990: 135–161.

40. See Kritzer, Sarat, et al., 1984: 587–591, for an analysis of the hourly rates charged by hourly fee lawyers.

41. Strictly speaking, it would be best to examine the relationship between the negotiation variables and success within the context of a full explanatory model for the three success indicators. I have in fact done that (see Kritzer, 1990: 135–161), and the simple bivariate results that I present here are generally consistent with that more extensive analysis. The one exception is that some weak relationships appearing in the bivariate analysis of lawyers' success disappear in the multivariate analysis. For reasons of space, I will not repeat the entire "success" analysis here.

42. Walton and McKersie (1965: 126) point out that most negotiation actually involves a mixture of cooperation and competition.

43. Lowenthal (1982: 75) uses a different set of characteristics to distinguish between what he labels competitive and collaborative negotiation:

—adherence to position: "Limited flexibility is an essential element of a negotiator's strategy in competitive bargaining" (ibid.: 75).

—the nature of the flow of information: the competitive negotiator seeks to restrict information flow with the goal of concealing from the opponent the negotiator's true "resistance point."

—the nature of communication: the competitive negotiator seeks to convince the opponent that the negotiator's desired outcome is in the opponent's best interest (with the communication marked by threats and arguments) in contrast with a collaborative search for a joint solution in both sides' interests.

—relationships between the negotiators: competitive negotiation is marked by suspicion and hostility compared with trust and concord in collaborative negotiation.

This scheme does tend to conflate means and goals, as pointed out by Menkel-Meadow (see note 44).

44. Part of the inconsistency may reflect the problem pointed out by Menkel-Meadow—that many analysts fail to recognize the *conceptual* distinction between ends and means of negotiations (1984: 818): ends can be either adversarial or what she terms "problem solving," and means can be either competitive or cooperative. Although this conceptual distinction is important, in practice I suspect there is a strong correlation between the two dimensions, with a high likelihood that negotiators who are oriented toward problem solving will adopt a cooperative style and negotiators who are oriented toward being adversary will adopt a competitive style. This empirical connection partly accounts for the frequent conflation of ends and means. For example, Gifford (1985) describes what he calls three strategies of negotiation: competitive, cooperative, and integrative. The last two differ not so much in tactics as in goals (the cooperative being zero sum, the integrative being positive sum). Gifford's three strategies fit almost perfectly into three of the cells of Menkel-

Meadow's fourfold table (1984: 818), combining the two categories of ends noted above and the two categories of means.

Chapter 3. Settlement, Negotiation, and Economics in Ordinary Litigation

1. This figure does not include tort claims settled before formal court filings, and it does not include cases handled in limited-jurisdiction courts.

2. This figure is by nature very crude. If one presumes that the institutional costs to the court system are roughly proportional to the total expenditures (both awards and transaction costs), this figure would be a significant underestimate, given that Kakalik and Ross (1983: xix) estimated that the institutional cost of tort cases accounts for less than 15 percent of the total costs of the civil courts. This figure rises to 18 percent if domestic relations, mental health, probate, and guardianship cases are excluded.

3. The approach described here is most often identified with Posner, even though Friedman's analysis, which appeared as a Note in the *Stanford Law Review,* was published three years before Posner's article, and Ross's book-length analysis of the process of out-of-court settlements with insurance companies was originally published two years before Posner's article. These analyses all build upon work on negotiation in the labor-relations area. See, in particular, the work of Walton and McKersie (1965).

4. The plaintiff's minimum and the defendant's maximum are normally referred to as the parties' resistance points—the points past which they will not move.

5. The multiplying of outcome by probability is the standard procedure in probability theory for obtaining what is technically known as the expected value. It is expected in the sense that if the "game" were played over repeated trials, on average the player could expect an outcome equal to the product. For example, in rolling a pair of honest dice, if the player is to receive $10 if either 7 or 11 results and no money otherwise, the expected outcome on a single roll is $2.22, because the probability of either 7 or 11 is .222 (.222 multiplied by $10 is $2.22).

6. Mathematically, this can be stated as follows:

A settlement is expected to occur if the following condition is met:

$$\pi_p D_p - C_p \le \pi_d D_d + C_d$$

where π_p = plaintiff's estimate of plaintiff's probability of winning at trial
where π_d = defendant's estimate of plaintiff's probability of winning at trial
where D_p = plaintiff's estimate of damages that would be awarded at trial
where D_d = defendant's estimate of damages that would be awarded at trial
where C_p = plaintiff's cost of going to trial
where C_d = defendant's cost of going to trial

A fairly simple mathematical manipulation of the equation above makes it clear that the condition for settlement will be met if the plaintiff's expected recovery $(\pi_p D_p)$ exceeds the defendant's expected loss $(\pi_d D_d)$ by an amount equal to or less than the sum of the costs of going to trial for the two sides:

$$\pi_p D_p - \pi_d D_d \leq C_p + C_d$$

7. There were also a number of pairs among the 20 for which no settlement was reached.

8. One feature of the experiment, intended to insure that the participants would take the process seriously, was that, after the agreements were reached, all the lawyers came together to reveal and discuss their results. Williams noted that the lack of consistency was "sobering" to the participants, but that the first reaction of each participant was to defend his own result as the right one.

9. These are my calculations from figures reported in Rosenthal's book (ibid.: 202–207).

10. It may be that the level of uncertainty associated with case evaluation has decreased in recent years with the increase both in the number of publications reporting jury verdicts and in informal communications among lawyers (see Daniels, 1986).

11. Mathematically, it would make the most sense to think in terms of a "distribution" of possible outcomes. For purposes of illustration, it is sufficient simply to consider some specific set of outcomes.

12. This approach could be further refined by allowing for the association of different transaction costs with each outcome.

13. Work at the Rand Institute for Civil Justice (Waterman and Peterson, 1981) sought to build on this image of negotiation and settlement (i.e., it depends upon the existence of a zone of overlap) by developing a "rule-based" model of the settlement process. The idea of this model is that decisions made by litigators regarding settlement (and other aspects of the litigation process) are guided by a series of rules that can be identified and combined in a series of if-then propositions. The major shortcoming of this approach is that it says little about how one arrives at the answers to the questions posed by each of the decision rules.

14. It should be noted that when considering transaction costs in this kind of analysis, only future costs are relevant, not sunk costs.

15. One might question the applicability of this kind of analysis when the plaintiff has retained an attorney on a percentage-fee basis, since the plaintiff's costs are then a fixed percentage of the outcome. However, as I will discuss below, in this situation it is the plaintiff's attorney who is in fact at risk for costs, and this serves to enhance the argument, because the costs as a percentage of the *attorney's* return are even greater.

16. Bebchuk (1984) provides a nice formalization of this kind of process, demonstrating mathematically that there is a clear trade-off between the extremity of the demand or offer and the likelihood of a settlement occurring. He uses his analysis to examine the impact of rules regarding who pays the costs of litigation (ibid.: 412),

and argues that the likelihood of settlement is greater under the American rule (where each side bears its own cost) than under the English rule (where the loser pays both sides' costs). However, this aspect of his analysis leaves out important dimensions in both systems: the likelihood that an individual plaintiff will be risk averse; the fact that in the United States it is the contingent-fee lawyer rather than the plaintiff himself that bears most of (if not all) the costs of litigation if no recovery is made (and that the plaintiff is almost totally dependent upon the lawyer for assessing what constitutes an appropriate settlement); the fact that in England there are effectively three sets of practices concerning costs in litigation—private funding (i.e., the plaintiff pays the fees directly), union funding (the plaintiff's union accepts all responsibility and risk for the costs of the litigation), and state funding through legal aid (where the cost is essentially shared by the state and the lawyer, since the lawyer must accept a lower fee for legal-aid cases).

Cooter and Marks (1982: 245), who also consider the trade-off between extremity of demands/offers and the likelihood of settlement, provide a more complex discussion of the implications of cost rules, considering the implications of both risk aversion and optimistic or pessimistic litigants. They do not, however, factor in the implications of representation by contingent-fee lawyers.

17. Galanter (1984: 268) refers to this shadow as "a compelling presence."

18. In an analysis of medical malpractice cases, Danzon and Lillard (1982) argue that there is good evidence to support the view that settlements occur in the shadow of the law. Applying a sophisticated econometric model, they found that settlements prior to trial are strongly influenced by the "shadow verdict," averaging 75 percent of that verdict. Furthermore, these authors found that judgments are strongly related to factors like the plaintiff's economic loss and the legal standards dealing with compensable damages.

Another recent study of settlements in private antitrust litigation (Perloff and Rubinfeld, 1987) considered the influence of legal rules affecting the magnitude of damages. Specifically, that research examined the influence of the antitrust law's triple-damage rule on the likelihood of settlement versus trial. The general conclusion of the study is that reducing the current damage multiplier "could increase substantially the fraction of litigated cases that go to trial" (ibid.: 170).

One problem with both of these analyses is that they deal with cases that probably fall outside the region of what I have labeled ordinary litigation. The typical malpractice case is at the margin of this region as I have described it, involving somewhat more in terms of stakes; the median malpractice verdict in the Rand civil jury study was $84,000 compared with $7,000 for all cases (Peterson and Priest, 1982: 28).

There is some evidence of shadows in ordinary cases. In a study of 582 civil cases involving rear-end automobile accidents in California during 1974–79, Wittman (1986: 162) found that "bargaining [i.e., offers and demands] by the plaintiff and defendant reflects the anticipated behavior of the jury." In divorce cases, an area that I am not directly addressing because of my sample design, Maccoby, Depner, and Mnookin (1988) examined child custody arrangements following divorces in California. They found a substantial increase in the frequency of agreements for joint custody arrangements in the wake of changes in California law in 1979 that established a presumption favoring joint custody and allowing judges to impose it even when one parent objected (ibid.: 93). In another study of divorce cases focusing on property and support issues, Seltzer and Garfinkel (1990) found that inequality in economic resources between the divorcing husband and wife limited the impact of the legal shadow on financial settlements that were reached; they conclude that for spouses with unequal resources, the primary determining factor in outcomes is not the legal shadow but is *either* the ability of one spouse to use the power in his or her (usually his) own self-interest *or* the father's altruistic concern for his children even when he did not obtain custody.

19. In other countries, such as England, where awards are set by a small cadre of judges, the amounts that might be expected to be paid in compensation for pain and suffering are known with more certainty than in the United States. In England, there is a standard reference, known as *Kemp and Kemp* (Kemp, 1986), that is used for determining likely payments in personal injury cases.

20. This argument assumes that each side bears its own costs. In a system where the loser must pay the winner's costs, this is, in theory, less of a problem. However, for the plaintiff in a small case, the advantage of the fee-shifting system must be weighed against the down-side risks that are created for the plaintiff in that system (see Kritzer, 1984b).

21. There is some evidence that creating risk in the settlement process is a conscious policy of insurance companies. In an article entitled "Creating Risk in Negotiation and Settlement Techniques," Clayton (1966: 472) provided the following advice for insurance claims adjusters: ". . . [T]he attorney will accept the offer, not because he feels that it is adequate, but because he recognizes that settling the case at that figure represents the most prudent means of eliminating the uncertainty of the outcome of the case. . . ."

22. By relative terms, I mean the ratio of the difference between the two points that represent the boundaries of the zone of overlap divided by the amount at stake.

23. The reasonableness of this assumption can be most clearly seen by stating it the other way around: as stakes increase, the costs rise, but not at a proportional rate. In other words, if a case involving $5,000 is expected to have transaction costs of $1,000, then a $10,000 case would be expected to involve greater costs, but not twice as great.

24. One could make an argument that one or both sides will tend to approach litigation in a pessimistic fashion, each side viewing his or her respective chances of prevailing more negatively than does the other side. However, given the risk that the contingent-fee plaintiff's lawyer takes on in accepting a case, it is likely that the lawyer will rigorously screen cases before accepting them, and take only cases that she believes to have high probabilities of yielding successful outcomes, particularly cases that can yield at best modest fees.

25. It is possible to come up with a situation where the zone of overlap will be larger in relative terms as stakes increase, but this requires that the rate of increase in

costs to the plaintiff be substantially greater than the rate of increase for the defendant.

26. Compare with Gifford (1985: 83): "In the small or medium-sized [tort] case, economic reality dictates settlement because the costs of litigation exceed the value of the claim."

27. There is an argument to be made that increasing zones of overlap might serve to *decrease* the likelihood of settlement. In a situation of shared information, if both sides can agree on the expected outcome for each side, settlement will be easiest if each side has exactly the same expected outcome. Once there is a *zone* of overlap (as distinct from a *point* of agreement), there is going to be the problem of deciding how to "share" the surplus that is generated by settling, though there is always the obvious choice of splitting the difference. The problem of how to share the surplus is unlikely to arise in the litigation context, because the two sides will not generally know the degree of overlap.

28. Some contingent-fee agreements call for an increased percentage to be paid to the lawyer if the case goes to trial (or is appealed); however, these marginal percentages seldom reflect the magnitude of the additional work required to carry through to trial.

29. Hensler and her colleagues (1990) report that only a third of injury victims who sought the assistance of lawyers in making a compensation claim through the tort system recall the lawyers mentioning estimates of the specific amounts of compensation the victims might obtain.

30. For this calculation, the primary transaction cost is the opportunity cost of the lawyer's time; one can ignore any transaction costs that are shifted to the client (e.g., filing and witness fees).

31. Yet another factor that would further enhance this analysis is risk preference. Most plaintiffs in ordinary civil litigation are individuals who are likely to be risk averse; that is, since most are one-shot players (see Galanter, 1974) who cannot expect to see the probability of winning balance out over a series of cases, one could reasonably expect those plaintiffs to be willing to accept less than the expected award minus transaction costs. This simply means that the plaintiff's side of the net expected outcome should be adjusted downward by a risk-aversion discount factor (see Wittman, 1988). If most defendants are repeat players who can expect winning and losing to balance out over time, no such discount should be applicable for them. The revised formulation of the settlement condition is then:

$$\pi_p D_p - C_p - R_p \leq \pi_d D_d + C_d$$

where the additional factor, R_p, is a discount factor for the plaintiff's risk preference. As I will discuss in the next chapter, differences in risk preference can led to "power" disparities between litigants.

In his analysis of settlement in product liability cases, Viscusi (1988; see also Viscusi, 1986) found evidence to support the presumptions that the probability of settlement increases as the level of risk (defined in terms of the degree of uncertainty about the size of payment) increases.

32. In Ross's sample the average compensation paid out was $1,500 in cases handled by solo lawyers; this rises to $2,225 for firm lawyers and $5,000 for lawyers specializing in negligence, the latter being defined by Ross (1980: 193) as those who are members of the American Trial Lawyers Association.

33. One major limitation in a general application of Carlin's analysis to ordinary litigation is the fact that most such litigation is not handled by lawyers in solo practice; only 18 percent of the lawyers in the CLRP sample were in solo practice (see Kritzer, 1990: 44). Carlin's results were specific to solo practitioners in Chicago (ca. 1960), but they probably were true of solo practitioners in other large cities across the United States.

34. This was expressed nicely by one of Carlin's respondents (1962: 79): "'Over the years if you deal with the same men, they know you're willing to fight and litigate, if necessary. You develop rapport. . . . They may settle with you where they won't with others, because of the regard they have for you, the fact that you treat them well, give them information. . . .'"

35. This phrase is taken from Jackson's (1974: 62–73) description of the approach to handling cases in a misdemeanor court.

36. It is important to note here that it may be the impression of the outcome rather than the actual outcome that is important. A number of years ago when I negotiated over a home purchase, the bargaining failed because the seller perceived an offer as negative sum when it was in fact zero sum. Specifically, the seller wanted to remain in the house for several months after the sale (because the new house that he was having built would not be ready, but he needed the money from the sale to finance the building). An offer was made to rent back the house at cost, which was essentially equal to the interest cost on the full purchase price (since I was going to have finance 100 percent of that price while waiting for the completion of the sale on my previous house), plus real estate taxes. The seller felt he was being "ripped off" because this came to 2.5 times his then-current mortgage payment (the difference reflected a combination of the increase in property values and the increase in interest rates), and no amount of explanation could persuade him otherwise.

37. One standard example of bilateral monopoly is a single employer dealing with a single supplier of labor; the problem for integrative bargaining is finding settlements that both sides see as advantageous. The role of tax laws with regard to fringe benefits is one clear example of how integrative solutions might be generated even where the two sides appear to have directly opposing interests. Another example involves providing employees with discounts on the employer's products (e.g., free or reduced-price travel for airline employees, employee discounts in retail stores); where the discount does not reduce the price below the employer's marginal cost and the employees' would not otherwise purchase the employer's product, the employer can increase not only the employees' compensation through the discount but also the employer's net income from the discounted sales.

38. Does this mean that a plaintiff would be better off paying a lawyer on some

basis other than a contingent fee? This is a difficult question, because the fees earned by contingent-fee lawyers in ordinary cases are relatively small, and it would not take a lot of effort on the part of a lawyer billing on an hourly basis to exceed those fees. The point here is simply that the elimination of an "uncontrollable" cost can lead to an integrative solution, whereas the elimination of a controllable cost simply avoids a negative-sum result.

39. These kinds of structured settlements often depend upon the fact that payments made in tort cases are not normally taxable as income, whereas investment income from a payment from a tort case is taxable. Thus, if the defendant purchases an annuity for the plaintiff, the payments are treated as nontaxable; the plaintiff and defendant can then share the tax savings (the defendant purchasing an annuity that yields a return greater than the after-tax return would be if the plaintiff were to purchase the annuity, but one that is less than what would be required to yield the same net return to the plaintiff).

40. Although I doubt that structured settlements would play much role in ordinary cases, the one empirical study of such settlements that I could find reported that 25 percent of the insurance companies responding would consider such a settlement for cases as small as $10,000, and some of them would consider much smaller cases. Overall, as of the early to mid-1980s, structured settlements occurred in substantially fewer than 1 percent of tort claims (AIRAC, 1983: 20).

41. Again, I should note that the lawyers representing the plaintiff class did not receive coupons as part of their fees and that one member of the plaintiff class who was unhappy with the settlement was reported to have suggested during a hearing that the lawyer *should* be paid partly in coupons.

42. The general issue of concession rates is one that is frequently considered in advice books on negotiation. For example, Karrass (1970: 18–20) draws on an experiment involving experienced negotiators to suggest that: "losers make the largest concession in a negotiation"; "people who make small concessions during negotiations fail less"; and "losers tend to make the first compromise." See Hamner and Yukl, 1977, for a general discussion of the experimental research concerning the effectiveness of various offer strategies and tactics in negotiation.

43. It is worth noting that directly preceding Ross's own statement (ibid.: 151–152), he quotes Carl Stevens (from Stevens, 1963: 63): "'The initial bargaining proposal is an information-seeking device. During the early stages of negotiation, each party, in addition to giving information about (and concealing) his preferences, is attempting to discover the true preferences of his opponent.'"

44. If one goes back to the case of Michael's wrist, described in chapter 1, it would seem (assuming that the lawyer's estimate of the likely settlement value was within the ball park) that Michael's initial demand of $1,700 served to set the bargaining range.

45. There is no reason that this argument need be limited to the low-intensity bargaining of ordinary litigation, but the advantages of being the first to impart information are probably clearest in this situation, given the uncertainties under which both sides must operate.

46. In some types of cases, such as contract disputes, the stakes may be quite clear, leaving little real room for bargaining give and take. In other cases, such as personal injury matters, stakes are frequently unclear (as I have described previously), and the initial offer/demand may set the bargaining range. Since the largest number of cases in the sample discussed in chapter 2 involves tort issues, the relatively small number of exchanges is probably more attributable to the effect of the initial demand or offer setting the bargaining range than to a lack of room for give and take.

Chapter 4. Power, Games, and Bargaining

1. See van Koppen, 1988, for an alternate discussion of power in the context of negotiation in civil litigation.

2. This assumes that the judgement is enforceable; if the defendant has no ability to satisfy the judgment (e.g., the defendant has no funds to pay a money judgment), then the power of the legal process is of little use.

3. Bargaining in other contexts also involves "shadows." Most obviously, traditional economic bargaining, when it concerns something like the sale of a house or a labor contract, functions in what might be called the shadow of the market; this simply means that the market constrains the kinds of outcomes that are likely to occur, just as in the litigation context the law and/or adjudication constraining whatever negotiated outcomes are likely to be reached.

4. In the previous chapter, I pointed out the tremendous range that appears to exist in the estimate of case worth in personal injury cases. This may have begun to narrow in recent years with the increasing prevalence of systematic reporting of jury verdicts (see Daniels, 1986).

5. Wittman's critique (1985) of Priest and Klein's work and Priest's response (1985) make it clear that there may be classes of cases that reach adjudication where contested issues have to do more with the magnitude of damages than with liability; in those cases liability will be decided predominantly in favor of the plaintiffs, but one would expect there to be greater differences in evaluations of case worth than is true for cases where settlements are reached.

6. The empirical evidence supporting the impact of the shadow of the law in divorce cases is mixed. Maccoby, Depner, and Mnookin (1988) provide evidence of the impact of the legal shadow on custody arrangements (in California), but Seltzer and Garfinkel (1990) can detect no legal shadow impacts on property and support settlements (in Wisconsin). In a multi-state comparison, Pearson, Thoennes, and Tjaden (1989) report at best a moderate change in child support agreements and orders in response to the imposition of various kinds of child support guidelines. Melli, Erlanger, and Chambliss (1988: 1147) argue that, "rather than a system of bargaining in the shadow of the law, divorce may well be one of adjudication in the shadow of bargaining"; this is based upon an analysis of child support agreements for which "the shadow of the law was cast by the agreements of the parties," not by adjudicatory decisions of judges.

7. Cooter and Marks (1982: 229) refer to the portion of the stakes that can be destroyed through litigation as the "surplus" that can be shared if a negotiated settlement is reached. The term "surplus" suggests a positive-sum game; however, the overall image is clearly more consistent with a negative-sum game.

8. Other areas, such as contracts, probably fall somewhere between the certainty concerning stakes associated with divorce cases and the uncertainty in tort cases.

9. The power asymmetries identified by Cooter and Marks may actually serve to obscure the impact of the legal shadow (see Seltzer and Garfinkel, 1990).

10. One exception is in the area of divorce (see Seltzer and Garfinkel, 1990; or Erlanger, Chambliss, and Melli, 1987). Also, it probably is the case that power derived from resource differences plays an important role in settlement negotiations in big-time contract disputes (or business regulation disputes, such as private antitrust actions) between business organizations of disparate sizes. Interestingly, a recent analysis of settlement in private antitrust litigation provides only minimal evidence that resource differences influence the likelihood of a settlement (Perloff and Rubinfeld, 1987: 162–163, 177).

11. Quite clearly, this ability to impose costs is related to rules concerning who bears the expense of litigation. In the United States, the norm is that each side pays its own lawyer; in most other countries, the norm is that the loser in litigation pays its own lawyer's fees plus some or all of the winner's lawyer's fees. There is tremendous variation in how this "indemnification" works in practice, but at least in theory, much of the argument above concerning imposing costs would have to be substantially modified in a system with "fee shifting," as it is called in the United States.

12. Systems of litigation with fee-shifting rules typically include some rules that allow a defendant to shift threats of costs to the plaintiff if the plaintiff seeks to take advantage of the defendant's cost risks by inflating demands. In the English system this involves making a formal settlement offer by depositing the amount of the offer with the court ("paying into court"). I would guess that at least part of the reason that the case of Michael's wrist led to an unexpectedly high offer by the insurance company was a concern about the potential costs of litigation if an attorney were to have become involved in the case.

13. I suspect that most organizations can provide anecdotal evidence of cases of this type having occurred.

14. What little evidence does exist indicates that lawyers are fairly rigorous in the screening of cases; Curran (1976: 9) reports one study of medical malpractice cases in which lawyers accepted only 12 percent of the claims they evaluated. My own conversations with defense attorneys for insurance companies do not provide indications that frivolous lawsuits are a frequent phenomenon, despite the occasional tales of crazy cases reported in the press.

15. The vast majority of *judgments* in civil courts in fact arise in these two types of cases—divorce cases because they all require a decree even when all conflictual issues have been resolved by negotiations, and collections cases because most end in default judgment for the plaintiff.

16. In tort litigation in many states, the nominal defendant may be an individual,

but the "real" defendant is the insurance company that is paying the defense attorney (thereby controlling the defense of the case and all settlement negotiations from the defense side) and that will pay any judgment or settlement that results in the case.

17. This statement would not apply to so-called you-bet-your-corporation litigation.

18. The technical definition of risk aversion is that a risk-averse player will accept less than the "expected value" of the gamble in lieu of playing the game; that is, given a 50–50 chance at $10, a risk-averse player will accept something less than $5 in lieu of playing the game. The degree of risk aversion is reflected in the level of discount the player is willing to accept. Obviously, a player could be a risk preferer, meaning that the player would demand a premium over the expected value in lieu of playing the game.

19. Discussions of risk preference typically fail to take into account asymmetries that may arise depending on whether the risk is one of winning a sum of money or losing a sum of money. A recent study by van Koppen (1990) in the Netherlands (f is the symbol for Dutch guilders) provides evidence that defendants may be more risk preferring than plaintiffs regardless of whether they are one-shot or repeat players. One group of subjects was presented with the following choice: a 45 percent chance to win f6,000 or a 90 percent chance to win f3,000. The expected value of both choices is winning f2,700. A second group was offered: a 45 percent chance to lose f6,000 or a 90 percent chance to lose f3,000. Again, the expected value of the two choices is equal, this time losing f2,700.

In the first group of subjects, 86 percent chose the *safe* alternative (the 90 percent chance to win f3,000), whereas in the second group 87 percent chose the *risky* alternative! Thus, it may be that defendants naturally tend toward risk seeking, and plaintiffs are naturally risk averse.

20. One of the most systematic efforts to develop a process approach for understanding negotiations in the dispute-processing context is to be found in the work of Gulliver (1979). Gulliver offers two complementary descriptions of negotiation (specifically within a dispute context). One model, which he labels the cyclical model, focuses on the offer-counteroffer image of negotiation; the second model, labeled the developmental model, focuses on the process of getting from initial contact to final outcome. Both models provide sets of categories for use in observing and interpreting an actual set of negotiations. The data I have available do not lend themselves to the kind of analysis that Gulliver envisioned, and I have some question about whether or not the elaborate processes he describes are particularly relevant to the cut-and-dried realities of negotiation in ordinary litigation.

21. A somewhat similar approach can be found in Gulliver's work (ibid.), which is described in note 20.

22. See Lowenthal, 1982, for an extensive discussion of the implications of competitive versus cooperative (which Lowenthal refers to as "collaborative") approaches to legal negotiations. Menkel-Meadow (1984: 818n250) points out that both Williams and Lowenthal "conflate the ends and means of negotiation." The conflation problem is even more acute in Gifford's (1985) delineation of three nego-

tiation strategies: competitive, cooperative, and integrative; the last two essentially distinguish between ends rather than means. In my discussion in this chapter, I use the competitive/cooperative dimension to refer to means or strategies rather than to the goals of negotiation.

23. Williams does not report the actual analyses (1983: 17–18); consequently it is not possible to draw conclusions about how his *operational* categories could be applied to the data upon which my analyses are based.

24. Williams seems to refer to "style" and "strategy" as interchangeable concepts, at least as they refer to his cooperative and competitive categories. As mentioned in note 22, this probably reflects, at least in part, the conflation of ends and means described by Menkel-Meadow (1984).

25. The balance of the cooperators were categorized as "average" negotiators.

26. In fact, elsewhere (Kritzer, 1990: 143–146) I have shown that the amount saved by defendants in payments to the plaintiffs (as measured by the plaintiffs' valuations of the cases), exceeded the legal fees paid by the defendants in about two-thirds of the cases.

27. Recall my comments in chapter 2 that, despite experimental evidence suggesting a linkage between bargaining behavior and psychological characteristics like risk preference, contentiousness, and personal efficacy (see Lowenthal, 1982:109–112), there are no apparent linkages of this sort for lawyers dealing in the world of ordinary litigation.

28. Genn suggests that the crucial point here may be the volume of litigation that is handled; she argues that general-practice solicitors who handle a small amount of litigation as part of a broad-ranging practice simply do not have the opportunity to create the kind of reputation that will allow them to be tough negotiators.

29. Actually, the Prisoner's Dilemma does not require the second of these characteristics for a single play of the game (see Rapoport, 1960: 173–177). The second requirement is necessary to make the repeated Prisoner's Dilemma nontrivial by eliminating the option of taking turns exploiting one another.

30. There is no requirement that the various payoffs for two players be identical, only that for each player the order and conditions of inequality be met.

31. Axelrod (ibid.: 44) modifies this last rule by limiting these defections to those that are "uncalled for," but he is not able to give a precise definition of "uncalled for."

32. Tit for Tat combined two other features that helped it succeed in a relative sense: it was easy to recognize *(clarity)*, and it did not do particularly badly against another rule *(robustness)*.

33. Later in this chapter, I will discuss one hypothesis suggested by Axelrod's analysis: there should be more cooperation in negotiation contexts where repeated play is most likely (i.e., tort cases); however, the data presented in chapter 2 do not support this hypothesis.

34. In his concluding chapter, "The Robustness of Reciprocity," Axelrod's discussion makes it clear that it is the ongoing relationship that makes reciprocity possible and desirable (ibid.: 169–191). Such an ongoing relationship is missing

from most ordinary litigation. Interestingly, in one area of ordinary litigation where an ongoing relationship between interested bargainers is likely, the data in chapter 2 indicate the stronger tendency is toward competitive rather than cooperative bargaining (I will discuss this later in the chapter).

35. The classic articles on game theory by Nash (1950, 1951, 1953) and Harsanyi (1956, 1965) are set in the context of the problem of bilateral monopoly. My description of the game relies heavily on Kahan (1983: 4–5).

36. Strictly speaking, one cannot definitively label bargaining in civil litigation as a positive-, zero-, or negative-sum game, because the nature of the payoff can vary from one "realization" of the game to another (i.e., from case to case). However, in ordinary litigation, I believe you can order the likelihood of the payoff taking one form or another: negative, zero, and, lastly, positive.

37. The model also assumes that if the case goes to trial, the court will always reach the "correct" decision (i.e., find for the plaintiff if the defendant is liable, and find for the defendant if he is not liable). P'ng reports having examined an extension of the game that allows for judicial error (ibid.: 545n); the implications of this extension depend heavily on the probability associated with judicial error.

38. Note that, in this game, it is the defendant who makes the settlement offer, to which the plaintiff must react. In an alternate game (P'ng, 1984), the plaintiff makes the settlement demand, which the defendant may accept or reject; if the demand is rejected, the plaintiff must decide whether to go to trial or drop the case.

39. P'ng also assumes that the litigants are risk neutral (1983: 542), which is clearly dubious in the context of ordinary litigation, given the difference between one-shot and repeat players (Galanter, 1974).

40. In fairness to P'ng it must be stated that he does *not* describe his analysis as a study of bargaining; however, what he does is representative of what are typically described as game-theoretic models of bargaining.

41. This heuristic value is most clearly seen in the brief consideration of frivolous suits (ibid.: 548–549).

42. It is instructive to note that, at the one point at which P'ng attaches numbers to his parameters, "all amounts are in millions" (ibid.: 548).

43. I would expect that many of the scholars working in this field would disagree with this characterization.

44. One might argue that, in situations where liability is assumed and damages are constrained to a known range that is relatively narrow, the desire to avoid transaction costs pushes the bargaining closer to the cooperative, or axiomatic, frame.

45. Optional or mandatory recourse to a third party is available in other kinds of bargaining situations, particularly in the labor arena. The generalization of this phenomenon is called the outside option (see Sutton, 1986: 712–715).

46. The technical definition of "extensive form" is more complex than this (see Luce and Raiffa, 1957: 47–49), but for purposes of this discussion, a less formal usage is adequate.

47. One could alternately diagram the game as having four branches at each

node: one that continues the game (opposing side rejects and makes an unacceptable counter), two that immediately terminate the game (opposing side accepts, and opposing side rejects and terminates game by going to trial), and one that "semi"-continues the game (opposing side rejects and responds with an acceptable counter).

48. These types of analyses are referred to as comparative statics. Sutton (1986: 712) describes these kinds of analyses as "one of the main attractions of the type" represented by noncooperative games.

49. See Jackson, 1977, for a detailed description of the structure of the English courts; I will discuss the English litigation system in more detail in the next chapter.

50. Many legally aided plaintiffs fall into the next category, where they bear no risk of costs; however, there is no ready way to distinguish between legally aided claimants who are partly protected and those who are fully protected. Consequently, in the discussion that follows, legally aided claimants are treated as though facing an intermediate level of risk, between privately funded and union supported.

51. The insulation from the indemnity rules arises from two principal forms of partial or complete third-party payment: legal aid and union sponsorship (see Genn, 1988: 92–94; Kritzer, 1989).

52. Swanson (1988: 11) reports that in his data "there was not a single reference to an offer of settlement by a plaintiff."

53. This argument is derived in part from an article intended as advice to insurance adjusters (Clayton, 1966: 472). The thesis of that article is that adjusters should take advantage of the uncertainty of trial.

54. Outside of divorce cases, individual plaintiffs almost always secure representation on a contingent-fee basis if the dispute is over something that can be reduced to a sum of money.

55. Still, given that the defendant will have to incur trial costs if the plaintiff will not accept his offer, the plaintiff's lawyer may be able to manipulate the defendant's risk preferences concerning those costs by refusing to accept a certain proportion of offers; if the logic of Swanson's model holds in the United States, then one might expect to find that the likelihood of rejecting an offer is constant across "rounds" (i.e., plaintiffs will reject the same proportion of second offers as they reject of first offers). Unfortunately, my data do not support this; the probability of acceptance for a second offer is much higher than the probability of acceptance for a first offer.

56. In his review of experimental studies of bargaining (most of which were conducted using a game-theoretic framework), Kahan (1983: 23–29) discussed research concerning the impact of representatives on the negotiation process. There was no reference in that discussion to repeated plays of the game.

57. See the discussion of the results presented in Table 2.16.

58. I previously listed a number of reasons why Axelrod's analysis probably did not apply in the ordinary litigation context; I suspect that this particular discrepancy has something to do with the positive-sum nature of the Prisoner's Dilemma. The benefits of cooperation are much clearer in a game with a high positive-sum payoff structure.

59. This is defined as the bottom of the plaintiff's settlement range, which is

equal to the expected verdict (verdict multiplied by probability of winning the judgment), minus the expected costs (costs for both sides multiplied by the probability of losing), minus a discount for risk aversion.

60. See Nalebuff, 1987, for a theoretical discussion of the issue of credibility of plaintiffs' settlement *demands* in a context that approximates the American litigation system.

61. Fenn makes the assumption that a plaintiff will not respond strategically by rejecting an offer above his or her minimum ask. He justifies this assumption on the basis of the asymmetry between plaintiff and defendant: the plaintiff will tend to be risk averse, and as a one-shot player, he has no reputational concerns that need to be demonstrated by threatening to go to court if a higher offer is not forthcoming. Thus, if the initial offer exceeds the plaintiff's minimum ask, he runs a risk of having to go to trial, where the expected outcome is only that minimum ask.

62. These probabilities are my estimates based on the results of Fenn's probit analysis; for purposes of obtaining these estimates, I set each of the damage variables in the equation to its mean value.

63. Strictly speaking, the last category is a residual that excludes the other three (no solicitor, privately funded solicitor, and trade union solicitor), but almost all the solicitors in the category will be paid, in whole or in part, by legal aid.

64. Swanson's data were extracted from the records of the English court officials responsible for reviewing claims for "costs" against a losing party. Cases that are rapidly settled with little difficulty seldom result in cost claims, unless certain specific circumstances are met.

65. Axelrod (1984: 124–141) draws on his results to suggest a variety of ways to increase cooperation: increase future interdependence of the bargainers, change the payoff structure, increase interpersonal caring, teach reciprocity, improve the ability of players to recognize an opponent's efforts to cooperate.

Chapter 5. The Structure of Economic Incentives for the Lawyer

1. In an interview, Chesley placed a value of $3.3 million on his time. That works out to an expected rate of approximately $175 per hour. In an earlier case, litigation arising from a fire at the Beverly Hills Supper Club in northern Kentucky, Chesley's firm earned a fee of $2.8 million for 7,459 hours work; that works out to about $375 per hour (*National Law Journal*, April 3, 1989, p. 47).

2. In fact, in the Bendectin litigation a group of lawyers representing some of the plaintiffs effectively torpedoed a proposed $120 million settlement because they had come to believe so passionately in the cause of their clients, and possibly because they believed that the defendant could be pressured into a higher settlement figure (see *Wall Street Journal*, July 16, 1984, p. 6; *National Law Journal*, July 30, 1984, p. 1, November 12, 1984, p. 3). The result was that the case went to trial on the issue of whether or not Bendectin did in fact cause the birth defects, and the jury returned a verdict exonerating the drug (*National Law Journal*, March 11, 1985, p. 6, March 25, 1985, p. 3; *New York Times*, March 13, 1985, p. 10).

3. In his study of American legal history, Lawrence Friedman (1973: 554) puts a more cynical cast on the same issue: "Most lawyers always served, mainly themselves, next their clients, last of all their conception of that diffuse, nebulous thing, the public interest."

4. An economist would point out that these concerns could be monetized in a straightforward way.

5. Interestingly, the example of Ms. Brown and Mr. Snead is based on a hypothetical case developed by the Legal Services Corporation, Office of Program Support, for training legal-services attorneys (Menkel-Meadow, 1984: 772n).

6. Possible alternative methods of compensating attorneys include fee shifting, whereby the defendant pays the plaintiff's attorney for her time, or payment from a central fund, created by "taxing" contingent fees, to which the lawyer could apply for compensation.

7. Another similar case involved a private antitrust suit brought by 150,000 lawyers in 23 states against Harcourt Brace Jovanovich (HBJ); the claim in that case was that HBJ refused to sell separately the materials developed for its bar review course (i.e., persons wanting those materials had to enroll in the course in order to obtain them). The settlement of that case involved a total cash payment of $2 million (less than $15 per claimant), plus discounts on HBJ's books and courses (*New York Times,* July 24, 1984, sec. 4, p. 1).

8. As with the example of the defective car, one can imagine solutions to this problem, such as fee-shifting.

9. In federal statutes authorizing the awarding of attorneys fees, the language is typically very nonspecific; for example, from the Civil Rights Attorneys Fee Awards Act: "the court, in its discretion, may allow the prevailing party, other than the United States, a reasonable attorney's fee as part of the costs" (42 USCS § 1988). Similar language is found in a wide variety of federal laws, including:
—the Freedom of Information Act, 5 USCS §552(a)(4)(E).
—the Clean Air Act, 42 USCS §7604(d).
—the Interstate Commerce Act, 49 USCS §11705(d)(3), §11708(a), §11710(a).
The issue of what is "reasonable" has not been a simple one (see Berger, 1977), and has generated substantial case law.

10. This is not necessarily the case. Class-action litigants, if they were in a real position to control the decisions regarding the litigation, may in fact be inclined to push further than contingent-fee lawyers representing the class (see Coffee, 1986).

11. It is probably the case that Joseph Jamail's fee in the Pennzoil-Texaco case was determined on a percentage basis. Even assuming a rate of $1,000 per hour, it is unlikely that Jamail and his firm could have put in the 300,000 hours needed to generate a $300 million fee.

12. For a general discussion of this issue, see the long feature section on fee awards in the *National Law Journal,* July 8, 1985, and a follow-up story on the lodestar question (April 9, 1990, pp. 13–14).

13. This holds both if the relationship is examined in a bivariate fashion (see chapter 2) or if a full, multivariate model is employed (see Kritzer, 1990: 141–143).

14. Elsewhere (Kritzer, 1990: 141–143), I have shown that the single most important predictor of effective hourly rates for contingent-fee lawyers is the number of hours worked, and that the relationship between these two variables is negative.

15. One problem with this entire analysis of outcomes is that it relies upon the lawyers' own evaluations of what is at stake. It may be that in modest cases the contingent-fee lawyer tends to underestimate what might be recovered, in order to facilitate the settlement process. In fact, typical success ratios (for the plaintiff, not the contingent-fee lawyer) for tort cases are much better for smaller cases than for cases involving $50,000 or more.

16. It is interesting to note that, although the median effective hourly rate for contingent-fee lawyers goes from $36 for cases with less than $10,000 at stake to $57 for cases involving $10,000–$50,000, the median rate for cases involving more than $50,000 is only $58. However, the third quartile for the big cases is $160 per hour compared with only $105 for the $10,000–$50,000 cases.

17. The one possible exception to this is simple debt-collection work, for which solicitors are permitted to accept payment on a "commission basis." There does exist a group of persons, known as claims assessors or loss assessors, who will negotiate a settlement with an insurance company for a client on a percentage-fee basis; these "assessors" are generally shunned by members of the legal profession (see Law Society, 1970).

18. There is a mechanism that allows a defendant who expects to lose in the sense of having to make some payment to the plaintiff to shift some of the risks of the costs to the plaintiff if the plaintiff refuses to accept what the defendant believes to be a reasonable settlement; this involves what is known as a payment into court. More detail on cost issues in the English litigation system can be found in Jackson, 1977.

19. See Rowe, 1984, for a symposium of articles that considers a variety of issues regarding fee shifting in the American context.

20. Recently, a study group of the governing body of the solicitor branch of the English legal profession advanced proposals that would create a mechanism with many of the characteristics of the American contingent-fee system, at least from the perspective of the plaintiff (Law Society, 1987; see also, Lord Chancellor's Department, 1989).

21. The impact of this downside risk has been dramatically illustrated in litigation in England over the arthritis drug Opren. The drug's manufacturer, Eli Lilly, played very tough in the litigation, and many of the members of the class decided to drop out of the litigation because of a fear of having to share in paying Lilly's estimated £6 million (U.S. $10 million) legal bill if Lilly had won the case (see, the *Guardian*, June 5, 1987, p. 19). In some interviews in connection with an entirely different research project, I asked several people in England to consider a hypothetical case in which they had suffered a broken leg in an automobile accident where it would appear that the other driver was entirely at fault. In this case, their solicitor had tried unsuccessfully to obtain a satisfactory offer of compensation from the other driver's insurance company, and was now asking the client whether to proceed to begin a formal lawsuit. I suggested that the solicitor described the case as involving the following set of parameters (I have converted the amounts from British pounds to

U.S. dollars here): the "going rate" for the injury is $10,000, and there is an 80 percent chance that if the case were to come to trial they would win (in which case the injured party's solicitor would be paid by the defendant); if the defendant were to prevail, the plaintiff could expect to have to pay $1,000 to his own solicitor plus perhaps $2,000 in costs to the defendant. When asked if they would instruct their solicitor to proceed or to drop the case, the tendency was overwhelmingly to drop the matter!

22. The set of categories used here differs from that used by Swanson (1988), but the two sets are closely related.

23. This sounds strongly reminiscent of the problem facing the privately paid criminal lawyer as described by Blumberg (1967).

24. One solicitor I spoke to in England told me that, when he had formerly been in private practice and had encountered clients who were going to have to pursue their cases on a privately funded basis but would have had problems in making payments "on account," he normally did not request such payments if he felt the cases were strong, expecting to be paid at the end of these cases by the defendants instead. When I asked him what had happened when a case was unsuccessful, he said that he had never encountered that situation. One must wonder whether he was simply very good at filtering out the weak cases, or whether he was under subtle pressures to accept the first offers that were made.

25. It is interesting to note that in Ontario, where on paper the system of costs (i.e., whether the loser pays some or all of the winner's legal fees) appears to be very similar to that in England, I was told that the issue of costs in settlement is treated as part of the settlement package, with some litigators believing that it is best to include an explicit "costs" component in the settlement and others feeling that it is best simply to cite a single settlement figure and leave it to the lawyer and his or her client to resolve the legal-fees issue.

26. Needless to say, in a fee-shifting system, not only is the lawyer reluctant to risk losing his or her fee because the client will not be able to pay it if the case is unsuccessful, but it is also the case that the client will be very fearful of the risk of losing the case and having to pay the other side's legal expenses as well as his own. The combination of the lawyers' concerns which tend to lead to recommendations to accept first or second settlement offers as reasonable and the clients' relief at avoiding the risk of losing altogether creates a powerful incentive to settle.

27. An American reader might think that this small percentage simply means that large numbers of claimants settle their claims directly with the insurance companies without involving solicitors or barristers, but that is not the case. Harris and his colleagues (1984: 81) found that the injured party was not represented by a solicitor in only 8 percent of the cases where damages were recovered. This largely reflects the reluctance of insurance companies to engage in direct settlements for the stated reason that a low settlement could later be thrown out by a court as an "unconscionable bargain" (see Genn, 1988: 14); a represented claimant who becomes dissatisfied with a settlement may sue his solicitor for negligence, but the original defendant is protected from further litigation because the claimant was

represented. A preliminary survey that was conducted as part of the Civil Litigation Research Project (partly reported in Miller and Sarat, 1980–81) showed that 78 percent of the tort claimants (with claims in excess of $1,000) obtained compensation without the assistance of attorneys (Kritzer, 1989: 170); this survey covered the period 1977 through 1979. A more recent American study (AIRAC, 1988), which covered the period October 1982 through December 1986, found that 65 percent of persons injured in automobile accidents resolved their claims directly with the opposing parties' insurance companies, though some of those persons had consulted attorneys.

28. This "discount" may be more important in theory than in practice. Conversations I had with a number of actors in the English system suggest that the 10 percent reduction requirement is often ignored. Still, what is important is the possibility of such a reduction rather than the frequency that such a reduction is enforced. However, a study of asbestos litigation in the United Kingdom reported that fees plaintiffs' solicitors obtained through legal aid were one half to two thirds of what would be billed to a union client or private client, or would be recovered directly from a defendant (Durkin, Dingwall, and Felstiner, 1990:20).

29. Generally, it appears that in England the plaintiff's costs that are paid by the defendant are not subject to negotiation; the defendant simply pays costs according to accepted scales (on occasion there is some negotiation over which scale will be used). In contrast, as I observed in note 25, in Ontario, which has a cost regime that in theory closely resembles the English system, a plaintiff's costs are part of the negotiating package. In tort cases, insurance companies typically will agree to pay the plaintiff's attorney 10–15 percent of the agreed damages as costs (see Kritzer, 1984b: 130–131). More interesting, however, is that, in talking to persons involved in litigation in Ontario, I found an accepted view that satisfying the lawyer's needs with regard to fees is a very important part of the settlement process; thus, negotiators in that context recognize the importance of attorney incentives as part of the overall negotiation context.

30. What is supposed to happen is that the loser pays the costs to the fund and the fund then pays the winner, even if the costs have been agreed between the parties (which can involve a higher rate than the fund might allow; see note 28) (Genn, 1988: 93).

31. The logic of this is that the winning party is better able to sustain the loss associated with the legal expense of fighting the case than is the legal aid fund.

32. As I previously noted, solicitors are under an ethical obligation to inform clients who are likely to qualify for legal aid.

33. The possibility of solicitors pursuing marginal cases under legal aid is not lost on the authorities who administer the fund; much of the delay associated with legal aid arises because of the requirement that cases be evaluated at various stages before proceeding, in order to insure that there is a reasonable chance that the legally aided client's position will eventually prevail.

34. The English system for compensating persons injured in the workplace combines elements of the general social security system to provide income replacement in

situations of disability (either temporary or permanent) or death (i.e., survivor benefits) and the tort system to compensate for pain and suffering (see Atiyah and Cane, 1987: 206–209, 327–354).

35. Notice that I have not talked about plaintiff's solicitors making demands. The strong norm in the English system is that the defendant will make offers, and the plaintiff will respond to those offers. The role of the plaintiff's solicitor is to state his client's case (usually in writing), with appropriate documentation, and then for the defendant to make an offer in response to that documentation. In contrast, 74 percent of the respondents in a recent survey of Wisconsin attorneys reported that in their most recent personal injury cases the first bargaining moves had been made by the plaintiffs (Kritzer, 1989: 173).

36. The £5 figure was quoted to me by an insurance broker in a small town in northern England. Although this cost may seem absurdly low at first, one has to keep in mind that in effect the insurance is only for *losing,* because if the insured person wins the case the other side will pay the fees of the winner's solicitor. There are some additional, minor costs associated with reviewing cases where ultimately no claim is lodged.

37. As stated by Schelling (1960: 29) in his essay on bargaining, "an 'agent' may be brought in as a principal in his own right, with an incentive structure of his own that differs from his principal's."

Chapter 6. The Forms of Negotiation: A "Sociological" Approach

1. For a brief discussion of the problems and issues in cross-cultural analyses of negotiation, see Weiss, 1987.

2. This kind of process approach is also found in Williams' (1983) study of negotiator effectiveness. As discussed in chapter 4, Williams describes a series of four stages: orientation and positioning, argumentation, emergence and crisis, and agreement or final breakdown.

3. See chapter 3 for a definition of integrative and distributive bargaining.

4. Although, as Menkel-Meadow notes (ibid.: 757n5), the conceptualization of problem-solving negotiation has been discussed by a number of authors, she provides a particularly cogent description of it. Specifically, it is based on the presumption that "[p]arties to a negotiation typically have underlying needs or objectives, . . . and by attempting to uncover those underlying needs, the problem solving model presents opportunities for discovering greater numbers of and better quality solutions. . . . [U]nearthing a greater number of actual needs of the parties will create more possible solutions because not all needs will be mutually exclusive" (ibid.: 795). Menkel-Meadow contrasts this to traditional zero-sum, distributive bargaining, which she labels adversarial negotiation (ibid.: 764–768).

5. See chapter 4 for a discussion of Williams' conceptualization of cooperative and competitive negotiators.

6. Gifford's discussion does not explicitly describe his analysis as crossing ends and means, but that in fact is what he does.

176 Notes to Pages 114–123

7. See also Williams, 1983: 54; Lowenthal, 1982: 82–83, 109–110; and Gifford, 1985: 60–62, for the discussion of asymmetric means.

8. In addition, the divided bar in England makes it possible for nonspecialist solicitors to obtain expert estimates of "quantum" by referring their cases to barristers specializing in tort cases.

9. Feeley (1979a: 462) suggests that the guilty-plea process does not so much resemble a bazaar in which buyer and seller haggle over a price as it resembles a "modern supermarket [where] prices for various commodities have been clearly established and labeled in advance." Customers can choose to take or leave a particular purchase: ". . . [They] may complain about prices, but they rarely 'bargain' to get them reduced."

10. For similar views, see Rosset and Cressey (1976: 15):

Undeniably, prosecutors and defenders sometimes use the adversary tactics of poker and chess in an attempt to win concessions from each other. . . . But in practice, most cases are disposed of in cooperative agreements reaching a consensus on facts and, therefore, an appropriate punishment.

Or Mather (1979: 93):

The attorneys each evaluated their cases to predict the likelihood of conviction and severity of punishment. Then they compared their expectations and negotiated to resolve differences.

Or Feeley (1979a: 462; see also Feeley 1982, 1983):

Arriving at an exchange . . . is not an explicit bargaining process—"you do this for me and I'll do that for you"—designed to reach a mutually acceptable agreement. To the extent that there is any negotiation at all, it usually focuses on the nature of the case and the establishment of relevant "facts."

11. In only one of the nine communities did substantial numbers of defendants obtain concessions in both the number of counts and the most serious charges (ibid.: 234–235).

12. Much of the recent move in the direction of determinate sentencing, particularly through the use of recommended sentences set by sentencing commissions, can be seen as efforts to institutionalize the going-rate system and to reduce the problems that inevitably occur when there are significant deviations from implicit sentencing norms (see Shane-DuBow, Brown, and Olson, 1985).

13. An informal survey of lawyers indicates that liability is at issue in perhaps only 20 percent of the "ordinary" cases the lawyers deal with.

14. These pairs of figures were selected because they are symmetric in the sense of being reciprocals: $1.33 = \frac{1}{0.75}$ and $2.00 = \frac{1}{0.5}$.

15. This is not to suggest that litigation, in the sense of initially resisting claims and forcing the invocation of the formal litigation process, is necessarily unprofitable. Analyses of outcomes from the perspective of the defendant suggest strongly that, in a large proportion of cases, defendant save more in payment to the plaintiff than they incur in legal fees (see Kritzer et al., 1987; Kritzer, 1990: 143–146).

16. There is certainly substantial potential for conflict of interest between

hourly fee lawyers and their clients (see Johnson, 1980–81; Kritzer et al., 1985); however, it may be that the greater sophistication of the organizational litigant who typically retains lawyers on an hourly fee basis is sufficient to offset this conflict, at least in regard to negotiation. It would be particularly useful to see how lawyers regularly representing organizational clients (particularly the same organizational clients on a frequent basis, such as lawyers doing defense work for insurance companies) interact with their principals regarding negotiations.

17. Compare the ritualistic nature of *pro forma* negotiation with the "cop-out" ceremony that often occurs as part of the acceptance of a guilty plea.

18. Compare with Lynn Mather's (1979: 65–66) description of the guilty-plea process in relatively minor felony cases in Los Angeles:

In "dead bang" cases [those with almost a 100 percent chance of conviction if they were taken to trial], agreement between prosecutor and defense attorney on a nontrial disposition was usually reached with little conflict; the D.A. knew that he would get a conviction as charged, while the defense attorney knew that his client would probably get a misdemeanor with no incarceration or time served. Most bargaining between the attorneys in these cases was implicit. That is, the attorneys operated on the basis of a shared understanding that predictably lenient treatment would accompany a nontrial disposition.

One of the judges interviewed by Mather suggested an example of this type of situation (ibid.: 71):

"The defense attorney comes into court and asks the D.A., 'What does Judge Hall give on bookmaking cases?' The D.A. asks if there are any priors. The attorney says, 'No,' and the D.A. says, 'He usually gives $150 fine on the first offense.' The attorney says, 'Fine. We'll enter a plea to count one.' . . . [N]o promise was made by anybody. It's just that everybody knows what customarily will happen."

19. In terms of second-party negotiation (i.e., that which occurs between an individual and her own insurance company), the transaction costs involved in handling small claims serve to create a substantial incentive to write policies with deductibles in order to avoid having to deal with such claims. Where deductibles do not exist in small claims, the negotiation is likely to be *pro forma*, with the insurance company operating at a disadvantage because of the transaction costs entailed in resolving such cases.

20. Many readers can probably recall similar events involving settlements with one's own insurance company. I recall an experience involving a fire in the stove in my childhood home. The stove was quite old, and the fire itself was minimal (in fact, after the fire department came and sprayed the smoldering oven with a carbon dioxide extinguisher, a fireman rescued the chicken that had been in the oven, and we had it for dinner that night as my mother had intended). My mother viewed the demise of her stove as a nuisance rather than a great loss, given that the stove was 13 years old and she had wanted to replace it for some time. She expressed the hope that the insurance company would give her at least $25. When the adjuster came to the house, my mother held her breath while he inspected the stove. After considering the situation for a few moments, the adjuster said to my mother, "Would you take $50?" My mother's one-word response was "Yes!"

21. Many insurance companies now offer an option of "replacement cost" coverage for property loss. Although this is marketed as an extra-cost feature, an alternative interpretation is that it is intended to minimize even more the already minimal negotiations that occur in small property loss claims; the extra amounts that are paid out are less than the costs of trying to reach agreement on the current value of smaller-price items, which are the subject of most property loss claims.

Chapter 7. Conclusion: The Need to Keep Negotiation in Perspective

1. Recent research on property and support settlements in divorce cases questions the shadow metaphor (Seltzer and Garfinkel, 1990; Melli, Erlanger, and Chambliss, 1988), at least as it applies to the content of the settlement, which was the focus on Mnookin and Kornhauser's (1979) original presentation of the shadow image. However, these later analyses do not negate the broader metaphor as I have used it throughout this book: settlements are reached because the court is there to impose an outcome on the parties if necessary. The critics of Mnookin and Kornhauser do not consider what would happen if, for example, a mother who has physical custody of children after a divorce could not go to court and obtain an order for payment of child support; many fewer noncustodial fathers would pay support if there were no legally enforceable obligation.

2. Elsewhere (Kritzer, 1987), I have pointed out that adjudication plays a significantly greater role in disposing of civil cases than is suggested by trial rates. Many cases are adjudicated in whole or in part without a formal trial, with partial adjudication typically leading to an agreement to resolve the issues that were not adjudicated.

3. One must keep in mind that actual litigation is only the tip of the dispute pyramid (see Miller and Sarat, 1980–81: 544–546). I suspect that those matters which are not about money tend to be dealt with in other ways (e.g., by bringing criminal complaints where possible), never get into the court (even if legal remedies are formally available), or get transformed in some way into issues where monetary compensation is possible (e.g., libel or slander). Few people of typical means would be prepared to put money into litigation where no financial return is possible, and even then, the natural risk aversion of the average person would dissuade him or her from litigation in the absence of the contingent fee or some other kind of subsidy for litigation if there were more than a minimal doubt about success.

4. The problem facing many of the players in these typical everyday cases is not unlike the situation I faced every time I took my 1968 Plymouth into the shop: Given what was at stake—a couple hundred dollars, the value of my old rusty car—was it worth the expenditure of a substantial portion of that value to try to improve upon what I might get? That is, should I have junked the car (I finally did in 1989) or spent $200 to have the clutch rebuilt? The answer to this kind of question often depends upon the alternatives: what would it have cost me to give up the higher potential payoff? Two hundred dollars might seem like a lot to put in an old car, but if the payments on a three-year-old used car would be $200 per month, then $200 to keep the old one going for another few months might be well worth it.

5. Much of the debate about contingent fees and the inherent conflict of interest they cause between lawyer and client (see MacKinnon, 1964; Franklin, Chanin, and Mark, 1961; Johnson, 1980–81; Clermont and Currivan, 1978; Schwartz and Mitchell, 1970; Kritzer et al., 1985; Miller, 1987; Rosenthal, 1974) fails to take into account that, under that fee arrangement, clients do not have a motivation to consider cost-benefit issues. The clients *do* have to consider the risks of losing entirely (or the costs of delay) that are associated with refusing offers of settlement, but they are not concerned about the amount of time and effort their lawyers must put in to continue a case. A client who is paying on an hourly basis, even under a contingency arrangement where the lawyer will be paid only if a recovery is made, might be very concerned about the costs of achieving a larger settlement (or award) if he were to decline an offer on the table. The limited use of contingent fees in Canada (see Kritzer, 1984b: 130) may reflect the fact that they are generally computed in essentially the same way as noncontingent fees, with the added proviso that they will be foregone if no recovery is made. However, this explanation is less than perfect, because in practice fees are generally closely related to the amounts at issue, particularly in cases involving insurance companies (ibid.: 131–132).

6. Sometimes these stories reflect incomplete or inaccurate reports of actual events; see "Tort Tales: Old Stories Never Die" (*National Law Journal,* February 16, 1987, p. 39).

7. As much as I would like to claim credit for this term, I can't; I first head it used by my colleague Ken Meier, who described some of the reactions to the supposed medical malpractice crisis as "legislation by anecdote."

8. In the early work of the Civil Litigation Research Project, we conceptualized litigation as a process of investment and focused our analysis on the key investment decision: the amount of effort expended by the lawyers (see Trubek, Grossman, et al., 1983: I-39–I-43).

9. It is worth noting that the context of this statement was an article on *corporate* alternative dispute resolution, and the conclusion drawn from this observation was that "organizations will have the same advantages and show the same margin of success over individuals in alternative dispute processing forums as they do in court" (ibid.).

10. In some specific areas this is *not* the case, but even where it is, the line between adjudication and settlement is not the clear dichotomy it is often presumed to be (see Kritzer, 1986).

11. Luban (1985: 404) misses this fundamental point in his review essay on negotiation and alternative dispute resolution: "Legal negotiation is successful, then, if it takes over the functions of trials. For only then can legal negotiation provide an alternative to adjudication." If one thinks of an alternative as one of two or more courses offered for one's choice, which necessarily entails the rejection of the other courses, then one cannot really think of negotiation as an alternative to trials, because trials are necessary to set the context for negotiations. On the other hand, adjudication *does* sometimes serve as an alternative to negotiation and settlement.

12. Compare this with Cavanagh and Sarat's observation (1979–80: 402):

There is no reason to think that the presence of courts as fora of last resort has acted to discourage the development of effective alternative dispute resolution mechanisms; given their highly tentative approach to related-party cases, and generally heartfelt willingness to hold up or forego decision where a settlement may be in prospect, judges can hardly be said to have displaced dispute resolution "competitors." As a result, it seems unlikely that alternatives to courts will suddenly blossom if only the prospect of judicial intervention can be removed. Indeed, the reverse could be true. Private sector dispute resolution mechanisms may actually be beneficiaries of the mutual incentive for trauma avoidance that court capacity limitations afford related-party disputants. Here as in the debtor-creditor context, the elimination of some manifestations of poor court performance could simply trigger new problems of equal or greater societal significance.

Or, in the words of Melli, Erlanger, and Chambliss (1988: 1143):

Negotiation is not just the typical outcome; it is also the *expected* mode of dispute resolution in the minds of the parties [to the divorce] and their lawyers. Contrary to the conventional view that the parties expect a judge to decide their case but *may* settle before trial, these parties saw settlement as the solution, and the judicial process [i.e., adjudication] as the alternative. . . . Only when negotiation failed did the parties turn to the alternative of a judicial solution.

13. There is another, closely related debate over the proper role of judges in the settlement process (see Galanter, 1985, 1986b; Bedlin and Nejelski, 1984; Resnik, 1982; Menkel-Meadow, 1985b; and Kritzer, 1982).

14. Galanter (1988), Bush (1989), and Luban (1989) provide catalogs and/or taxonomies of factors that might be used in judging the quality of outcomes; see Esser (1989), for a review of extant literature on the quality issue, and Tyler (1989), for a discussion of some of the empirical problems of research on quality of dispute-processing outcomes.

References

Administrative Office of the United States Courts. 1985. *Analysis of the Workload of the Federal Courts for the Twelve Month Period Ended June 30, 1985.* Washington, D.C.: Government Printing Office.

All-Industry Research Advisory Council (AIRAC). 1983. *Structured Settlements: Use and Characteristics of Structured Settlements in the Property-Casualty Insurance Industry.* Oak Brook, Illinois: All-Industry Research Advisory Council.

All-Industry Research Advisory Council (AIRAC). 1988. *Attorney Involvement in Auto Injury Claims.* Oak Brook, Illinois: All-Industry Research Advisory Council.

Alschuler, Albert W. 1968. "The Prosecutor's Role in Plea Bargaining." *University of Chicago Law Review* 36: 50–112.

Alschuler, Albert W. 1975. "The Defense Attorney's Role in Plea Bargaining." *Yale Law Journal* 84: 1179–1206.

Alschuler, Albert W. 1976. "The Trial Judge's Role in Plea Bargaining, Part I." *Columbia University Law Review* 76: 1059–1154.

Alschuler, Albert W. 1981. "The Changing Plea Bargaining Debate." *California Law Review* 69: 652–723.

Alschuler, Albert W. 1983. "Implementing the Criminal Defendant's Right to Trial: Alternatives to the Plea Bargaining System." *University of Chicago Law Review* 50: 931–1050.

Alschuler, Albert W. 1986. "Mediation with a Mugger: The Shortage of Adjudicative Services and the Need for a Two-Tier Trial System in Civil Cases." *Harvard Law Review* 99: 1808–1859.

Atiyah, P.S., and Peter Cane. 1987. *Accidents, Compensation and the Law.* 4th ed. London: Weidenfeld and Nicolson.

Axelrod, Robert. 1984. *The Evolution of Cooperation.* New York: Basic Books.

Bacharach, Samuel B., and Edward J. Lawley. 1981. *Bargaining: Power, Tactics, and Outcomes.* San Francisco: Jossey-Bass.

Banks, Jeffrey S. 1986. "Liability Rules and Pretrial Settlement." California Institute of Technology, Social Science Working Paper 608.

Barton, John. 1975. "Behind the Legal Explosion." *Stanford Law Review* 27: 567–584.

Bartos, Otomar. 1974. *Process and Outcome of Negotiations.* New York: Columbia University Press.

Bebchuk, Lucian Arye. 1984. "Litigation and Settlement under Imperfect Information." *Rand Journal of Economics* 15: 404–415.

Bebchuk, Lucian Arye. 1988. "Suing Solely to Extract a Settlement Offer." *Journal of Legal Studies* 17: 437–450.

Bedlin, Howard, and Paul Nejelski. 1984. "Unsettling Issues about Settling Civil Litigation: Examining 'Doomsday Machines,' 'Quick Looks,' and Other Modest Proposals." *Judicature* 68: 9–29.

Bellow, Gary, and Bea Moulton. 1981. *The Lawyering Process: Negotiation.* Mineola, New York: The Foundation Press.

Benson Commission. 1979. *The Royal Commission on Legal Services: Final Report.* London: HMSO.

Berger, Samuel R. 1977. "Court Awarded Attorneys' Fees: What Is 'Reasonable'?" *University of Pennsylvania Law Review* 126: 281–328.

Blumberg, Abraham S. 1967. "The Practice of Law as a Confidence Game: Organizational Cooptation of a Profession." *Law & Society Review* 1: 15–39.

Bovbjerg, Randall R., Frank A. Sloan, and James F. Blumstein. 1989. "Valuing Life and Limb in Tort: Scheduling 'Pain and Suffering'." *Northwestern University Law Review* 83: 908–976.

Brazil, Wayne D. 1980. "Views from the Front Lines: Observations by Chicago Lawyers about the System of Civil Discovery." 1980 *American Bar Foundation Research Journal* 217–251.

Brazil, Wayne D. 1985. *Settling Civil Suits: Litigators' Views about Appropriate Roles and Effective Techniques for Federal Judges.* Chicago: American Bar Association.

Burger, Warren E. 1982. "Isn't There a Better Way?" *American Bar Association Journal* 68: 274–277.

Bush, Robert A. Baruch. 1989. "Defining Quality in Dispute Resolution: Taxonomies and Anti-Taxonomies of Quality Arguments." *Denver University Law Review* 66: 335–380.

Carlin, Jerome E. 1962. *Lawyers on Their Own: A Study of Individual Practitioners in Chicago.* New Brunswick: Rutgers University Press.

Cartter Report. 1977. "The Cartter Report on the Leading Schools of Education, Law, and Business." *Change* 9 (February/March): 44–48.

Cavanagh, Edward D. 1988. "Attorneys' Fees in Antitrust Litigation: Making the System Fairer." *Fordham Law Review* 57: 51–110.

Cavanagh, Ralph, and Austin Sarat. 1979–80. "Thinking about Courts: Toward and Beyond a Jurisprudence of Judicial Competence." *Law & Society Review* 14: 371–420.

Center for Public Resources. 1980. *A Manual of Innovative Corporate Strategies for the Avoidance and Resolution of Legal Disputes.* New York: Center for Public Resources.

Chatterjee, Kalyan. 1985. "Disagreement in Bargaining: Models with Incomplete Information." Pp. 9–26 in *Game-Theoretic Models of Bargaining,* ed. Alvin Roth. Cambridge: Cambridge University Press.

Chatterjee, Kalyan, and Larry Samuelson. 1987. "Bargaining with Two-sided Incomplete Information: An Infinite Horizon Model with Alternating Offers." *Review of Economic Studies* 14: 175–192.

Chatterjee, Kalyan, and Jacob W. Ulvila. 1982. "Bargaining with Shared Information." *Decision Sciences* 13: 380–404.

Church, Thomas W., Jr. 1982. *Examining Local Legal Culture: Practitioner Attitudes in Four Criminal Courts.* Williamsburg, Virginia: National Center for State Courts.

Church, Thomas W., Jr. 1985. "Examining Local Legal Culture." *American Bar Foundation Research Journal,* no. 3: 449–518.

Church, Thomas W., Jr., Alan Carlson, Jo-Lynne Lee, and Teresa Tan. 1978. *Justice Delayed: The Pace of Litigation in Urban Trial Courts.* Williamsburg, Virginia: National Center for State Courts.

Clayton, Paul. 1966. "Creating Risk in Negotiation and Settlement Techniques." *Insurance Law Journal,* no. 523: 465–472.

Clermont, Kevin M., and John D. Currivan. 1978. "Improving on the Contingent Fee." *Cornell Law Review* 63: 529–639.

Coffee, John C., Jr. 1986. "Understanding the Plaintiff's Attorney: The Implications of Economic Theory for Private Enforcement of Law through Class and Derivative Actions." *Columbia Law Review* 86: 669–727.

Cohen, Herb. 1982. *You Can Negotiate Anything.* New York: Bantam.

Cohen, Richard M., and Jules Witcover. 1974. *A Heartbeat Away: The Investigation and Resignation of Vice President Spiro T. Agnew.* New York: The Viking Press.

Condlin, Robert J. 1985. "Cases on Both Sides: Patterns of Argument in Legal-Dispute Negotiations." *Maryland Law Review* 65: 65–136.

Conley, John M., and William M. O'Barr. 1988. "Hearing the Hidden Agenda: The Ethnographic Investigation of Procedure." *Law and Contemporary Problems* 51: 181–197.

Cooter, Robert, and Stephen Marks (with Robert Mnookin). 1982. "Bargaining in the Shadow of the Law: A Testable Model of Strategic Behavior." *Journal of Legal Studies* 11: 225–251.

Cross, John G. 1969. *The Economics of Bargaining.* New York: Basic Books.

Curran, Barbara A. 1986. "American Lawyers in the 1980's: A Profession in Transition." *Law & Society Review* 20: 19–51.

Curran, William J. 1976. *How Lawyers Handle Medical Malpractice Cases: An Analysis of an Important Medicolegal Study.* Washington, D.C.: National Center for Health Services Research.

Dahl, Scott S. 1988. "Ethics on the Table: Stretching the Truth in Negotiations." *Review of Litigation* 8: 173–202.

Daniels, Stephen. 1986. "Civil Juries, Jury Verdict Reporters, and the Going Rate." Paper presented at 1986 Annual Meeting of the Law & Society Association, Chicago Hilton Hotel, Chicago, Illinois, May 29–June 1.

Danzon, Patricia Munch, and Lee A. Lillard. 1982. *The Resolution of Medical Malpractice Claims: Modeling the Bargaining Process.* Santa Monica: The Rand Corporation.

Danzon, Patricia Munch, and Lee A. Lillard. 1983. "Settlement Out of Court: The Disposition of Medical Malpractice Claims." *Journal of Legal Studies* 12: 345–377.

Durkin, Tom, Robert Dingwall, and William L. F. Felstiner. 1990. "Plaited Cunning: Manipulating Time in Asbestos Litigation." Unpublished paper, American Bar Foundation.

Ebener, Patricia A., and Donna R. Betancourt. 1985. *Court-Annexed Arbitration: The National Picture.* Santa Monica: The Rand Corporation.

Eisenberg, Melvin A. 1976. "Private Ordering through Negotiation: Dispute-settlement and Rulemaking. *Harvard Law Review* 89: 637–681.

Eisenberg, Theodore, and Stewart Schwab. 1987. "The Reality of Constitutional Tort Litigation." *Cornell Law Review* 72: 641–693.

Eisenberg, Theodore, and Stephen C. Yeazell. 1980. "The Ordinary and the Extraordinary in Institutional Litigation." *Harvard Law Review* 93: 465–517.

Eisenstein, James, and Herbert Jacob. 1977. *Felony Justice: An Organizational Analysis of Criminal Courts.* Boston: Little, Brown.

Eisenstein, James, Roy B. Flemming, and Peter F. Nardulli. 1988. *The Contours of Justice: Communities and Their Courts.* Boston: Little, Brown.

Engel, David M. 1980. "Legal Pluralism in an American Community: Perspectives on a Civil Trial Court. *American Bar Foundation Research Journal,* no. 3: 425–454.

Engel, David M., and Eric H. Steele. 1979. "Civil Cases in Society: Process and Order in the Civil Justice System." *American Bar Foundation Research Journal,* no. 2: 295–346.

Erlanger, Howard S., Elizabeth Chambliss, and Marygold Melli. 1987. "Participation and Flexibility in Informal Processes: Cautions from the Divorce Context." *Law & Society Review* 21: 563–584.

Esser, John P. 1989. "Evaluations of Dispute Processing: We Do Not Know What We Think and We Do Not Think What We Know." *Denver University Law Review* 66: 499–562.

Feeley, Malcolm M. (ed.). 1979a. "Special Issue: Perspectives on Plea Bargaining." *Law & Society Review* 13: 197–687.

Feeley, Malcolm M. 1979b. *The Process Is the Punishment.* New York: Russell Sage Foundation.

Feeley, Malcolm M. 1982. "Plea Bargaining and the Structure of the Criminal Process." *The Justice System Journal* 7: 338–354.

Feeley, Malcolm M. 1983. *Court Reform on Trial: Why Simple Solutions Fail.* New York: Basic Books.

Feinberg, Kenneth R., and John S. Gomperts. 1986. "Attorneys' Fees in the Agent Orange Litigation: Modifying the Lodestar Analysis for Mass Tort Cases." *New York University Review of Law & Social Change* 14: 613–631.

Felstiner, William L. F., Richard L. Abel, and Austin Sarat. 1980-81. "The Emergence and Transformation of Disputes: Naming, Blaming, Claiming . . ." *Law & Society Review* 15: 631–654.

Fenn, Paul. 1988. "Bargaining Behavior by Defendant Insurers: An Economic Model." Paper presented at the Joint EALE/Geneva Association Conference on Professional Liability Insurance.

Fine, Ralph Adam. 1986. *Escape of the Guilty.* New York: Dodd, Mead.

Fisher, Roger, and William Ury. 1981. *Getting to Yes: Negotiating Agreement without Giving In.* Boston: Houghton-Mifflin.

Fiss, Owen. 1984. "Against Settlement." *Yale Law Journal* 93: 1072–1090.

Flango, Victor Eugene, Robert T. Roper, and Mary E. Elsner. 1983. *The Business of State Trial Courts.* Williamsburg, Virginia: The National Center for State Courts.

Flemming, John. 1976. "Search for Settlement: Evidence on a Model of Payment in and Litigation in Personal Injury Cases." Unpublished mimeo.

Franklin, Marc A., Robert H. Chanin, and Irving Mark. 1961. "Accidents, Money and the Law: A Study of the Economics of Personal Injury Litigation." *Columbia University Law Review* 61: 1–39.

Friedman, Alan E. 1969. "An Analysis of Settlement." *Stanford Law Review* 22: 67–100.

Friedman, Lawrence. 1973. *A History of American Law.* New York: Simon and Schuster.

Fuller, Lon. 1981. "The Forms and Limits of Adjudication." Pp. 86–124 in *The Principles of Social Order: Selected Essays of Lon Fuller,* ed. Kenneth I. Winston. Durham, North Carolina: Duke University Press.

Galanter, Marc. 1974. "Why the 'Haves' Come Out Ahead: Speculations on the Limits of Legal Change." *Law & Society Review* 9: 95–160.

Galanter, Marc. 1983. "Reading the Landscape of Disputes: What We Know and Don't Know (and Think We Know) about Our Allegedly Contentious and Litigious Society." *UCLA Law Review* 31: 1–71.

Galanter, Marc. 1984. "Worlds of Deals: Using Negotiation to Teach about Legal Process." *Journal of Legal Education* 34: 268–276.

Galanter, Marc. 1985. "'. . . . . A Settlement Judge, Not a Trial Judge': Judicial Mediation in the United States," *Journal of Law and Society* 12: 1–18.

Galanter, Marc. 1986a. "The Day after the Litigation Explosion." *Maryland Law Review* 46: 3–39.

Galanter, Marc. 1986b. "The Emergence of the Judge as a Mediator in Civil Cases." *Judicature* 69: 256–262.

Galanter, Marc. 1988. "The Quality of Settlements." *Journal of Dispute Resolution* 1988: 55–84.

Genn, Hazel. 1988. *Hard Bargaining: Out of Court Settlement in Personal Injury Actions.* Oxford: Oxford University Press.

Gifford, Donald G., 1985. "A Context-Based Theory of Strategy Selection in Legal Negotiation." *Ohio State Law Journal* 46: 41–94.

Gould, John P. 1973. "An Economic Analysis of Legal Conflicts." *Journal of Legal Studies* 2: 279–300.

Grady, John F. 1976. "Some Ethical Questions About Percentage Fees." *Litigation* 2(4): 20–26.

Green, Eric D. 1986. "Corporate Alternative Dispute Resolution." *Ohio State Journal on Dispute Resolution* 1: 203–297.

Green, Jonathon (comp.). 1982. *Morrow's International Dictionary of Contemporary Quotations.* New York: William Morrow.

Grossman, Joel B., Herbert M. Kritzer, Kristin Bumiller, Austin Sarat, Stephen McDougal, and Richard E. Miller. 1982. "Dimensions of Institutional Participation: Who Uses the Courts and How?" *Journal of Politics* 44: 86–114.

Grossman, Sanford J., and Motty Perry. 1986. "Sequential Bargaining under Asymmetric Information." *Journal of Economic Theory* 39: 120–154.

Gulliver, Paul H. 1979. *Disputes and Negotiations: A Cross Cultural Perspective.* New York: Academic Press.

Hamner, W. Clay, and Gary A. Yukl. 1977. "The Effectiveness of Different Offer Strategies in Bargaining. Pp. 137–160 in *Negotiation: Social Psychological Perspectives,* ed. D. Druckman. Beverly Hills: Sage Publications.

Handler, Joel, 1967. *The Lawyer and His Community.* Madison: University of Wisconsin Press.

Harris, Donald, Mavis Maclean, Hazel Genn, Sally Lloyd-Bostock, Paul Fenn, Peter Corfield, and Yvonne Brittan. 1984. *Compensation and Support for Illness and Injury.* Oxford: Clarendon Press.

Harsanyi, John C. 1956. "Approaches to the Bargaining Problem Before and After the Theory of Games." *Econometrica* 24: 144–157.

Harsanyi, John C. 1965. "Bargaining and Conflict Situations in Light of a New Approach to Game Theory. *American Economic Review* 55: 447–457.

Hause, John C. 1989. "Indemnity, Settlement, and Litigation, or I'll Be Suing You." *Journal of Legal Studies* 18: 157–179.

Hensler, Deborah R. 1984. *Reforming the Civil Litigation Process: How Court Arbitration May Help.* Santa Monica, California: The Rand Corporation.

Hensler, Deborah R., M. Susan Marquis, Allan F. Abrahamse, Sandra H. Berry, Patricia A. Ebener, Elizabeth G. Lewis, E. Allan Lind, Robert J. MacCoun, Willard G. Manning, Jeannette A. Rogowski, and Mari E. Vaiana. 1990. *Compensation for Accidental Injuries in the United States.* Santa Monica, California: The Rand Corporation.

Heumann, Milton. 1975. "A Note on Plea Bargaining and Case Pressure." *Law & Society Review* 9: 515–528.

Heumann, Milton. 1978. *Plea Bargaining: The Experiences of Prosecutors, Judges, and Defense Attorneys.* Chicago: University of Chicago Press.

Hoffer, Peter Charles. 1989. "Honor and the Roots of American Litigiousness." *American Journal of Legal History* 33:295–319.

Ilich, John. 1973. *The Art and Skill of Successful Negotiation.* Englewood Cliffs, New Jersey: Prentice-Hall.

Jackson, Donald Dale. 1974. *Judges: An Inside View of the Agonies and Excesses of an American Elite.* New York: Atheneum.

Jackson, R. M. 1977. *The Machinery of Justice in England.* Cambridge: Cambridge University Press.

Jacob, Herbert. 1979. "Related Party Disputes in Criminal Courts: Some Data and Speculations about Alternative Functions." Pp. 15–28 in *The Study of Criminal*

Courts: Political Perspectives, ed. Peter F. Nardulli. Cambridge, Massachusetts: Ballinger Publishing Company.

Jenkins, John A. 1989. *The Litigators.* New York: Doubleday.

Johnson, Earl, Jr. 1980–81. "Lawyers' Choice: A Theoretical Appraisal of Litigation Investment Decisions." *Law & Society Review* 15: 567–610.

Kahan, James P. 1983. "Experimental Studies of Bargaining as Analogues of Civil Disputes." Rand Paper Series, Rand Corporation.

Kakalik, James S., and Nicholas M. Pace. 1986. *Costs and Compensation Paid in Tort Litigation.* Santa Monica: The Rand Corporation.

Kakalik, James S., and Randy L. Ross. 1983. *Costs of the Civil Justice System: Court Expenditures for Various Types of Civil Cases.* Santa Monica: The Rand Corporation.

Karrass, Chester L. 1970. *The Negotiating Game.* New York: World Publishing Company.

Karrass, Chester L. 1974. *Give and Take: The Complete Guide to Negotiating Strategy and Tactics.* New York: Thomas Y. Crowell.

Kemp, David A. M. 1986. *Kemp and Kemp: The Question of Damages in Personal Injury and Fatal Accident Claims.* London: Sweet & Maxwell.

Kennedy, Gavin. 1983. *Everything Is Negotiable: How to Get a Better Deal.* Englewood Cliffs, New Jersey: Prentice-Hall.

Kritzer, Herbert M. 1980–81. "Studying Disputes: Learning from the CLRP Experience." *Law & Society Review* 15: 503–524.

Kritzer, Herbert M. 1982. "The Judge's Role in Pretrial Case Processing: Assessing the Need for Change." *Judicature* 66: 28–38.

Kritzer, Herbert M. 1984a. "The Civil Litigation Research Project: Lessons for Studying the Civil Justice System." Pp. 30–36 in *Proceedings of the Second Workshop in Law and Justice Statistics 1983,* ed. Alan Gelfand. Washington, D.C.: U.S. Department of Justice, Bureau of Justice Statistics.

Kritzer, Herbert M. 1984b. "Fee Arrangements and Fee Shifting: Lessons from the Experience in Ontario." *Law and Contemporary Problems* 47: 125–138.

Kritzer, Herbert M. 1986. "Adjudication to Settlement: Shading in the Gray." *Judicature* 70: 161–165.

Kritzer, Herbert M. 1987. "Fee Arrangements and Negotiation: A Research Note." *Law & Society Review* 21: 341–348.

Kritzer, Herbert M. 1989. "A Comparative Perspective on Settlement and Bargaining in Personal Injury Cases" (a review essay of *Hard Bargaining: Out of Court Settlement in Personal Injury Actions,* by Hazel Genn). *Law & Social Inquiry* 14: 167–185.

Kritzer, Herbert M. 1990. *The Justice Broker: Lawyers and Ordinary Litigation.* New York: Oxford University Press.

Kritzer, Herbert M., and Jill K. Anderson. 1983. "The Arbitration Alternative: A Comparative Analysis of Case Processing Time, Disposition Mode, and Cost in the American Arbitration Association and the Courts," *Justice System Journal* 8: 6–19.

Kritzer, Herbert M., Austin Sarat, William L. F. Felstiner, and David M. Trubek. 1985. "The Impact of Fee Arrangement on Lawyer Effort." *Law and Society Review* 19: 251–278.

Kritzer, Herbert M., Austin Sarat, David M. Trubek, and William L. F. Felstiner, 1987. "Winners and Losers in Litigation: Does Anyone Come Out Ahead?" Pp. 29–81 in *The Civil Litigation Research Project: Final Report,* Part C, David M. Trubek, Joel B. Grossman, William L. F. Felstiner, Herbert M. Kritzer, and Austin Sarat. Madison, Wisconsin: University of Wisconsin Law School, Institute for Legal Studies. Portions reprinted in *American Court Systems: Readings in Judicial Process and Behavior,* ed. Sheldon Goldman and Austin Sarat, 516–524. New York: Longman.

Kritzer, Herbert M., Joel B. Grossman, Elizabeth McNichol, David M. Trubek, and Austin Sarat. 1984. "Courts and Litigation Investment: Why Do Lawyers Spend More Time on Federal Cases?" *Justice System Journal* 9: 7–22.

Kritzer, Herbert M., Austin Sarat, David M. Trubek, Kristin Bumiller, and Elizabeth McNichol. 1984. "Understanding the Costs of Litigation: The Case of the Hourly Fee Lawyer." *American Bar Foundation Research Journal,* no. 3: 559–604.

Landes, William M. 1971. "An Economic Analysis of the Courts." *Journal of Law and Economics* 14: 61–107.

Landon, Donald. 1985. "Clients, Colleagues, and Community: The Shaping of Zealous Advocacy in Country Law Practice." *American Bar Foundation Research Journal,* no. 1: 81–112.

Law Enforcement Assistance Administration (LEAA). 1973. *National Survey of Court Organization.* Washington, D.C.: Department of Justice.

Law Enforcement Assistance Administration (LEAA). 1982. *National Survey of Court Organization* (rev. ed.). Washington, D.C.: Department of Justice.

Law Society. 1970. *Memorandum on Maintenance and Champerty: Claims Assessors and Contingency Fees.* London: The Law Society.

Law Society. 1987. *Improving Access to Civil Justice: The Report of the Law Society's Working Party on the Funding of Litigation.* London: The Law Society.

Leubsdorf, John. 1981. "The Contingency Factor in Attorney Fee Awards." *Yale Law Journal* 90: 473–513.

Lieberman, Jethro. 1981. *The Litigious Society.* New York: Basic Books.

Lieberman, Jethro. 1982. "The Public Processing of America's Disputes: The Capacities and Capabilities of Our Courts and Other Formal Public Dispute Resolution Institutions." Paper presented at National Conference on the Lawyer's Changing Role in Resolving Disputes, Harvard Law School.

Lowenthal, Gary T. 1982. "A General Theory of Negotiation Process, Strategy, and Behavior." *University of Kansas Law Review* 31: 69–114.

Lord Chancellor's Department. 1989. *Contingency Fees.* London: HMSO.

Luban, David. 1985. "Bargaining and Compromise: Recent Work on Negotiation and Informal Justice." *Philosophy and Public Affairs* 14: 397–415.

Luban, David. 1989. "The Quality of Justice." *Denver University Law Review* 66: 381–417.

Luce, R. Duncan, and Howard Raiffa. 1957. *Games and Decisions: Introduction and Critical Survey.* New York: John Wiley and Sons.

Maccoby, Eleanor E., Charlene D. Depner, and Robert H. Mnookin. 1988. "Custody of Children Following Divorce." Pp. 91–114 in *Impact of Divorce, Single Parenting and Step-Parenting on Children,* ed. E. Mavis Hetherington and Josephine D. Arasten. Hillsday, New Jersey: Lawrence Erlbaum Associates.

MacKinnon, F. 1964. *Contingent Fees for Legal Services.* Chicago: Aldine Publishing.

McThenia, Andrew W., and Thomas L. Shaffer. 1985. "For Reconciliation." *Yale Law Journal* 94: 1660–1668.

Mann, Kenneth. 1985. *Defending White-Collar Crime: A Portrait of Attorneys at Work.* New Haven: Yale University Press.

Manning, Bayless. 1977. "Hyperlexis: Our National Disease." *Northwestern University Law Review* 71: 767–782.

Marvell, Thomas B. 1985, "Civil Caseloads: The Impact of the Economy and Trial Judgeship Increases." *Judicature* 69: 153–156.

Marvell, Thomas B. 1987. "Caseload Growth—Past and Future Trends." *Judicature* 71: 151–161.

Matheny, A. R. 1980. "Negotiation and Plea Bargaining Models." *Law & Policy Quarterly* 2: 267–284.

Mather, Lynn. 1979. *Plea Bargaining or Trial? The Process of Criminal Case Disposition.* Lexington, Massachusetts: Lexington Books.

Mather, Lynn, and Barbara Yngvesson. 1980–81. "Language, Audience, and the Transformation of Disputes." *Law & Society Review* 15: 775–821.

Maynard, Douglas W. 1984a. "The Structure of Discourse in Misdemeanor Plea Bargaining." *Law & Society Review* 18: 75–104.

Maynard, Douglas W. 1984b. *Inside Plea Bargaining: The Language of Negotiation.* New York: Plenum Publishing.

Melli, Marygold S., Howard S. Erlanger, and Elizabeth Chambliss. 1985. "The Process of Negotiation: An Exploratory Investigation in the Divorce Context." University of Wisconsin, Institute for Legal Studies, Dispute Processing Research Program, Working Papers, Series 7.

Melli, Marygold S., Howard S. Erlanger, and Elizabeth Chambliss. 1988. "The Process of Negotiation: An Exploratory Investigation in the Context of No-Fault Divorce." *Rutgers Law Review* 40: 1133–1172.

Menkel-Meadow, Carrie J. 1983. "Review Essay: Legal Negotiation: A Study of Strategies in Search of a Theory." *American Bar Foundation Research Journal,* no. 4: 905–937.

Menkel-Meadow, Carrie J. 1984. "Toward Another View of Legal Negotiation: The Structure of Problem Solving." *UCLA Law Review* 31: 754–842.

Menkel-Meadow, Carrie J. 1985a. "The Transformation of Disputes by Lawyers:

What the Dispute Paradigm Does and Does Not Tell Us." *Missouri Journal of Dispute Resolution* 1985: 25–44.

Menkel-Meadow, Carrie J. 1985b. "For and Against Settlement: Uses and Abuses of the Mandatory Settlement Conference." *UCLA Law Review* 33: 485–514.

Merry, Sally Engle. 1990. *Getting Justice and Getting Even: Legal Consciousness among Working-class Americans.* Chicago: University of Chicago Press.

Merry, Sally Engle, and Susan S. Silbey. 1984. "What Do Plaintiffs Want? Reexamining the Concept of Dispute." *Justice System Journal* 9: 151–178.

Miller, Geoffrey P. 1987. "Some Agency Problems in Settlement." *Journal of Legal Studies* 16: 189–215.

Miller, Richard E., and Austin Sarat. 1980–81. "Grievances, Claims, and Disputes: Assessing the Adversary Culture." *Law & Society Review* 15: 525–565.

Mnookin, Robert H. 1985. "Divorce Bargaining: The Limits of Private Ordering." *University of Michigan Journal of Law Reform* 18: 1015–1037.

Mnookin, Robert H., and Lewis Kornhauser. 1979. "Bargaining in the Shadow of the Law: The Case of Divorce." *Yale Law Journal* 88: 950–997.

Nalebuff, Barry. 1987. "Credible Pretrial Negotiation." *Rand Journal of Economics* 18: 198–210.

Nardulli, Peter F., James Eisenstein, and Roy B. Flemming. 1988. *The Tenor of Justice: Criminal Courts and the Guilty Plea Process.* Urbana: University of Illinois Press.

Nardulli, Peter F., Roy B. Flemming, and James Eisenstein. 1985. "Criminal Courts and Bureaucratic Justice: Concessions and Consensus in the Guilty Plea Process." *Journal of Criminal Law & Criminology* 76: 1103–1131.

Nash, John F. 1950. "The Bargaining Problem." *Econometrica* 18: 155–162.

Nash, John F. 1951. "Non-Cooperative Games." *Annals of Mathematics* 54: 286–295.

Nash, John F. 1953. "Two-Person Cooperative Games." *Econometrica* 21: 128–140.

National Center for State Courts. 1978. *State Court Caseload Statistics: The State of the Art.* Washington, D.C.: Law Enforcement Assistance Administration.

National Center for State Courts. 1985. *State Court Caseload Statistics: Annual Report 1981.* Williamsburg, Virginia: National Center for State Courts.

Nelson, Robert. 1981. "Practice and Privilege: Social Change and the Structure of Large Law Firms." *American Bar Foundation Research Journal,* no. 1: 95–140.

Nelson, Robert. 1985. "Ideology, Practice and Professional Autonomy: Social Values and Client Relations in the Large Law Firm." *Stanford Law Review* 37: 503–555.

Nelson, Robert. 1988. *Partners in Power.* Berkeley: University of California Press.

Nierenberg, Gerald I. 1968. *The Art of Negotiating.* New York: Cornerstone Library.

Nierenberg, Gerald I. 1973. *Fundamentals of Negotiating.* New York: Hawthorn Books.

Ordover, Janusz A., and Ariel Rubinstein. 1983. "On Bargaining, Settling, and Litigation: A Problem in Multistage Games with Imperfect Information." New

York University, C. V. Starr Center for Applied Economics, Economic Research Report 83-07.

Packer, Herbert L. 1964. "Two Models of the Criminal Process." *University of Pennsylvania Law Review* 113: 1–68.

Pearson, Jessica, Nancy Thoennes, and Patricia Tjaden. 1989. "Legislating Adequacy: The Impact of Child Support Guidelines."*Law & Society Review* 23: 569–590.

Pen, Jan. 1952. "A General Theory of Bargaining." *American Economic Review* 42: 24–42.

Perloff, Jeffrey M., and Daniel L. Rubinfeld. 1987. "Settlements in Private Antitrust Litigation." Pp. 149–184 in *Private Antitrust Litigation,* ed. Lawrence White. Cambridge: MIT Press.

Perschbacher, Rex R. 1985. "Regulating Lawyers' Negotiations." *Arizona Law Review* 27: 75–138.

Peters, Geoffrey. 1987. "The Use of Lies in Negotiation." *Ohio State Law Journal* 48: 1–50.

Peterson, Mark A. 1987. *Civil Juries in the 1980's: Trends in Jury Trials and Verdicts in California and Cook County, Illinois.* Santa Monica: The Rand Corporation.

Peterson, Mark A., and George L. Priest. 1982. *The Civil Jury: Trends in Trials and Verdicts, Cook County, Illinois, 1960–1979.* Santa Monica: The Rand Corporation.

Phillips, Jenny, Keith Hawkins, and John Flemming. 1975. "Compensation for Personal Injuries." *Economic Journal* 84: 129–134.

P'ng, I. P. L. 1983. "Strategic Behavior in Suit, Settlement, and Trial." *Bell Journal of Economics* 14: 539–550.

P'ng, I. P. L. 1984. "Liability, Litigation, and Incentives to Take Care." Center for Economic Policy Research Technical Report, Stanford University.

Posner, Richard A. 1972. "The Behavior of Administrative Agencies." *Journal of Legal Studies* 1: 305–347.

Posner, Richard A. 1973. "An Economic Approach to Legal Procedure and Judicial Administration." *Journal of Legal Studies* 2: 399–455.

Posner, Richard A. 1985. *The Federal Courts: Crisis and Reform.* Cambridge, Massachusetts: Harvard University Press.

Priest, George L. 1985. "Reexamining the Selection Hypothesis: Learning from Wittman's Mistakes." *Journal of Legal Studies* 14: 215–243.

Priest, George L., and Benjamin Klein. 1984. "The Selection of Disputes for Litigation." *Journal of Legal Studies* 13: 1–55.

Pruitt, Dean. 1981. *Negotiation Behavior.* New York: Academic Press.

Raiffa, Howard. 1982. *The Art and Science of Negotiation.* Cambridge, Massachusetts: Belknap Press.

Rapoport, Anatol. 1960. *Fights, Games, and Debates.* Ann Arbor: University of Michigan Press.

Reinganum, Jennifer, and Louis L. Wilde. 1986. "Settlement, Litigation and the Allocation of Litigation Costs." *Rand Journal of Economics* 17: 557–566.

Resnik, Judith. 1982. "Managerial Judges." *Harvard Law Review* 96: 374–448.

Rosenberg, D., and S. Shavell. 1985. "A Model in Which Suits Are Brought for Their Nuisance Value." *International Review of Law & Economics* 5: 3–13.

Rosenberg, Maurice. 1972. "Let's Everybody Litigate?" *Texas Law Review* 50: 1349–1368.

Rosenberg, Maurice. 1980–81. "Civil Justice Research and Civil Justice Reform." *Law & Society Review* 15: 473–483.

Rosenthal, Douglas. 1974. *Lawyer and Client: Who's in Charge?* New York: Russell Sage.

Ross, H. Laurence. 1980. *Settled Out of Court: The Social Process of Insurance Claims Adjustment,* rev. 2nd ed. Chicago: Aldine.

Rosset, Arthur, and Donald R. Cressey. 1976. *Justice by Consent: Plea Bargains in the American Courthouse.* Philadelphia: J. P. Lippincott.

Roth, Alvin E. (ed.). 1985. *Game-Theoretic Models of Bargaining.* Cambridge: Cambridge University Press.

Rowe, Thomas D., Jr. (ed.). 1984. "Attorney Fee Shifting" *Law & Contemporary Problems* 47: 1–354 (entire issue).

Rubin, J. Z., and B. R. Brown. 1975. *The Social Psychology of Bargaining and Negotiation.* New York: Academic Press.

Salant, Stephen W. 1984. "Litigation of Settlement Demands Questioned by Bayesian Defendants." California Institute of Technology, Social Science Working Paper 516.

Salant, Stephen W., and Gregory Rest. 1982. "Litigation of Questioned Settlement Claims: A Bayesian Nash-Equilibrium Approach." Rand Paper, The Rand Corporation.

Samuelson, Robert J. 1986. "The Litigation Explosion: The Wrong Question." *Maryland Law Review* 46: 78–85.

Samuelson, William. 1983. "Negotiation vs. Litigation." Discussion Paper, Boston University School of Management.

Sarat, Austin. 1981. "The Role of Courts and the Logic of Court Reform: Notes on the Justice Department's Approach to Improving Justice." *Judicature* 64: 300–311.

Schelling, Thomas. 1956. "An Essay on Bargaining." *American Economic Review* 46: 281–306.

Schelling, Thomas. 1960. *The Strategy of Conflict.* Cambridge: Harvard University Press.

Schuck, Peter H. 1986. *Agent Orange on Trial: Mass Toxic Disasters in the Courts.* Cambridge, Massachusetts: Belknap Press.

Schulhofer, Stephen J. 1984. "Is Plea Bargaining Inevitable?" *Harvard Law Review* 97: 1037–1107.

Schulhofer, Stephen J. 1985. "No Job Too Small: Justice without Bargaining in the Lower Criminal Courts." *American Bar Foundation Research Journal,* no. 3: 519–598.

Schwab, Stewart J., and Theodore Eisenberg. 1988. "Explaining Constitutional Tort

Litigation: The Influence of the Attorney Fees Statute and the Government as Defendant." *Cornell Law Review* 73: 719–784.

Schwartz, Murray L., and Daniel J. B. Mitchell. 1970. "An Economic Analysis of the Contingent Fee in Personal-Injury Litigation." *Stanford Law Review* 22: 1125–1162.

Seltzer, Judith A., and Irwin Garfinkel. 1990. "Inequality in Divorce Settlements: An Investigation of Property Settlements and Child Support Awards." *Social Science Research* 19: 82–111.

Selvin, Molly, and Patricia A. Ebener. 1984. *Managing the Unmanageable: A History of Civil Delay in the Los Angeles Superior Court.* Santa Monica: The Rand Corporation.

Shane-Dubow, Sandra, Alice P. Brown, and Erik Olsen. 1985. *Sentencing Reform in the United States: History, Content and Effect.* Washington, D.C.: National Institute of Justice.

Shanley, Michael G., and Mark A. Peterson. 1983. *Comparative Justice: Civil Jury Verdicts in San Francisco and Cook Counties, 1959–1980.* Santa Monica, California: The Rand Corporation.

Shannon, James. 1988. *Texaco and the $10 Billion Jury.* Englewood Cliffs, New Jersey: Prentice Hall.

Shavell, Steven. 1982. "Suit, Settlement and Trial: A Theoretical Analysis under Alternative Methods for the Allocation of Legal Costs." *Journal of Legal Studies* 11: 55–82.

Sherwood, David R., and Mark A. Clarke. 1981."Toward an Understanding of 'Local Legal Culture.'" *Justice System Journal* 6: 200–217.

Slovak, Jeffrey S. 1979. "Working for Corporate Actors: Social Change and Elite Attorneys in Chicago." *American Bar Foundation Research Journal,* no. 3: 465–500.

Slovak, Jeffrey S. 1980. "Giving and Getting Respect: Prestige and Stratification in a Legal Elite." *American Bar Foundation Research Journal,* no. 1: 31–68.

Slovak, Jeffrey S. 1981a. "Influence and Issues in the Legal Community: The Role of a Legal Elite." *American Bar Foundation Research Journal,* no. 1: 141–194.

Slovak, Jeffrey S. 1981b. "The Ethics of Corporate Lawyers: A Sociological Approach." *American Bar Foundation Research Journal,* no. 3: 753–794.

Smigel, Erwin O. 1964. *The Wall Street Lawyer.* New York: Free Press.

Sobel, Joel. 1985. "Disclosure of Evidence and Resolution of Disputes: Who Should Bear the Burden of Proof?" Pp. 341–361 in *Game-Theoretic Models of Bargaining,* ed. Alvin E. Roth. New York: Cambridge University Press.

Spulber, Daniel F. 1985. "Negligence, Contributory Negligence and Pre-Trial Settlement Negotiation." University of Southern California, Department of Economics, Modelling Research Group Working Paper M8511.

Stevens, Carl M. 1963. *Strategy and Collective Bargaining Negotiations.* New York: McGraw-Hill.

Strauss, Anselm. 1978. *Negotiations: Varieties, Contexts, Processes and Social Order.* San Francisco: Jossey-Bass.

Sudnow, David. 1965. "Normal Crimes: Sociological Features of the Penal Code in a Public Defender Office." *Social Problems* 12: 255–276.

Sutton, John. 1986. "Non-Cooperative Bargaining Theory: An Introduction." *Review of Economic Studies* 53: 709–724.

Swanson, Timothy. 1988. "The Repeat Player in Dispute Resolution: Its Impact upon Civil Litigation." Unpublished mimeo, Department of Economics, University College, London.

Tocqueville, Alexis de. 1945. *Democracy in America*. Edited by P. Bradley. New York: Alfred Knopf.

Tribe, Lawrence. 1979. "Too Much Law, Too Little Justice: An Argument for Delegalizing America." *Atlantic Monthly* (July): 25–30.

Trubek, David M., Herbert M. Kritzer, Karen Holst, and William L. F. Felstiner. 1984. "Costs, Processes, and Outcomes: Lawyers' Attitudes towards Courts and Other Dispute Processing Options." Report to the National Institute for Dispute Resolution, Madison, Wisconsin: Disputes Processing Research Program, University of Wisconsin Law School. (Available as a DPRP Working Paper 1984-9.)

Trubek, David M., Joel B. Grossman, William L. F. Felstiner, Herbert M. Kritzer, and Austin Sarat. 1983. *The Civil Litigation Research Project: Final Report*. 2 vols. Madison, Wisconsin: University of Wisconsin Law School, Institute for Legal Studies.

Trubek, David M., Austin Sarat, William L. F. Felstiner, Herbert M. Kritzer, and Joel B. Grossman. 1983. "The Costs of Ordinary Litigation." *UCLA Law Review* 31: 72–127.

Tullock, Gordon. 1980. *Trials on Trial: The Pure Theory of Legal Procedure*. New York: Columbia University Press.

Tyler, Tom R. 1989. "The Quality of Dispute Resolution Procedures and Outcomes: Measurement Problems and Possibilities." *Denver University Law Review* 66: 419–436.

Utz, Pamela. 1978. *Settling the Facts: Discretion and Negotiation in Criminal Court*. Lexington, Massachusetts: Lexington Books.

van den Haag, Ernest. 1975. *Punishing Criminals: Concerning a Very Old and Painful Question*. New York: Basic Books.

van Koppen, Peter J. 1988. "Justice and Power in Civil Law Negotiations." *Social Justice Research* 2: 137–153.

van Koppen, Peter J. 1990. "Risk Taking in Civil Law Negotiations." *Law and Human Behavior* 14: 151–167.

Victor, Mark B. 1985. "The Proper Use of Decision Analysis to Assist Litigation Strategy." *Business Lawyer* 40: 617–629.

Viscusi, W. Kip. 1986. "The Determinants of the Disposition of Product Liability Claims and Compensation for Bodily Injury." *Journal of Legal Studies* 15: 321–346.

Viscusi, W. Kip. 1988. "Product Liability Litigation with Risk Aversion. *Journal of Legal Studies* 17: 101–121.

von Neumann, John, and Oskar Morgenstern. 1944. *Theory of Games and Economic Behavior.* (2nd ed., 1947). Princeton: Princeton University Press.

Wallach, E. Robert. 1979. "Settlement in a Personal Injury Case: The Imperfect Art." *Litigation* 5(1): 35–39, 60.

Walton, Richard E., and Robert B. McKersie. 1965. *A Behavioral Theory of Labor Negotiations: An Analysis of a Social Interaction System.* New York: McGraw-Hill.

Wanner, Craig. 1974. "The Public Ordering of Private Relations, Part One: Initiating Civil Cases in Urban Trial Courts." *Law & Society Review* 8: 421–440.

Wanner, Craig. 1975. "The Public Ordering of Private Relations, Part Two: Winning Civil Court Cases." *Law & Society Review* 9: 293–306.

Waterman, D. A., and Mark A. Peterson. 1981. *Models of Legal Decisionmaking.* Santa Monica, California: The Rand Corporation.

Weiss, Stephen E. 1987. "Negotiation and Culture: Some Thoughts on Models, Ghosts, and Options." *Dispute Resolution Forum* (September): 3–5.

White, James J. 1980. "Machiavelli and the Bar: Ethical Limitations on Lying in Negotiation." *American Bar Foundation Research Journal,* no. 4: 921–938.

Williams, Gerald R. 1983. *Legal Negotiation and Settlement.* St. Paul: West Publishing.

Wittman, Donald. 1985. "Is the Selection of Cases for Trial Biased?" *Journal of Legal Studies* 14: 185–214.

Wittman, Donald. 1986. "The Price of Negligence under Differing Liability Rules." *Journal of Law & Economics* 29: 151–163.

Wittman, Donald. 1988. "Dispute Resolution, Bargaining, and the Selection of Cases for Trial: A Study of the Generation of Biased and Unbiased Data." *Journal of Legal Studies* 17: 313–352.

Yngvesson, Barbara. 1988. "Making Law at the Doorway: The Clerk, the Court, and the Construction of Community in a New England Town." *Law & Society Review* 22: 409–448.

Yngvesson, Barbara, and Patricia Hennessey. 1975. "Small Claims, Complex Disputes: A Review of the Small Claims Literature. *Law & Society Review* 9: 219–274.

Young, Oran (ed.). 1975. *Bargaining.* Urbana: University of Illinois Press.

Zartman, William. 1975. "Negotiations: Theory and Reality." *Journal of International Affairs* 9: 69–77.

Zemans, Frances Kahn. 1980. "Coercion to Restitution: Criminal Processing of Civil Disputes." *Law & Policy Quarterly* 2: 81–105.

Zemans, Frances Kahn. 1984. "Fee Shifting and the Implementation of Public Policy." *Law and Contemporary Problems* 47: 187–210.

Zemans, Frances Kahn, and Victor G. Rosenblum. 1981. *The Making of a Public Profession.* Chicago: American Bar Foundation.

Zeuthen, Frederik. 1930. *Problems of Monopoly and Economic Warfare.* London: G. Routledge.

Index

Abel, Richard L., 23, 47
Adjudication: contrast to settlement, 3–4, 136–37, 141$nn5,6$, 179$nn10,11$; threat of, 130–31
Administrative Office of the United States Courts, 14,15
Adversarial negotiation, 100–3, 112–16. *See also* Competitive, approach to negotiations; Distributive bargaining
Agent Orange, 7–10, 30, 71, 103, 141$nn10,11$
Agents: lawyers as, 123–24
Aggressive approach to negotiations: effect on outcome, 54–56, 79. *See also* Competitive
Agnew, Spiro, 10
All-Industry Research Advisory Council (AIRAC), 163$n40$, 174$n27$
Alschuler, Albert W., 5, 137
Alternative dispute resolution (ADR), 136–37, 143$n20$, 179$n9$
Anderson, Jill K., 143$n20$, 147$n43$
Appropriate-result, consensus-oriented negotiations, 14, 118–25, 127–29, 134
Area of law: change in demands and offers by, 51–52; contact intensity by, 32–33; content of demands and offers by, 42–43, 47; exchange intensity by, 38–39; first offers/first demands by, 48–49
Asbestos litigation, 174$n28$
Atiyah, P. S., 175$n34$
Attitudes (of lawyers): change in demands and offers by, 52; contact intensity by, 34; variation in, 26–28
Axelrod, Robert, 80–82, 95, 167$nn31,33,34$, 169$n58$, 170$n65$
Axiomatic models of bargaining (game theory), 87

Bacharach, Samuel B., 72–73
Banks, Jeffrey S., 89, 92

Barristers, 107
Barton, John, 3
Bartos, Otomar, 68–69
Bebchuk, Lucian Arye, 75, 88, 92, 158$n16$
Bedlin, Howard, 180$n13$
Bellow, Gary, 142$n15$
Bendectin litigation, 99, 170$n2$
Benson Commission, 99
Big cases: negotiation in, 6–10
Bilateral monopoly: applications to bargaining, 66, 162$n37$; game, 83–84, 168$n35$
Blumberg, Abraham S., 173$n23$
Blumstein, James F., 142$n15$
Bovbjerg, Randall R., 142$n15$
Brazil, Wayne D., 142$n13$, 152$n17$
Brown, Alice P., 176$n12$
Brown, B. R., 81, 129
Bruce, Lenny, 141$n7$
Burger, Warren E., 3
Bush, Robert A. Baruch, 180$n14$

Canada: litigation in, 173$n25$, 174$n29$, 179$n5$
Cane, Peter, 175$n34$
Carlin, Jerome E., 65–66, 95, 148$n45$, 162$nn33,34$
Cartter Report, 148$n46$
Case-oriented negotiation, 71
Case worth: ambiguity of, 58–59, 73–74, 121, 133–34, 164$n46$
Cavanagh, Edward D., 103
Cavanagh, Ralph, 179$n12$
Centre for Socio-Legal Studies (Oxford), 107
Chambliss, Elizabeth, 137, 141$n8$, 144$n25$, 164$n6$, 165$n10$, 178$n1$, 180$n12$
Chanin, Robert H., 179$n5$
Chatterjee, Kalyan, 86, 87, 92
Chesley, Stanley, 99, 170$n1$
Church, Thomas W., Jr., 35
Civil justice reform. *See* Reform of the civil justice system

197

Civil Litigation Research Project (CLRP), 4, 10, 14–17, 54, 122, 127, 143*n17*
Civil rights. *See* Area of law
Clarke, Mark A., 35
Clayton, Paul, 160*n21*, 169*n53*
Clermont, Kevin M., 179*n5*
Coffee, John C., Jr., 103, 171*n10*
Cohen, Richard M., 10
Collaborative negotiators, 113, 116, 166*n22*
Competitive: approach to negotiations, 55–56, 114, 155*n33*; type of negotiator, 77–80, 113, 116. *See also* Maximal-result, concessions-oriented negotiation
Complexity (of case): change in demands and offers by, 51–52; contact intensity by, 32–34; content of demands and offers by, 44; exchange intensity by, 39–40; first demands/first offers by, 48–49; measurement of, 152*n9*
Concessions. *See* Learning models; Maximal result, concessions-oriented negotiation
Condlin, Robert J., 112
Conley, John M., 23, 47
Consensus. *See* Appropriate-result, consensus-oriented negotiation
Content of demands and offers. *See* Demands and offers, content of
Contingent fee: absence of in England, 93; agent, lawyers using as 123–24; concern about outcome, effect on, 53–54; defense of by lawyers, 110–11; economic incentives created by, 100–5, 179*n5*; economics of settlement, implications for, 63–64; frequency of, 169*n54*; monetary nature of demands and offers, relationship to 45, 100–3; potential for integrative bargaining, effect on, 67; relative advantage of plaintiff and defendant when used, 74–75; repeat player (contingent fee lawyer as), 95, 105; tactical bargaining, relationship to, 100–3; use of 169*n54*
Contracts. *See* Area of law
Cooperative: approach to negotiations, 55–56, 114; game-theoretic models, 87; type of negotiator, 77–80, 113, 116. *See also* Appropriate-result, consensus-oriented negotiations

Cooter, Robert, 60–61, 74, 92, 159*n16*, 165*nn7,9*
Court records, 16
Court reform. *See* Reform of the civil justice system
Cressey, Donald R., 176*n10*
Criminal justice system: models of, 128; negotiations in, 116, 120–21, 125, 131, 154*n23*; sentencing reform, 176*n12*. *See also* Guilty plea process
Cross, John G., 66, 68, 87, 119
Curran, Barbara A., 148*n45*, 149*n49*
Curran, William J., 165*n14*
Currivan, John D., 179*n5*
Cyclical model of negotiation, 113

Dahl, Scott S., 142*n15*
Damages. *See* Case worth
Demands and offers: change during negotiation, 49–52; content of, 41–47, 154*n28*; contingent fees and, 100–3; effect on outcome, 54–56, 79; first move, 153*n20*, 175*n35*; initial, 47–49
Daniels, Stephen, 158*n10*, 163*n43*
Danzon, Patricia Munch, 137, 142*n12*, 159*n18*
de Tocqueville, Alexis, 141*n1*
Dependency relationships: effect on power in bargaining situations, 73
Depner, Charlene D., 144*n25*, 159*n18*, 164*n6*
Developmental model of negotiation, 113
Dingwall, Robert, 174*n28*
Discrimination: content of demands and offers in cases involving claims of, 42–43. *See also* Area of law
Dispute pyramid, 178*n3*
Distributive bargaining: assumption of in bilateral monopoly game, 84; defined, 66; as description of bargaining in litigation, 67–68; type of negotiation, 113
Divorce cases: exchange intensity in, 39; shadow of the law in, 74, 164*n6*, 178*n1*; studies of negotiation in, 16, 141*n8*, 144*n25*, 159*n18*, 165*nn10,15*. *See also* Area of law
Durkin, Tom, 174*n28*

Ebener, Patricia A., 36

Economics of settlement, 58–66, 157*n*6;
    effect of contingent fees on, 63–64
Eisenberg, Melvin A., 61
Eisenberg, Theodore, 142*nn*12,13
Eisenstein, James, 6, 116, 121, 126, 129,
    131, 153*n*18, 154*n*23
Eli Lilly, 172*n*21
Elsner, Mary E., 145*n*37
Engel, David M., 137, 141*n*4
England: asbestos litigation in, 174*n*28;
    studies of negotiation in, 55–56, 78–79,
    93–98, 105–10, 114–15, 153*n*19
Erlanger, Howard S., 137, 141*n*8, 144*n*25,
    164*n*6, 165*n*10, 178*n*1, 180*n*12
Esser, John P., 180*n*14
Ethics: negotiator, 142*n*15
Expected outcome. *See* Economics of
    settlement
Experience (of lawyers), 25
Expertise (of lawyers), 25. *See also* Spe-
    cialization

Fee arrangement: relationship to monetary
    nature of demands and offers, 45. *See also*
    Contingent fee
Fee awards, 171*nn*9, 12
Feeley, Malcolm M., 6, 131, 176*nn*9,10
Feinberg, Kenneth R., 8, 103
Felstiner, William L. F., 23, 47, 174*n*28
Fenn, Paul, 95–97, 142*n*12, 170*nn*61,62
Financing of litigation: effect on settlement
    in England, 106–10
Fine, Ralph Adam, 5
Fisher, Roger, 136, 147*n*44
Fiss, Owen, 5, 137
Flango, Victor Eugene, 145*n*37
Flemming, John, 93, 96
Flemming, Roy B., 6, 116, 121, 126, 131,
    153*n*18, 154*n*23
Franklin, Marc A., 179*n*5
Friedman, Lawrence M., 171*n*3
Friedman, Alan E., 58, 157*n*3
Frivolous lawsuits, frequency of: game-
    theoretic analyses of effect of rule
    changes on, 92; impact of transactions
    costs, 75
Function of negotiation, 117

Galanter, Marc, 3, 4, 61, 75, 126, 130, 137,
    141*n*5, 145*n*37, 159*n*17, 161*n*31,
    168*n*39, 180*nn*13,14
Game theory, 80–98
Garfinkel, Irwin, 144*n*25, 160*n*18, 164*n*6,
    165*nn*9,10, 178*n*1
Garment, Leonard, 141*n*10
Genn, Hazel, 55–56, 70, 78–79, 95,
    105–10, 114–15, 116, 133, 135,
    169*n*51, 173*n*27, 174*n*30
Getty Oil. *See* Pennzoil v. Texaco
Gifford, Donald G., 78, 114, 116, 156*n*44,
    161*n*26, 166*n*22, 175*n*6, 176*n*7
Going rates, 39, 71
Gomperts, John S., 103
Gould, John P., 58
Government: lawyers, 17; as litigant,
    151*n*6; party and effect on contact
    intensity, 32
Grady, John F., 99
Green, Jonathan, 141*n*7
Green, Eric D., 136
Grossman, Joel B., 4, 17, 34, 76, 136,
    179*n*8
Grossman, Sanford J., 87, 90
Guilty-plea process, 5–6, 10, 71, 121, 126,
    131, 176*nn*9,10, 177*n*18
Gulliver, Paul H., 113, 166*nn*20,21

Hamner, W. Clay, 163*n*42
Handler, Joel, 148*n*45
Hard bargaining, 55–56, 114
Harris, Donald, 96, 107, 153*n*19, 173*n*27
Harsanyi, John C., 168*n*35
Hause, John C., 92
Hawkins, Keith, 93, 96
Hennessey, Patricia, 154*n*27
Hensler, Deborah R., 161*n*29
Heumann, Milton, 6, 126, 131
Heydebrand, Wolf, 15
Hoffer, Peter Charles, 23
Hyperlexis. *See* Litigiousness

Incomplete information. *See* Uncertainty
Indemnity rule: effect on settlement analysis
    92; in England, 105–6
Individuals as litigants: effect on negotia-
    tion, 75–76; risk aversion and, 161*n*31
Information: bargaining as the exchange of,
    66–71, 119, 163*n*43; incomplete, 85, 87,
    92, 96. *See also* Uncertainty

Insurance companies: in England, 173*n*27; lawyers representing, 111; role in settlement, 65–66
Insurance: legal expense in England, 109–10, 175*n*36
Integrative bargaining: bilateral monopoly game requirement of, 84; contingent fees and, 67; defined, 66–67; role in economic theories of bargaining, 67–68; type of negotiation, 113–14. *See also* Appropriate-result, consensus-oriented negotiation
Intensity: contact, 31–36; definition, 30–31; exchange, 36–40; function of negotiation and, 128; impact on success of, 54
Interviews, 16–17

Jackson, Donald Dale, 162*n*35
Jackson, R. M., 169*n*49, 172*n*18
Jacob, Herbert, 129, 147*n*42
Jamail, Joseph, 99, 171*n*11
Jenkins, John A., 99
Johnson, Earl, Jr., 63, 100, 104, 177*n*16, 179*n*5
Judicial districts: characteristics of, 15; contact intensity by, 35–36; research sites, 14; variation by, 18
Jury verdicts: typical size of, 142*n*13, 145*n*34

Kahan, James P., 82, 168*n*35, 169*n*56
Kakalik, James S., 57, 157*n*2
Karrass, Chester L., 163*n*42
Kemp, David A. M., 160*n*19
Klein, Benjamin, 73, 164*n*5
Kornhauser, Lewis, 61, 72, 73, 130, 144*n*25, 178*n*1
Kritzer, Herbert M., 4, 34, 52, 54, 63, 104, 110, 123, 124, 130, 132, 137, 141*n*5, 143*n*20, 144*n*28, 147*n*43, 154*n*22, 155*n*35, 156*nn*39,40,41, 162*n*33, 167*n*26, 169*n*51, 171*n*13, 172*n*14, 174*nn*27,29, 175*n*35, 176*n*15, 177*n*16, 178*n*2, 179*nn*5,10, 180*n*13

Landes, William M., 119
Landon, Doinald, 129
Law firm size: contact intensity by, 35
Law school: types attended and performance in, 24

Lawyer effort, 31
Lawyers: attitudes of, 26–28, 150*nn*53, 54,55; characteristics of and contact intensity, 34–35; description of, 24–29, 147*n*45; economic incentives (effect of), 99–110; experience of, 25; expertise of, 25–26; 149*n*51; gender of, 147*n*45, income of, 147*n*45, 149*n*49,50; law school attended by, 24, 148*nn*46,48
Law Society, 172*nn*17,20
Lawley, Edward J., 72–73
Legal aid: effect on settlement in England, 107–10, 174*n*30
Legal issues. *See* Areas of law
Legal practice, 26
Learning models: inapplicability to bargaining in ordinary litigation, 67–69
Leubsdorf, John, 103
Liability: uncertainty concerning, 94–95, 121
Lieberman, Jethro, 3, 145*n*37
Lillard, Lee A., 137, 142*n*12, 159*n*18
Litigiousness, 3
Litigotiation, 4–5, 137
Lord Chancellor's Department, 172*n*20
Lowenthal, Gary T., 78, 113, 116–17, 155*n*33, 156*n*43, 166*n*22, 167*n*27, 176*n*7
Luban, David, 179*n*11, 180*n*14
Luce, R. Duncan, 168*n*46

Maccoby, Eleanor E., 144*n*25, 159*n*18, 164*n*6
MacKinnon, F., 99, 179*n*5
Mann, Kenneth, 125
Manning, Bayless, 3
Mark, Irving, 179*n*5
Marks, Stephen, 60–61, 73, 92, 159*n*16, 165*nn*7,9
Marvell, Thomas B., 3
Mathematica Policy Research (MPR), 16
Matheny, A. R., 119
Mather, Lynn, 23, 47, 176*n*10, 177*n*18
Maximal-result, concessions-oriented negotiation, 14, 118–25, 127–29, 134
Maynard, Douglas W., 6, 126, 154*n*23
McKersie, Robert B., 156*n*42, 157*n*3
McThenia, Andrew W., 137
Medicine: comparison to incentives in practice of, 100

Mega-cases. *See* Big cases
Meier, Kenneth, 179*n*7
Melli, Marygold S., 137, 141*n*8, 144*n*25, 164*n*6, 165*n*10, 178*n*1, 180*n*12
Menkel-Meadow, Carrie J., 23, 47, 100–102, 112–14, 116–17, 135, 136, 147*n*44, 156*nn*43,44, 166*n*22, 167*n*24, 171*n*5, 175*n*4, 180*n*13
Merry, Sally Engle, 23, 47, 146*n*39, 147*n*42
Miller, Richard E., 141*n*3, 143*n*20, 147*n*43, 174*n*27, 178*n*3
Miller, Geoffrey, P., 63, 104, 123, 156*n*38, 179*n*5
Mitchell, Daniel J. B., 179*n*5
Mnookin, Robert H., 61, 72, 73, 130, 144*n*25, 159*n*18, 164*n*6, 178*n*1
Monetary nature of cases, 20–24, 131–32, 154*n*26, 178*n*3
Morgenstern, Oskar, 80
Moulton, Bea, 142*n*15
Moving the business: economic incentives to, 64–66

Nalebuff, Barry, 170*n*60
Nardulli, Peter F., 6, 116, 121, 126, 131, 153*n*18, 154*n*23
Nash, John F., 168*n*35
National Center for State Courts, 145*n*37
Negotiator effectiveness (as defined by Williams), 76–77
Nejelski, Paul, 180*n*13
Nelson, Robert, 148*nn*45,47
Nonmonetary content of demands and offers, 46–47
Nonmonetary goals sought, 146*nn*39,40, 41, 147*n*43, 154*n*25

O'Barr, William M., 23, 47
Offers. *See* Demands and offers
Olsen, Erik, 176*n*12
One-shot players: in the negotiation process, 75–76, 93–94, 126–27; risk aversion of, 161*n*21
Opren, 172*n*21
Optimal hardness, 60
Ordinary cases: examples of settlement and negotiation in, 10–13
Ordover, Janusz A., 88, 92
Organizations: as litigants, 75–76

Outcome of cases. *See* Success

Pace, Nicholas, 57
Packer, Herbert L., 128
Pain and suffering: problems of valuing, 61
Payoffs: in Prisoner's Dilemma, 80–81
Pearson, Jessica, 164*n*6
Pen, Jan, 66
Pennzoil v. Texaco, 6–7, 99, 141*n*9, 171*n*11
Perloff, Jeffrey M., 159*n*18, 165*n*10
Perry, Motty, 87, 90
Perschbacher, Rex R., 156*n*38
Peters, Geoffrey, 142*n*15
Peterson, Mark A., 142*n*13, 145*n*34, 158*n*13, 159*n*18
Phillips, Jenny, 93, 96
Plea bargaining. *See* Guilty plea process
P'ng, I. P. L., 75, 84–85, 88, 168*nn*37, 38,39,40,41,42
Position-oriented negotiation, 71
Positive-sum game. *See* Integrative bargaining
Power: role in negotiation, 72–76, 165*nn*9,10
Posner, Richard A., 3, 58, 119, 157*n*3
Priest, George L., 73, 142*n*13, 145*n*34, 159*n*18, 164*n*5
Prisoner's Dilemma: game-theoretic analysis of, 80–82, 167*n*29, 169*n*48; repeat player in litigation and, 95
Problem solving negotiation, 100–103, 112–16, 156*n*44, 175*n*4. *See also* Cooperative approach to negotiation; Integrative bargaining
Pro forma negotiations, 14, 125–29, 132, 134, 177*n*19,20
Property. *See* Area of law
Pruitt, Dean, 69
Punishment. *See* Prisoner's Dilemma

Raiffa, Howard, 6, 57, 59, 70, 92, 113, 116–17, 136, 147*n*44, 168*n*46
Rapoport, Anatol, 167*n*29
Reform of the civil justice system, 135–38
Regulation. *See* Area of law
Reinganum, Jennifer, 89
Repeat players, 75–76, 93–94, 126–27
Reputation of negotiator: effect on outcome, 79
Resistance points, 157*n*4

Resnik, Judith, 180*n13*
Rest, Gregory, 92
Rhetoric (theory of): as framework for analysis of negotiation, 112–13
Risk analysis: use in economic analysis of settlement, 59–60
Risk preference: assymetries in, 115, 166*n19*; definition of, 166*n18*; discount for, 97; effect on relative power of parties, 75–76, 160*n21*; element in stakes, 144*n31*; lawyer's and change in demands and offers, 52; lawyers's and contact intensity, 34; litigant's, 161*n31*; measurement of 152*n13*
Roper, Robert T., 145*n37*
Rosenberg, Maurice, 3, 143*n17*
Rosenberg, D., 64, 92
Rosenblum, Victor G., 148*n46*, 149*n48*
Rosenthal, Douglas, 59, 123, 134, 135, 156*n38*, 158*n9*, 179*n5*
Ross, H. Laurence, 58, 65, 69–70, 119, 162*n32*, 163*n43*
Ross, Randy L., 95, 132, 157*nn2,3*
Rosset, Arthur, 176*n10*
Roth, Alvin E., 87
Routinization: effect on content of demands and offers, 44–45
Rowe, Thomas D., Jr., 92, 172*n19*
Rubin, J. Z., 81, 129
Rubinfeld, Daniel L., 159*n18*, 165*n10*
Rubinstein, Ariel, 88, 92
Rule-based model of settlement, 158*n13*

Salant, Stephen W., 89, 92
Sampling: of cases, 14–16; cases excluded, 16
Samuelson, Robert J., 92
Samuelson, Larry, 86, 87
Sarat, Austin, 4, 17, 23, 31, 32, 34, 47, 132, 136, 141*n3*, 142*n13*, 143*nn17,20*, 147*n43*, 154*n22*, 155*n35*, 174*n27*, 178*n3*, 179*n12*
Schelling, Thomas, 73, 123, 175*n37*
Schuck, Peter H., 7
Schulhofer, Stephen J., 6, 131
Schwab, Stewart J., 142*n12*
Schwartz, Murray L., 179*n5*
Seltzer, Judith A., 144*n25*, 160*n18*, 164*n6*, 165*nn9,10*, 178*n1*
Selvin, Molly, 36
Seron, Carroll, 15

Settling the facts, 120, 123
Shadow: of adjudication, 61; of the law, 61, 72–73, 130, 164*n6*, 165*n9*; in nonlitigation contexts, 164*n3*
Shaffer, Thomas L., 137
Shane-DuBow, Sandra, 176*n12*
Shanley, Michael G., 142*n13*
Shannon, James, 141*n9*
Shapiro, David, 8
Shavell, Steven, 75, 92
Sherwood, David R., 35
Silbey, Susan S., 23, 47, 146*n39*, 147*n42*
Simulation: of Prisoner's Dilemma, 81–83
Sloan, Frank A., 142*n15*
Slovak, Jeffrey S., 148*n47*
Smigel, Erwin O., 148*nn45,47*
Sobel, Joel, 92
Solicitors. *See* England
Specialization (of lawyers): change in demands and offers by, 51–52; content of demands and offers by, 44–45; exchange intensity by, 39; measurement of, 154*n22*
Sponsoring organizations, 116
Spulber, Daniel F., 89, 92
Stakes: change in demands and offers by, 51; contact intensity by, 32–34; content of demands and offers by, 43–44; definition of, 18–20, 144*nn31,32*; economics of settlement and, 61–66; 144*nn31,32*; exchange intensity by, 30–40; first demands/first offers by, 49–50; nonmonetary, 21–23; variation in, 20–21, 145*n38*. *See also* Case worth
Steele, Eric H., 137, 141*n4*
Stevens, Carl M., 163*n43*
Strauss, Anselm, 116–17
Structured settlements, 68, 163*nn39,40*
Success: frequency of, 167*n26*, impact of negotiation on, 54–56, 172*n15*; measurement of, 52–54
Sucker. *See* Prisoner's Dilemma
Sudnow, David, 120
Sutton, John, 87, 168*n45*, 169*n48*
Swanson, Timothy, 76, 93–94, 97, 142*n12*, 169*nn52,55*, 170*n64*, 173*n22*

Tactics: change in offers and demands, 49–52; contingent fees and, 100–103; first offer/first demand, 47–49, 122; impact on success, 54

Temptation. *See* Prisoner's Dilemma
Texaco. *See* Pennzoil v. Texaco
Thoennes, Nancy, 164*n6*
Tit for Tat: strategy in Prisoner's Dilemma, 82, 167*n32*
Tjaden, Patricia, 164*n6*
Torts. *See* Area of law
Trade unions: funding of litigation in England, 109, 120, 125
Transaction costs: function of negotiations and, 124; game-theoretic analyses of, 86; imposition of, 74–75, 165*n11*; role in economics of settlement, 59–61, 130–32, 159*n16*
Tribe, Lawrence, 3
Trubek, David M., 4, 17, 31, 32, 132, 136, 142*n13*, 147*n43*, 179*n8*
Tullock, Gordon, 92
Tyler, Tom R., 180*n14*

Ulvila, Jacob W., 92
Uncertainty: concerning case worth, 58–59, 73–74, 121; differences regarding in England, 94–95; impact on negotiation, 85, 87, 92, 96
Unions. *See* Trade unions
Ury, William, 136, 147*n44*
Utz, Pamela, 6, 120, 131

van Koppen, Peter J., 115, 122, 164*n1*, 166*n19*
van den Haag, Ernest, 5

Victor, Mark B., 59
Viscusi, W. Kip, 142*n12*, 161*n31*
Von Neumann, John, 80

Wallach, E. Robert, 6
Walton, Richard E., 156*n42*, 157*n3*
Wanner, Craig, 75
Waterman, D. A., 158*n13*
Weinstein, Jack B., 8–10
Weiss, Stephen E., 175*n1*
White, James J., 142*n15*
Wilde, Louis L., 89
Williams, Gerald R., 55–56, 58, 76–78, 116–18, 135, 158*n8*, 166*nn22,23,24*, 175*nn2,5*, 176*n7*
Witcover, Jules, 10
Wittman, Donald, 75, 159*n18*, 161*n31*, 164*n5*

Yeazell, Stephen C., 142*n13*
Yngvesson, Barbara, 23, 47, 147*n42*, 154*n27*
Young, Oran, 84, 86
Yukl, Gary A., 163*n42*

Zemans, Frances, 103, 147*n42*, 148*n46*, 149*n48*
Zero-sum games. *See* Distributive bargaining
Zeuthen, Frederik, 66
Zone of overlap. *See* Economics of settlement